the Agents' Game

The Stories of Australian Football Agents

the Agents' Game

The Stories of Australian Football Agents

Peter Paleologos

FAIRPLAY
PUBLISHING

First published in 2024 by Fair Play Publishing

PO Box 4101, Balgowlah Heights, NSW 2093, Australia

www.fairplaypublishing.com.au

ISBN: 978-1-925914-73-3

ISBN: 978-1- 925914-79-5(ePub)

Design and typesetting by Leslie Priestley

Front cover photograph by Billion Photos

All inquiries should be made to the Publisher via hello@fairplaypublishing.com.au

NATIONAL
LIBRARY
OF AUSTRALIA

A catalogue record of this book is available from the National Library of Australia.

Contents

Love them or hate them, football agents are a fundamental cornerstone of the international transfer system. Football agents work with clubs and players to achieve their professional goals and assist clubs in building teams to deliver on-field success.

While the headlines are hogged by the biggest transfer fees, highest agent commissions, and deals involving the best players, the industry's untold reality is that most agents put in thousands of hours of work behind the scenes to help deliver successful outcomes for their clients.

The Agents' Game tells those stories - and more - through the eyes of Australia's leading and most impactful football agents.

James Kitching, former Director of Football Regulatory, FIFA

We often hear about talented Australian football players aspiring to play overseas at major clubs. Yet, what is frequently overlooked in the Australian football landscape is the crucial role that Australian football agents play in making these opportunities a reality. Positioned far from the heart of the global football industry, the agents tirelessly drive negotiations, forge pathways, and secure outcomes for Australian players and coaches.

The hard work behind the scenes—overcoming fixed perceptions of Australian talent, navigating constant travel, building relationships with football directors and clubs, and managing the complexities of dealmaking—rarely receives the attention it deserves.

In The Agents' Game, Peter Paleologos brings together the untold stories of Australian football agents, shedding light on a business that is both uncompromising and deeply compelling. This book fills a gap in football literature, offering valuable insights into the pivotal role that football agents play in influencing the game, both in Australia and internationally.

*Craig Moore, former Australian International and FIFA Football Agen*t

Chapter 1:
The Business —
An Introduction to the
Australian and International
Football Agents Industry

The Australian football agents' story needed to be written. It is a story that is often overlooked by many in football circles, as agents are generally seen through a suspicious lens. In telling part of the Australian agent story, I wanted to not only provide insights into the industry and events from my own personal experience but also find sincere, honest and genuine stories from those agents who have a positive story to tell. This book is based on interviews with them and chronicles their significant contributions.

The initial idea for the book emanated from a meeting I attended with a fellow agent and colleague, Lou Sticca, on behalf of the Australian Football Agents Association Inc (AFAA). The meeting was with Ben Buckley (CEO) and Lyall Gorman of the then Football Federation Australia (FFA). It turned out to be a sliding-doors moment. At the time, Lou and I were in negotiations with FFA to set up a memorandum of understanding between both entities. During this meeting, it became apparent to me that key figures in the game were not aware of the contribution, presence and support that Australian agents give to all stakeholders in the local football industry. Further, the FFA and the A-League clubs were not fully cognisant of the value agents collectively had created for the A-League, the players and the clubs. This value was not just about agents representing players but in the investment that agents make in promoting Australian football, generating player transfers (both local and internationally), and scouting and backing Australian talent.

To provide a balanced insight to the story of the agents interviewed for this book, I have taken a two-fold approach. Firstly, I have researched the background of each agent and provided my observations on their unique, niche and nuanced contribution to Australian football, focusing on some of the player deals they have engaged in and how they have influenced the football market. Secondly, I provided each agent with an opportunity to articulate their story in their own words and provide anecdotes, personal views and experiences within a frank interview. This approach provides a different context to the story of Australian agents. I have also analysed important regulatory milestones and set out the business environment that affects agents. Finally, I have provided a roundtable platform for the agents to give their unique insights into the always trending topic of Australian player development and pathways.

Who are the agents?

Football agents carry many labels. Player agent, football agent, football intermediary, manager, adviser, talent identification scout, mentor, fixer, consultant, dealmaker and broker. In reality, all of these labels are intrinsic to what agents do and touch the narratives of their business.

What is the agent's business?

"Being a football agent is not a complicated job, but it is the most complicated job in the world."
— Stijn Francis, Belgium sports lawyer and football agent.

The international football transfer market and recruitment of players has become an industry within an industry, with agents being key players. Yet the player representation business is recognised as a difficult, precarious and unscrupulous one. For an agent to succeed, they must be able to provide a whole suite of services and professionalism. Further, agents must build long-lasting relationships with clients. This is challenging within a football market which is constantly affected by the pull factor and glamour of bigger European agents, the difficulties of finding clubs for an oversupply of players, the cutthroat competition of the industry and the ever-shifting loyalties of clients.

Agent services

Essentially, football agents provide comprehensive player agent and management services to players and other client segments (clubs and coaches). Their services include both a business aspect and a regulatory advice aspect.

In terms of the business aspect, the agent will:

- Negotiate a player's contract, salary and bonuses.
- Negotiate managerial or coaching contracts.
- Market a player to clubs.
- Understand what makes a successful player. Profiling is key.
- Provide talent management and CV services.
- Review player contract renewal option arrangements.
- Negotiate pre-contracts (so a player can join a designated club in the future).
- Facilitate player transfers and loans between clubs and leagues.
- Negotiate a player's commercial/endorsement contracts and image rights contracts (including assignments and licences).
- Make financial planning and investment/real estate referrals to professionals on behalf of clients.
- Handle the media training, press activations and assist with curating player content on social media platforms.
- Facilitate boot deals and sponsorships.
- Monitor career development and post-career planning for clients.
- Mentor and be a sounding board for the player.
- Be a type of life coach, or just a shoulder to cry on, particularly for young players or those from overseas who are away from their families.
- Provide talent identification and scouting services for clubs.
- Research club and coaches' tactical styles and player type requirements.
- Monitor their players' performances, keep players accountable and give them honest feedback when they are not delivering on the pitch.

Additionally, the agent must provide relevant guidance and support to players. For instance, agents will support younger players in getting help with education options, language training, targeted training, mental resilience coaching and managing social media profile risks.

Agents need to negotiate player contract demands/requests from a player's perspective. These may include negotiations on an agreed salary, percentage of a future transfer fee, and add-on benefits like flight tickets, accommodation, medical insurance, transport/car and possible driver, school fees, tax arrangements and any bank guarantees. Additionally, agents need to balance any endorsement aspects of the player's deal (there are up to 63 types of image rights to be negotiated[1]) as well as protect the privacy rights of the player in performance and biometric data. Agents must also pay attention to the informally pre-agreed contractual details and terms with clubs, which usually occur on WhatsApp or via text message and are then formalised into written employment contracts.

Nowadays, the structure of playing deals/contracts are more complex than ever and agents must ensure that incentives or bonuses are payable (e.g., through team or individual success) or negotiate any sign-on fees. In longer player contracts, there is an opportunity to include a transfer fee amount in the form of a buy-out, transfer clause, sell-on clause or release clause. These clauses trigger the transfers of contracted players. Agents must also attempt to limit the notorious liquified damages or penalty clauses that international clubs may request be put into a contract should a player want to terminate their contract unilaterally.

In terms of regulatory advice, agents are required to understand the different frameworks that apply to football player movements, employment and transfers.

These include:

- Preparing mandates with other football agents and players.
- Handling and resolving disputes and providing tribunal support.
- Dealing with crisis, risk management and legal issues.
- Providing football league transfer window and player registration advice.
- Providing guidance to players on compensation for breaches of their contract.
- Advising on how club training compensation and solidarity payments affect a young player's transfer to a new club.
- Solving work permit and immigration issues.
- Protecting players from nefarious activities engaged in by clubs. For example, the practice of lofting which is to force a player to leave or sign a new contract.2
- Being aware of the validity of their player representation contracts in each jurisdiction.
- Understanding different league and federation contractual requirements (player entitlements and obligations).
- Understanding how to represent minors and having the working with children check.
- Monitoring agent industry trends and the agent 'chatosphere' (what is happening with the market and competitors).
- Maintaining an awareness of doping and match fixing regulations.
- Understanding FIFA transfer regulations and national association/league player registration regulations.

For Australian agents, there is a triumvirate of regulations that they must fully comprehend at all times. Internationally, all agents must know and comply with the FIFA Regulations on the Status and Transfer of Players (RSTP).[3] These regulations cover the key pillars of the football transfer market including player registrations, player and club contractual stability, loan regulations and player transfer rules. Secondly, Australian agents must be across Australian regulations including A-League salary caps, Football Australia registration regulations, A-League, Matilda and Socceroo collective bargaining agreements, and professional player contracting regulations. Thirdly, agents must be informed of agent-specific regulations such as the various agent or intermediary regulations that FIFA has implemented since 1994, as well as those of national federations or professional leagues. Being an agent is not just about negotiating player deals. Regulatory compliance needs to be at the forefront of an agent's thinking.

Further, in Australia and other common law countries like England, agents must ensure they follow the common law principle of the duty of care owed to each client and always follow their instructions. A client's wishes and interests must come first. Agents must avoid conflicts of interest, the non-disclosure of fees, and ensure that they negate any unfavourable contractual terms affecting their clients.

The emergence of agents in football — 1st generation

Agents have been present within the English and Scottish football leagues since the 1960s and 1970s. "At that time, the role of an agent was confined mainly to that of a club representative tasked with discovering new talent."[4] However, professional advisers were starting to emerge in football player representation as well as offering services in law and accounting. Across the Atlantic, the Americans were the pioneers of sports agency during the 1960s. Mark McCormack, an attorney with a law degree from Yale "ushered in the modern era of sports management and marketing. McCormack, founder of International Management Group (IMG), believed the popularity and marketability of athletes could transcend borders, cultures, language, even sports itself."[5] He branched into tennis and other sports with a global footprint and was involved in Pelé coming to the United States and the New York Cosmos.

In Europe, the use of agents by players grew as the commercial opportunities and international market for players expanded.[6] In England, Dennis Roach was regarded as the first-ever football agent. In 1979, Roach negotiated and finalised the world's first £1,000,000 transfer fee when Trevor Francis moved from Birmingham

City to Nottingham Forest. Previously, he famously undertook the transfer negotiations of Dutch superstar Johann Cruyff to Barcelona in the 1970s. On an inter-country level, Italian agent Gigi Peronace first started engaging as a broker in player transfers between English and Italian clubs on a large scale. Gigi was initially a translator for British managers (coaches) who moved to Italy. He saw a market opportunity as there was a considerable wage disparity between Italian clubs who could offer more tempting deals than English clubs who faced wage caps (at the time) which would limit a players' earnings.

In Australia, it was not the agents but the successful immigration programs that allowed historic local and ethnic clubs (with well-connected presidents and committees) to bring players as migrants to Australia. Unfortunately, in 1960 the Australia Soccer Association's membership was suspended by FIFA after disobeying its mandate on recruiting foreign players without a transfer fee.

In South America, Jorge Cyterszpiler was one of the first agents tasked with making significant player deals happen. Cyterszpiler was Diego Maradona's lifelong friend and first agent/manager. There was also an entrepreneur Ruben Horacio Gaggioli, the agent involved in bringing Lionel Messi to Barcelona. Gaggioli is known for the famous quote that "all the fathers believe they have a Diego Maradona, but it doesn't always work out."[7] Fast forward five decades later, the growth of agents and agency activity correlates with the number of international transfers conducted in the worldwide football market. Players are transferring to new clubs more frequently during their career and the average age of an international transfer by a player is decreasing. In 2023, agents acted on behalf of players in a record total of 3,353 transfers.[8] Football agents tend to appear more frequently in transfers with greater player salaries and for younger players and professionals moving to better leagues or elite and higher-level clubs.

The rise of both agents and money in football player transfers necessitated a formal response from FIFA. FIFA international regulations on the transfer of players and agents became the main set of governance rules that apply worldwide.

With FIFA being the chief regulator (and national associations co-regulating at a local level), the agent profession has been impacted by the slow, spasmodic, inconsistent and layered growth of regulations. FIFA's end game was to initially develop a robust, licensed agent model (between 1994 and 2014); yet in 2015 FIFA suddenly scrapped their model and essentially removed the need for licences. Consequently, somewhat of a Wild West emerged in the agent's industry. FIFA subsequently backflipped (and begrudgingly admitted its error) by bringing a new suite of regulations into effect in October 2023.

The 2nd generation of agents — 1994 FIFA regulations

The 1994 Players' Agents Regulations (PAR)[9] were the first international player agent regulations. They required a person wanting to provide player agent services to be in possession of a licence issued by a national football association. Clubs and players were under an obligation to only engage the services of "FIFA Licensed Agents" during transfers or new contract negotiations. This licence designation was highly sought after, as there were not many recognised agents in the worldwide football market at the time.

To obtain the FIFA licence, candidates were required to undertake an interview to ascertain their knowledge of football regulations and employment contract laws. They were also required to provide proof that they had no criminal record and could provide a bank guarantee deposit of 200,000 Swiss francs (CHF). Prospective agents attended FIFA's offices in Zurich, Switzerland to undertake their licensing interview with officials. FIFA recorded 214 players' agents worldwide in 1996.[10] Representation agreements between a licensed agent and a player were set for a maximum period of two years. Disputes involving agents were heard by FIFA's Players' Status Committee.

The 3rd generation — 2001 FIFA regulations

The 2001 FIFA Players' Agent Regulations retained the obligation for player agents to hold a licence issued by the competent national association. For a licence to be issued, the candidate was required to have an "impeccable reputation" and then take a written multiple-choice examination at their local national association offices. The change from interview to an exam was a major shift. The agent was also required to take out a professional liability insurance policy or deposit a bank guarantee to the amount of CHF 100,000. This lower amount allowed more people to afford setting up a licensed agent business. There were 613 licensed players' agents worldwide in February 2001.[11]

The 4th generation — European Union licence changes

In 2002, FIFA made a technical amendment to the regulations by stating that nationals and citizens of the European Union (EU) and European Economic Area (EEA) must make their application for a licence to the national association of their home country or their country of residence. The changes ensured that the regulations complied with EU competition law. By 2003, there were close to 1500 licensed agents and by 2004 that figure expanded to about 1800.[12]

The 5th generation — 2008 FIFA regulations

The 2008 FIFA Players' Agent Regulations (2008 PAR) brought significant changes to the definition of the agent's business. The PAR defined an agent as "a natural person who, for a fee, introduces players to clubs with a view to negotiating an employment contract or introduces two clubs to one another with a view to concluding a transfer agreement." Other services offered by agents, such as image rights, consulting, sponsorship, social media and marketing work, were not covered by the 2008 PAR.

Candidates who wanted to become licensed agents, had to undertake a written multiple-choice exam.[13] In most countries, the exam consisted of two parts. One set by FIFA on international regulations and one by the home association on its regulations. If the candidate passed the exam, they had to obtain professional liability insurance and sign a code of professional conduct. It was then the national association (such as Football Australia) who issued a personal and non-transferable licence, and the agent was entitled to use the title "Players' agent licensed by the football association of [country]." Another key change was that the remuneration of an agent acting for a player was calculated on the player's annual basic gross income. In December 2011, there were 6,082 licensed players' agents operating worldwide.[14]

The 6th generation — FIFA's regulations on working with intermediaries

The sixth generation of agents were completely different to the previous five. FIFA brought in the Regulations on Working with Intermediaries (RWWI) which came into force on 1 April 2015. There has been much speculation on why FIFA undertook such a drastic change but some of the justification for the need to reform the 2008 PAR stemmed from a statistic produced by FIFA that "only 25-30% of transfers are managed by official FIFA licensed agents." There were too many unlicensed agents involved in transfers of players. Many experienced agents were incensed with FIFA as they preferred that the 2008 PAR just be properly enforced.

The key features of the RWWI were: [15]

- The regulations referred to agents as intermediaries.
- An intermediary could be a natural person or a legal entity. This was the first-time companies could be an agent through their intermediaries.

- Intermediaries were no longer required to have a licence or to sit an exam. In Australia,[16] intermediaries had to certify that they had no conflicts of interests and an impeccable reputation.
- Each time an intermediary was involved in a transaction, they were required to be registered with the national association to which the club was affiliated. In Australia, Football Australia allowed intermediaries to register as pre-lodged intermediaries to avoid duplicity.
- Intermediaries could not be remunerated for employment contracts (in most countries) and/or transfer agreements if the player concerned was a minor.

The shift from agents to intermediaries was a game-changer for the industry as it removed the universality of the agents' licence. Worldwide, it was estimated that there were between 8,000 to near 10,000 active intermediaries in this generation.

Interestingly, post the 2015 regulatory change, a survey was undertaken by leading English sports law firm Brabners with chief executives, heads of recruitment and academy managers at 22 English Premier League and English Football League clubs. It revealed "that less than a quarter of agents and intermediaries had a good working knowledge of the transfer market and the relevant regulations."[17]

The 7th generation — FIFA's 2023 regulations

FIFA has brought in new regulations (fully effective from October 2023) that principally revert to a combination of the earlier agent licensing frameworks. The basic tenets underpinning these new FIFA Football Agent Regulations (FFAR) include:

A mandatory licensing system — the exam is back as is the need to hold a FIFA agent licence.

Dual representation of clients is limited, with agents only permitted to act as an agent for a player or a player and engaging club.

New commission caps on agent fees (which are being challenged).

Representation agreements between the agent and the player are set for a maximum period of two years whilst agreements between agents and clubs have no period limit.

Transparency (reporting and compliance requirements and the application of the new FIFA clearing house to process transactions).

New dispute resolution system (The Agents Chamber) to hear agent disputes that feature an international dimension.

Lawyers and parents are not exempt from holding an agent's licence.

Continuous professional development (CPD) — Agents must undertake compulsory professional development courses offered by FIFA.

Over 7,440 agents have been licensed worldwide under these regulations as of June 2024.

The most contentious issue with the new FIFA regulations is the introduction of fee commission caps which apply on football service and player transaction activity. Fee caps may have a significant effect on the next generation of agents, especially many middle and smaller agents who may find it difficult to operate in financially capped environments. Several agents and agent associations worldwide litigated against the introduction of the FFAR, believing that the caps may infringe anti-trust/ anti-competition laws in certain national jurisdictions.

The recent outcomes of this litigation have seen court injunctions stopping the application of some of the FFAR provisions in Germany, Brazil and Spain. An arbitration tribunal also disallowed the implementation of commission caps in England by the Football Association.

The implementation of the FFAR is now in a state of flux. For most of Europe at least, it depends on the European Court of Justice's future decision on the legality of commission caps and other limitations imposed by FIFA on agents. For England, China, Australia and the United States, local competition law does not necessarily allow the introduction of commission's caps. Inevitably, we may end up having an 8th generation of agents!

Types of agents

"People have the wrong idea about agents. Being an agent means many different things. I am someone normal; I'm working hard every day. I have ambition, determination, and (value) being honest and doing the right things."
— Jorge Mendes, super-agent and former representative of Ronaldo.[18]

Generally, agent services are intrinsically influenced by whether a player wants just an end service (a new deal) or day-to-day representation. There are different types of agents within this context, including the super-agent, club agent, traditional player agent, the intermediary, the smaller independent agent, and trainee agents (runners).

The **super-agent** refers to the likes of Mino Raiola (RIP), Jorge Mendes, Jonathan Barnett (who represented close to 800 players[19]), Giovanni Branchini, Roger Wittman, Rafaela Pimenta, Pere Guardiola, Federico Pastorello, Pini Zahavi and Volker Struth. They all have so much influence in so many big clubs and/or big name players in club dressing rooms. Super-agents are always leveraging players and contract situations. Moreover, they have about 50-60 client clubs in Europe that they deal with who can meet their client's wage expectations and the high transfer fees (plus China was a recent market and Major League Soccer and Saudi Arabia are a new emerging client base). The emergence of the super-agent coincided with one of the major pillars of change in the player transfer market — Real Madrid's campaign to sign all the 'Galacticos' (footballers who are deemed to be superstars or boast ability levels that are 'out of this world').

Clubs often accuse big agents of manipulating players, but privately, many club directors seek out the super-agents like Jorge Mendes. As Tor-Kristian Karlsen, Monaco's former sporting director, articulated regarding Mendes, "He's charismatic, good company and can connect with people at any level. He is also well-dressed, a gentleman — significant in a world where fine suits and good looks matter. Most importantly, he controls the game's essential commodity: talent. No club official can match his network".[20]

In his book *The Deal*, Jon Smith writes that "only a tiny fraction of the 1,600 plus UK agents make the kind of money that annoys people." To those easily upset, he counters. "Don't be influenced by a big number. If you are trading commodities or foreign exchange in the City (London's financial district) and making huge commissions, no one minds. But they seem to object to football agents being paid a few million pounds when they've made someone millions of pounds. Big players want big services, so the bigger agencies are benefiting."[21]

Club agents bring players to clubs on trial or pre-contracts and help clubs shift players who have outstayed their welcome. Many are well-connected and networked agents who have a contacts book that is invaluable to both clubs and coaches for player recruitment. Just like players, some agents are better than others. Therefore, top clubs must compete to get the services of agents who have an in-demand and talented player management portfolio or access to top players.

The **traditional player agent representative** deals with players day to day and manages most aspects of their career. They are an all-rounder type of agent. A traditional player representative agent will have a valuable portfolio of players. Clubs come to them to discuss established players who have good track records and an upside. [For] their younger talented players who are on the cusp of a career, the agent will push and hustle to promote them during the transfer window periods, where football agency is a 7-days a week and 24-hour a day business."[22]

An **intermediary type** agent likes to act both on behalf of clubs and players and does not always want to manage players day to day. An intermediary is generally self-referential in their expertise on certain clubs and leagues. They are like consultants. Further, there is the intermediary type of agent who is more transactional and brings together clubs, other agents and players for transfer deals; they are like a matchmaker. Some intermediaries act like brokers and are mandated by clubs to find suitable players. The intermediary also puts players or their agents directly in contact with interested clubs.

Many **smaller independent agents** generally focus on national or regional markets and they do not always charge players for their first professional contract. They need to get the player a good deal to gain their trust going forward. Generally, a good smaller agent would know the price for a player in their local transfer market and work hard to build a portfolio of playing talent that they seek to manage.

The **runner or trainee agents** are mostly focused on recruiting younger players and looking for the player's first professional contract. They may be employed, mentored or trained by more experienced agents or agencies.

Recently, the agent scene has seen the emergence of the **mega football player agencies** like Sports Entertainment Group (SEG) from the Netherlands, Rogon from Germany, Gestifute from Portugal, Creative Artists Agency (CAA) Base Soccer, CAA Stellar, Wasserman and Roc Nation. CAA, Wasserman and Roc Nation have major offices in the United States and the United Kingdom. These mega agencies have cornered a considerable portion of the largest European football markets and hold huge sway with elite coaches, club boards and football directors. Many super-agents are at the helm of mega football agencies. Further, mega agent agencies or groups do not only seek to control the player deal. They also aim to control their intellectual property content creation and management. From being just agent groupings, they have emerged as talent managers.

It is essential for all types of agents to avoid outsourcing when things go wrong. An agent needs to be personally on top of any client issues which need to be resolved quickly. They must be effective problem-solvers and able to distil player data. An important attribute for agents is the ability to weigh up a player's future employment options and see several moves ahead.

Further, all types of agents must be competent at feeding information to media writers about players to shape stories in their client's interests. Anecdotally, the English and Italian media are acknowledged as leaders in getting player deal information and transfer news out into the football market and the public. Football journalists like Gianluca di Marzio, Fabrizio Romano and David Ornstein's X (Twitter) accounts and articles are followed obsessively by fans and clubs. They are the elite in reporting player and club transfer news, including the involvement of agents in high profile deals. There are also important football-specific broadsheets or magazines like *France Football, Kicker* (Germany*), La Gazzetta dello Sport* (Italy) and *Marca* (Spain).

The Australian agent context and landscape

A unique aspect of Australian agents is that they operate in a local salary-capped league environment. The A-League Men's salary cap affects both their agents' fees (which are partly included in the salary cap) as well as the player salaries that agents can negotiate. Further, Australian agents suffer considerable travel costs as they are located well away from Europe, North and South America, and Asia. Interestingly, and surprisingly, recent research indicates Australian players have one of the highest levels of agent demand as an overall percentage worldwide. One or more agents (intermediaries) were involved on their behalf in 43.5% of 115 international transfers in 2019. Players from Norway (42%) and Canada (41.9%) completed the top 3 positions.[23] Minors and younger players have the highest level of agent representation in transfers (23.5% worldwide), and this also applies to Australia where young players and their parents are consistently contacting agents for representation. Most Australian agents also operate as the scouts in Australia, as there is no true player and club scouting ecosystem.

Taking on players as clients

Every football agent is looking for a super-talented client who we often call a "baller."[24] This is a footballer who plays the beautiful technical way, full of confidence and swag, has done the hard work and has a top career pathway ahead of them. However, these top players are few and far between, and a plethora of agents will chase them and their families for their signature, including the mega agencies.

On the other hand, a reputable agent will not normally advertise for players as their track record, good organisational habits and word-of-mouth are the biggest drivers of getting better players to sign to their agency. Many youth players are referred to these agents. However, many are wary of taking on a young player, especially if the young player's parent is toxic and tries to control the player pathway. Agents lose their value, cachet and influence if they let too many people into the player pathway decision-making process.

Ultimately, an agent can only do so much to create opportunities. It is common to have an expectation mismatch. Further, patience can sometimes be hard to find in the football business, as everyone wants instant outcomes. From an agent's perspective, the client/player must be playing and cannot be someone who dips in and out of the first team sheet. For players to garner club attention, it is about games and appearances and not just a mere contribution here or there or some off-the-bench impact. Agents cannot forecast whether a player will make it. Nor can clubs. Circumstances in football can change in a moment.

Finally, the experienced agents understand the industry well enough to know that 95% of professional players are not in a position of power to dictate terms to clubs in terms of the value of their contract. Only the top 5% of the top players have that leverage due to the competitive demand by big and successful clubs for their playing services. You also have the geographic equation to consider. Coming from a certain geographic region or country as a player may be seen by some club decision-makers as an initial obstacle (perception-wise) if that place has not been historically strong in producing quality players.

Managing player expectations

I have heard it so many times, as have most agents, "Get me a good deal or otherwise I will be disappointed and turn to another agent."

The management of player expectations is integral to success in player agency. Meet the player's remit and most players will stick with their agent. Generally, players want to go to a club to be a more important player. However, managing this move and motivation is not easy as there are not that many jobs available. In 2016, the Fédération Internationale des Associations de Footballeurs Professionnels (FIFPRO) published its global employment report into the "Working Conditions in Professional Football." They identified that on a global level, 45 per cent of players earned less than USD $1000 a month in wages[25] and that at any one time, 45 per cent of professional players are free agents[26] (uncontracted) during the important transfer window periods. With opportunities limited in the bigger leagues for most players, Australian agents must work very hard to get players better opportunities. Both player and agent must bring something to the negotiating table. For the agent to manage a player's transfer expectations, it is a must to listen to the player's wishes, yet also advise what is realistic. For the player, they need to be prepared to seize an opportunity when it arises by being in full fitness and top form.

The primary aim when negotiating a new contract is for the agent to know the player's value and generally make the first offer to the club (as good agents have a ballpark value based on similar players). In terms of advice, the agent must advise players on two aspects. The financial side of the deal versus the sporting side (i.e., are you going to play?).

Smaller agents need to show players that they can get them to a bigger club, otherwise players have doubts. Players will often feel that "if he or she believes another agent can help them get a better contract, then they may leave."[27] Then there is the challenge that if the player performs at the bigger club, more high-profile agents will look to move in on the player after the smaller agent has done a lot of hard work opening opportunities.

Alternatively, managing successful players brings other challenges. In bigger European leagues, players can find themselves in a dressing room full of people spending a lot but not wisely. It is sometimes difficult to stop a successful player's spending pattern, as the short- term culture is common in football. When a player receives an amount of money that they have not had to deal with before; it can be tempting to spend it. Further, there is also the entourage issue to deal with, where hangers-on use their friendship with the player to benefit themselves. Some intermediaries or their entourage will try to persuade top players to invest in shady property investments or cryptocurrency deals. The entourage member may earn a commission from a malicious intermediary when they convince a player to make risky investments.[28] Agents must aim to protect their players from these risky moves and the influence of troublesome entourages.

Agents and clubs — a complicated relationship

Generally, many clubs have a neutral relationship with agents. They must deal with them to contract or employ players. Many clubs receive a barrage of emails or contacts and may only reply to a small number of agent queries. Additionally, many agents who have no relationship with clubs will harass coaches, managers, football directors and CEOs by asking them to look at CVs of players who they do not control.[29] Conversely, some clubs or their directors of football only wish to deal with preferred agents or ones they have a long-standing relationship with. The stronger-networked agents have insider club contacts who can get their players in front of the decision-makers. Top agents are always talking to club football or sporting directors or coaches or even club physiotherapists about players. For example, many Australian agents have strong contacts within A-League clubs and with coaches and football directors, which provides value to the clubs in several ways.

For instance, agents can provide a myriad of value-added services to clubs, including player market valuations as well as knowing the mentality of the player and whether he/she is a good fit for the club.

Conversely, agents also must educate themselves on the financial conditions at different clubs and the type of strategy a club may employ to recruit players. The question often faced by agents is will the club take care of the player and his or her family? At English clubs, there may be up to 20 staff working to have players perfectly integrated into the club and provide player care. In fact, many English clubs have a team of experts for transitions, player care and they know where the responsibility of the club rests. For players, there is a lot of administration involved with moving to another country, including local bank and real estate rental matters, tax consequences, spouse comfort, visas, working permits and sorting out a pre-contract medical fitness test. Agents must be across these issues and ascertain what the clubs can provide to the player in assisting with the transition. Anecdotally, clubs in Spain, Italy, France and Germany seem to offer less support than English clubs. In fact, in Germany if a player gets injured, the Bundesliga clubs only pay their salary for six weeks (of the injury period), whereas in many other leagues - clubs will pay for six months. In Italy, negotiations between clubs and agents about players can often turn into a show, where sometimes a club president may want to shout in the boardroom to feel like they have had the final say in any deal. In Turkey, some clubs try to reduce the agent fee. In Asia, it can be slow work to get a player deal over the line due to hierarchical decision-making structures; agents need patience and the right local agent to work with.

Moreover, clubs now do a lot more due diligence internationally on agents, and if the agent is obscure with no track record, they may not deal with them. Many club staff take the approach that if they don't know them (the agent) and they don't trust them, then they don't want to hear from them. When agents do get access to decision-makers, they must continually cultivate the relationship.

Finally, player agents are prohibited from approaching any player who is under contract to a club with the aim of persuading him or her to terminate their contract prematurely or to violate any obligations stipulated in the employment contract.[30] It's a fine line getting players out of a club and agents must ensure they do not cross the breach of employment contract line.

Dealing with other agents in different leagues and markets

Football agency is a collaborative business. Different agents in different countries will have a different strategy and mindset. There are differing international business languages and cultural nuances, as well as different legal frameworks. Agents worldwide collaborate on transferring players. Yet these collaborations are also dictated by who holds the contacts and networks. For instance, some Italian agents are not always easy to deal with, as they have passed more vigorous tests and barriers of entry to the agent profession and wish to control the deal from the Italian club's side. Many other international agents prepare six months before the transfer windows open and will not take on new players during that time, as they need to get their own players signed with clubs.

Within some European markets, there is significant interference in deals by some agents who engage in dishonest practices. This may include agents trying to convince the player and the agent of the player that they have an official mandate of the club. Alternatively, some wily agents try to convince a player that a club is interested in them but refuse to work with the player's agent. Further, some agents are commission sellers where they garner interest in a player then push clubs to make a move for them.

Regardless of these challenges, an overseas network is a 'must have' for any agent. Many Australian agents have overseas agent partnerships based on longstanding relationships and a solid record of player transfers. In many Asian markets, Australian agents have stronger connections and networks than many of their European counterparts.

Agent's commissions and fees

"I cannot go into a club and force them to pay more (to a player) than they want to do. It's a fallacy."
— Jonathan Barnett, CAA Stellar super-agent

Some critics, fans and pundits perceive agents as opportunists who only care for their fees and do not give much back to football. This is a total misrepresentation of good agents. The commission and fees that agents can be paid vary greatly depending on the league, player, country and club. However, in a business where there are no hourly rates, very few retainers, even fewer stable salaries and significant operating costs to cover cash flow, agent income can be very spasmodic. An agent's income is directly linked to the quality of their players and a return on their investment and time is sometimes never realised. Most of the work agents undertake is not fee-based, with only the contract negotiation for a new deal, an extension of a contract or a transfer of player being a billable service in the agent contract agreement.

The range of agent commission generally averages between 6.8 per cent, as noted by European Football Agents Association research, and 5.8 per cent, reported by recent FIFA research into agent fees. The 2019 European Commission report[31] into agent fees indicated the average agent fee was around 6–7 per cent of the player's salary or transfer fee. Of course, there are exceptions, with many agents charging over 10 per cent and some big agents much more than that. Interestingly, 80 per cent of agent commissions worldwide are paid cumulatively in 6 countries (France, Italy, England, Spain, Germany and Portugal). In fact, over 96 per cent of all agent commission worldwide is paid by European clubs (however, this may change with the recent Saudi Arabia Pro League activity). Australian agents must work hard to get deals in those European club markets.

English agents are generally more commercially aggressive as English clubs pay the highest commissions, while in Spain, most agents are paid generally a 5 per cent fee. Further, Spanish agents are known to be a bit more flexible about when they receive their payments. In more than 90 per cent of cases, club intermediaries receive commissions of under USD $1 million, with USD $10,000 to $100,000 being the most common scenario.[32] Generally, many agents will say that they are not paid enough as the current regulations result in much of the commission needing to be shared around to other partners in the deal. As noted by former English Association of Football Agents (AFA) chairperson Mike Miller, "to get a licence across Europe you need to register in nearly every country and if you use a local agent that is half your fee gone."[33] Further, there have been unfortunate circumstances where a player deal will not go through because the agents cannot agree on their fee with the club.[34]

For their players to understand the value of their work, many agents will list, itemise and document all their work for each player. At present, the agent business income model has shifted. To make an income, agents may need to be part of a large multinational player agency or a small dynamic grouping with three to four well-connected agents. Alternatively, to remain financially viable, agents must either have loyal players as clients or find a couple of young talented players who very quickly transition to the better leagues and clubs. Offering other services like scouting, CV drafting, marketing and sponsorship deals can also generate fees.

To finish, the football agent experience is complex, challenging, rewarding, dynamic and multidimensional with a lot of moving parts. This experience has also influenced and fashioned the various significant Australian football agents – whom I now explore and enter a conversation with in the next chapters.

Chapter 2:
The Pioneer –
George Christopoulos

It was 17 February 1997 and the football media had just reported that George Christopoulos had won FIFA's approval to join "an elite global club of player agents." Was this the beginning of the football agency industry in Australia? I needed to find this out and phoned him in early 2021.

George's story requires us to be aware of the impact of the 1995 Bosman ruling which opened the transfer market for international player movement.[35] It allowed a player to leave a club on a free transfer as soon as their contract expired, meaning they had leverage to demand bigger sign-on fees and salaries from new clubs or their current club. The (player's) power, "as Alex Ferguson (legendary Manchester United coach) puts it, was handed to the player, in-turn giving rise to the agent."[36]

Australian football talent was not going to be left behind in this new transfer market reality and their goal was to seek professional opportunities abroad. Bosman was also the catalyst for the fledgling football agent industry to emerge as a more active player in the international football ecosystem. Agent advisers were now able to grow their business and move players more freely to new clubs, with the magnetism of European moves becoming attractive. Therefore, it was inevitable that football agency would finally take off in Australia. And it was George Christopoulos who was officially the first player agent in Australia (and Oceania).[37]

Background

George saw an opportunity at a time when the Australian football agent industry was in its infancy. He was a debutant at 17 years and 182 days for the Socceroos and a successful hospitality business operator. He brought a fresh entrepreneurial spirit to player agency by building his business on being innovative and not just on European agent criteria. It was a time where the National Soccer League (NSL) had

16 clubs and there was even an Australia player transfer system in place where big clubs at the time like Sydney Olympic FC would pay transfer fees for players to move from smaller clubs like Inter Monaro. George was the first agent to be a consultant to two NSL clubs. Therefore, he had competing things on his agent agenda in that he represented players (player's agent) while helping build club player rosters (club agent).

During his time as an agent, George became the football consultant for South Melbourne Football Club and was influential in rebuilding the playing group after it lost some key squad members over a short period of time. Local NSL star players like Con Boutsianis, Andy Vlahos, Goran Lozanovski and Simon Colosimo had all moved on and John Anastasiadis had retired. George explained to Ed Wyatt of *SBS TV* that "considering that we had a plan in progress with regards to young players coming through, we don't see value in offering big contracts to other 30-year-old players."[38] This approach was part of George's agent philosophy. He wanted to support the club to get rewarded financially on the emerging transfer market, as well as work on the agent model of getting young Australian players opportunities.

Further, George was passionate about the development of young players through the MVP (Most Valuable Player) academy he set up during his time at South Melbourne FC. Basically, George was the first in Australia who understood the player transfer model; where you bring young players through to consolidate potential large transfer opportunities. At the time, sharper agents overseas were about buying and selling players and making a commission, yet George was pioneering an innovative agency model where he focused on nurturing young player talent.

In an interview George gave to the *FNR Football Extra* podcast show on March 27, 2018, he commented that during the NSL period, his pioneering vision did not suit the landscape as there was no real football industry at the time.[39] Clubs were semi-professional and there was no player association like the Professional Footballers' Australia (PFA) as a support mechanism. George sought to remedy the situation and was driven by building player pathways and developing the profile of the Australian football industry. George believed in the holistic nature of player management, one to one support for elite young players and scouting the State football Institutes around Australia for talent. He was also involved in Carlton Soccer Club where he drove the academy model. He wanted young Australian 16 to 18-year-olds to be knocking on the door of the senior team squads to showcase their talents at that level. George wanted contracted players to develop under good club programs. He helped build links with the Victorian Institute of Sport (VIS) and the Australian Institute of Sport (AIS), which at the time were some of the pioneering (and leading) young player development academies worldwide. Uniquely though, George was one of the sole voices in Australia's football agency who wanted players released at an earlier age by both Institutes to play for their clubs.

In terms of building the profile of Australian soccer, George organised and promoted the FIFA All-Star game in Sydney in 1999. He brought major sponsors like Ansett and Adidas on board and ensured he obtained Tag Heuer signature watches for all the players to mark the occasion. FIFA invited high-profile players to the fixture, including Leonardo from Brazil. The All-Star game sold 88,000 tickets as the FIFA promoters promised George that Ronaldo Nazario would also be coming. Unfortunately, not all the promised players participated in the game.

Subsequently, George was also responsible for organising and promoting the Leeds United versus Colo Colo (Chilean club powerhouse) game at Melbourne Docklands Stadium in 2002 where Mark Viduka and Harry Kewell were invited to showcase their talent to Australian fans. Unfortunately, there was an issue concerning the state of pitch which affected the flow of the match. As in all things, there are always inherent risks in football but George was willing to undertake new football marketing, event and player academy ventures that were ahead of their time.

As an agent pioneer, George was the first to understand the potential that Australian football had and the ongoing challenges. Here is George's agent story in his own words.

In his own words[40]

On transitioning from playing football to George's interest in the emerging Australian sport business

Unfortunately, my career finished pretty early, and obviously during the time I was playing in Australia, it was still part-time. I was a full-time footballer at AEK Athens from Greece when I returned from overseas. I was involved in hospitality after that time, and I operated a pub here (Melbourne), the Rose and Crown. I had that from 1987 and operated it through to 2000. By 1987 I had pretty much finished playing. I tried to make a comeback after my injury, but the business was too busy and there was no money in the game here. It wasn't worth doing. But by around 1995, I started getting itchy feet. I wanted to do things (in soccer). So, the great thing about the pub business was that I had a lot of sports administrators and executives that used to come in as customers. Ron Barassi (Australian Rules Football legend) used to come in and I had quite a flow of Australian Football League (AFL) people and many were from Carlton Football Club. They started talking to me about the Carlton experience. That was a lightbulb moment and I subsequently put in a proposal to AFL clubs about doing this super club competition, where they were multisport clubs also offering soccer, basketball and swimming, like they have in Spain. I'm not saying I created the idea, but if you look at a sport, it was a way of getting soccer into the more professional arena and not having to compete with AFL or cricket. In fact, I persisted with the idea and spoke with Eddie McGuire (ex-Collingwood Football Club president and media personality) and people that he knows from his network. I actually recall that I said to Eddie that he should create a football (soccer) operation as Collingwood had a netball team at the time. Further, I told Eddie that he should go beyond AFL and bring a swim team, (and) an athletics team, because we were losing ground in the Olympic sports in Australia.

I also suggested to him, why not have a basketball team? The Greeks community here are crazy about basketball! And you don't know which sport is going to be popular at any given time. So that was the discussion that spawned my early ideas on the football (soccer) business.

I also enjoyed catching up with people like John Constantine and Tony Labozzetta (both former presidents and CEOs of Soccer Australia). In previous years it had been Sam Papasavvas (ex-South Melbourne Football Club president), before his untimely death. I would say to them, you've got to change the structure (of the NSL). I went to Canberra to study in the early days when the AIS started, and it was the first sports management and marketing course of its kind in Australia. There were three streams. There was sports marketing and business, there was journalism and there was sports science. I was one of the first graduates to come out of the sports marketing, along with Craig McClatchey, who was unfortunately injured within three months of coming out of the AIS football program. But Craig stuck to his studies and then ended up being head of Australian swimming. He was the CEO of the Australian Olympic Committee during the Sydney Games and has gone on to live in Switzerland.

On becoming Australia's first FIFA player's agent

I always kept contacts in football and Craig McClatchey (who was developing a strong C-suite career in sports business) kept taunting me to come back into sport. I used to attend most Olympic Games competitions and whilst in Barcelona and Atlanta, I continued meeting people.

For instance, one of my ex-teammates was (former Australian youth international) Ian Rowden. Ian became vice-president of Coca-Cola worldwide (and was one of the protagonists behind the Sydney Rovers A-League bid). When we went to the Atlanta Olympic Games, I visited him at this amazing mansion and he's now a big worldwide advertising executive. So, here I was dealing at that professional level, it was very sad every time you came to Australia and saw the amateurism. Back then the world game was steeped back in a somewhat mix of ethnic and other politics. Also, the host network *SBS TV* (Special Broadcasting Service), in my opinion, at the time just kept flip flopping on how they handled it (football).

The meetings with McClatchey and Rowden inspired me to pursue sports business in Australia. I wondered how I could participate in the game and make it more professional and successful. So, the obvious answer was to become an independent player agent.

No one's doing it (at the time). And I felt I could without influence from the clubs, federations and politics. So, I went ahead and did it. I contacted the NSL but I also went directly to FIFA and got all the required information.

And back then you had to have a comprehensive understanding of all the FIFA regulations. I passed the FIFA requirements for being an agent and then I provided a 250,000 Swiss franc bank guarantee to FIFA. That was in 1996. I was the first licensed FIFA agent in Australia, if not in Asia, at the time.

On George's agency role in setting up the Carlton Soccer Club

Simultaneously, there had been a bit of action going on with Carlton Football Club in the background in setting up Carlton Soccer Club. So, I spoke to Carlton Football Club about how we best work together. By this time, Lou Sticca has come on the Carlton scene via a different connection.

I'd never met Lou Sticca at the time. I'd never been involved in soccer administration circles. Being a player agent, I couldn't have a formal role with the club. So, we decided that Jack Riley would become the president of the new entity being Carlton Soccer Club. Lou would become the CEO and I'd be the consultant adviser. I would also be the player agent that was supporting the club and recruiting the players. At the time, it was also about recruiting Eddie Krncevic (ex-Australian international) as the coach.

We created a lean board that had to report to John Elliott (president of Carlton Football Club). That board had good people on it, like John Valmorbida, mainly AFL people that were not on the AFL board but saw this new venture as a stepping stone. Nike came in as apparel sponsor in a really big way. They were already getting involved in soccer, but they saw this as an amazing way to get involved in football and Carlton simultaneously. And it was good proof of what I was trying to say to these super AFL clubs, that you're going to get better bang for your buck if you can add more product. We had a sizeable budget, more than any other club in the NSL I believe. Parmalat (the Italian dairy giant) came on as sponsors. I recall they had a

Brazilian CEO in Australia, and they were buying out milk companies around the country. The timing was just right to get these big-name brands involved with the sport (football). We were able to run as a professional club (in Australia as Carlton Soccer Club), which I believe no one had ever done before.

On his focus as an agent in bringing talented Australian youth players to Carlton Soccer Club and South Melbourne FC

We put in a strong development program (at both clubs), with the idea being to develop players and then I would help market and transfer them (to bigger clubs, in particular (in) Europe).

Everything was done in a very professional way. I also brought in former NSL goalkeeper Jeff Olver. We ran the (youth) academy and then later years we transferred it to South Melbourne under another arrangement that I did with them. With Carlton Soccer Club, we made it to the grand final in the first year. Everything in agency and Carlton Soccer Club was all new at the time, but I think we were involved in ground-breaking pioneer stuff (with me as the club agent). I had a direct influence in developing and bringing in excellent young players like Vince Grella, Simon Colosimo and Mark Bresciano.

One of the other young talented players I was chasing as an agent to get him to Carlton was Brett Emerton (ex-Blackburn Rovers and Australian International). I had a lot of close communication and support from Ron Smith of the AIS and others telling me Brett was from a good family and that they would advise the family I was a good agent. I thought if we could get Brett Emerton in that Carlton team (as well with Colosimo, Grella and Bresciano), it would be a game-changer. As it subsequently happened, all four players were to be an integral part of the Socceroos in (the) Germany 2006 World Cup except for Simon Colosimo, who had a mishap with injury. As a passionate agent I fought so hard, and in the end, I was so disappointed not to sign Brett Emerton. I recall (maybe prematurely) I organised Brett a Nike endorsement contract because that was part of what I built up as my agent offering.

On the tension with both the AIS and VIS management about whether young talented players should stay with the Institutes or join clubs

Fortunately, I still had my connections at the Australian Institute of Sport (AIS) (as a former football graduate). Vince Grella was still with the AIS, as were Simon Colosimo, and Mark Bresciano. So, I was able to talk to the AIS coaches Ron Smith and Steve O'Connor about them coming to the clubs I worked with.

The Victorian Institute of Sport (VIS) football program was headed by Frank Pike. He developed and ran the sports marketing course I completed in Canberra previously. So, I knew Frank Pike very well. However, I had some issues down in Melbourne, Victoria with Ernie Merrick (head coach of VIS) because Vince Grella was a scholar with both the VIS and the AIS. I had verbal tussles with Ernie Merrick on the topic of when should (timing) VIS players join clubs. It's amusing because Ernie later became a top senior club coach. So, I was saying to Ernie Merrick and Frank Pike (and Ron Smith and Steve O'Connor) that these young players, if they're good enough, they shouldn't be with an Institute program — they should be with a club (Merrick's view at the time was polar opposite to mine on this issue).

During my time as a player, I trained with the AIS, but I was playing with South Melbourne, so I was commuting every week from Canberra and joining South Melbourne and playing and then going back to the AIS. In my view, the AIS and the VIS should have been a supporting layer. You should give scholarships to players but they should still be participating with their clubs. You can support them in a sport science way, in an education way (via the Institutes). However, Ernie was adamant that he wanted to keep these players at the VIS and eventually I had to (try and fight this policy) but ultimately it was the player's decision. We had this same issue with Kristian Sarkies (former South Melbourne and A-League player). Kristian, who we were trying to get across to a club, decided he was very loyal to Ernie, so he stuck with the VIS program.

I recall at the time that the VIS subsequently decided that they would take players into their program at a younger age. The idea was that Ernie Merrick would pick them at 14 years of age, and he would have them in a development program until they were 16. Then he may contact the AIS and say, these two, I think can go there. The idea was to develop more players. But I kept insisting that the Institute system was wrong because players needed to belong to clubs — they don't belong to institutions. In fact, my idea that I proposed at the time was for the Institutes to offer scholarships and the players can attend intensified camps. My idea also included putting a little AIS emblem on their playing shirt or team apparel to indicate AIS or VIS support in creating that player. In my opinion, talented players should be with clubs, and part of the role of the AIS should have been to help clubs build better development programs.

On his agency's endorsement offering being unique at the time
in the agent world

Whenever a player signed with me as an agent at MVP, they got access to our endorsement offering. I had documented a lot of our agency structure and had a business plan which focused on sponsorship and endorsement as one of our major pillars of the business. This endorsement suite offering through an agency was not all happening by accident (in fact, it was ahead of its time not just in Australia but internationally). So as soon as a player signed on with us, they immediately were introduced to Nike for sponsorship and inevitably Nike would agree with the player we put forward (most of the time). The trust we had with Nike led us to put the players on contracts that were performance-based.

Our model was players would receive a base level pay. But once you played 'X' number of games for the Socceroos and then went overseas, the idea was that Nike would follow their career. We'd also take the player who signed with my agency to the local Tag Heuer watch shop. The player chose a watch, there was a limited budget ceiling on which one they could choose when they joined the agency, but obviously as the player met their performance KPIs, they could get a more valuable watch.

On organising the FIFA All-Stars match at Sydney's new Olympic Stadium

I recall that a colleague informed me that the New South Wales government was looking for a major event to open the new Olympic Stadium in Sydney.

Apparently, there was interest from rugby league and AFL to hold an opening game (sports I enjoy). I thought in my head, "That's got to be bullshit." They're not even Olympic sports. I then created the idea/concept of getting a FIFA world team to come and play against Australia.

The interest in this idea grew exponentially. Graham Halbish, who had just finished up at the Australian Cricket Board, was having lunch with another good contact of mine from Ansett, (who were also Olympic Games sponsors). Both were aware of the NSW government interest.

I told Graham about my idea and before we knew it, we had formed a joint company. We then bid for the opening game event. By this time, I'd had a little bit of contact with FIFA through my player agency arrangements. Sepp Blatter's (former FIFA president) daughter (Corinne Blatter) was working in Sydney at the time and we spoke about the concept and she relayed it back to her father. Channel Seven came on board as a sponsor, as did Tag Heuer and Toohey's beer.

To undertake event management initiatives, you've got to be a businessperson or have that mindset. You've got to have strong networks to know what you're doing, and you've got to know how to piece people together. So, for one year in my agency, we focused on that event. It was around nine months before the Olympics.

We had to do a TV broadcast deal, sell the rights here and overseas and have the sponsorship deal sorted. We had to negotiate with FIFA to get the guest players. They promised us Ronaldo from Brazil and in the end, players were pulling out left, right and centre. We had issues with some in the media; calling us 'possible frauds' because the players we were advertising were not coming. However, despite these issues, the game went ahead.

We brought back the epic Australian band INXS to play after the death of Michael Hutchence. So that also drew massive international interest. The event also cemented my relationship with Soccer Australia at the time because we made them an official partner.

They (Soccer Australia) wanted tickets. They wanted corporate tables (boxes), they wanted to meet FIFA executives. Yet we wanted them to remain a little bit out of being the prime focus or garnering too much attention, as the NSL (National Soccer League) was struggling at that time in Australia.

On why talented young Australian players were in demand during George's agency career

As one of the earliest agents in Australia, I was starting to get divergence on player transfer strategies from clubs. I recall that with Brett Emerton, the reason he didn't sign with me as an agent was that Sydney Olympic decided to manage his future transfer. The player did belong to Olympic. But a club cannot solely manage a player transfer and give advice on an international transfer. This is not how it is done in agency.

In the meantime, I'm fielding off phone calls from overseas agents and clubs regarding Australia's talented players. Some of my players were ringing me saying, "So-and-so is calling me from overseas." They would say words to the effect that "he's (the agent has) got a representative in Portugal. I can go play for Porto." The players were suddenly getting anxious, they're 17 or 18 or 19 years of age, hardly played a season in the NSL, and already they're wanting to be world-beaters as agents in Europe are starting to call them. I am a big believer that players need to wait for the right opportunity. Similarly, some footballer's parents can be very, very naive. But when someone random in the agent's game rings a parent and says, "I don't know who your boy's agent is, but your boy should be playing for Liverpool, your boy should be doing this, I can arrange it, a parent thinks that's possible." This hurts us agents who have a plan and are trying to do the right thing. However, I realised at the time that we had issues with the way the whole agency thing worked due to these enticements by unregulated agents' elements and the mindset of some clubs, players and parents.

The Bosman decision had already come through at the time when I was an agent and everyone thought that these large transfer fees would disappear as players can (now) leave for free from a club at the end of their contract. Yet the trend at the time I was an agent was that transfer fees were only becoming bigger and bigger for currently contracted players.

On difficulties in the football agent space in Australia

Initially, I felt new to the agency game. I contacted Arthur Cox from Newcastle United (who I knew), who was the assistant coach to Kevin Keegan at Manchester City. He introduced me to this person and that person in the agent business and clubs. With my agency business, I tried to stay at the premium end of the market in terms of the clubs I was dealing with and that's how I got Simon Colosimo to Manchester City.

We had some very bad experiences with other players, because we sent them in good faith to partner agents in Europe. And those players, even though they had contracts with us, somewhat alienated the relationship. We created the contact, but the contact sometimes 'screwed' us over and I don't even think some of those agents were licensed.

So, in the early days of FIFA agents, the whole thing was a bit of a shambles (maybe because it was new). Worldwide, the licensing of agents was a mixed bag to a degree. And I saw things in the media with big English clubs in court against European agents as allegedly there were secret commissions getting paid. I did see it sometimes as a dirty part of the sport and agency at the time.

On the MVP Academy (Australia's first real elite academy outside of the AIS)

We were starting to work on an academy concept. Ange Postecoglou (coach at South Melbourne FC at the time) and George Vasilopoulos (president of South Melbourne FC) rang and were interested in what we were trying to achieve. Postecoglou had developed many players at South Melbourne.

He was successful. He had won Championships. He had done well with nowhere near the sort of budget that we had at Carlton Soccer Club. Postecoglou could see what we were putting together at the MVP agency — it really was some really good building blocks for player development and pathways. I met with Ange and George and despite the fact that Ange was leaving the club, they were interested in working together.

The plan was for me to have complete influence over all the playing wages, staff, who comes and goes, and developing players, not just buying them. That plan was to make the club transfer fee money in the long run. I felt MVP at the time had a good brand reputation (as well) — as we were the only ones providing a variety of services within the player agency space.

I brought back Jeff Olver and we chose Mickey Peterson as the coach. We brought Simon Colosimo to South Melbourne for a short stint and then we sold him to Manchester City.

We had a track record as an agency. With the help of my player agency, we got Carlton Soccer Club into the grand final in one season and lost to South Melbourne Soccer Club. Then with the assistance of my agency, we got South Melbourne to the grand final in one season and lost again. However, by this time, the NSL was starting to fail.

My role at every South Melbourne board meeting was to talk about the team activities and players and keep them informed, keep them positive. At the same time, we at MVP were funding the academy. We reversed the concept. We were now actually working for the club now, not just for the player. We could represent the player once they left, but we were actually helping the club develop and sell players. And we were going to share that commission with the club. (But) In the end, I was left out of pocket. Some clubs fell over in the NSL and the league collapsed as well.

On when young players should be playing senior football
to make it as a professional

They should be playing (for clubs) if you're a talented 16-year-old. I played for Australia when I was 17. In my view in Australia, if you're not playing at A-League level before you're 21-years-old, you're not going to make it overseas.

On current Australian player development

Parents of kids at age 12 and 14, thinking they are good enough to go overseas, is a problem. But this is what some agents nowadays will tell them. Sadly, they are just a number. I always look at the statistics. How many Australian players are overseas now? If you look at where they're playing now and how much game time they're getting and what they're earning, it ebbs and flows. However, it is difficult at the moment.

On investment in clubs and player development going forward

We lack investment in Australia. I used to think a lot about what has happened with Manchester City coming here (buying Melbourne Heart FC). I talked to Newcastle United (from the EPL) about investment in Australia with the people that I knew. I used to say to them, "maybe take an investment stake in a local Australian club and from that relationship, you can implant the sort of thing that the Manchester City (City Football Group) people are doing." However, with some of the financial losses in Australian football, it would be hard for clubs to accept these sorts of losses.

Alternatively, clubs should forget about the idea that selling one player pays for everything. We need to spend money and get the inside information on how Belgium suddenly became a great footballing country. I own a Belgian Beer Café in Melbourne, so I've spent a bit of time in Belgium and met the owners of Anderlecht and spoken to them. Their success has all come through development (Belgium is known for excellent youth academies). They stuck to a development program (we are seeing some recent green shoots of this approach from Central Coast Mariners and Adelaide United). Their clubs are not big, yet they have affiliations with super clubs.

Many great players in Italy and England have come through Belgium and the Netherlands. Ajax Amsterdam is probably what our clubs should be looking at as a model. They're a professional club, but they are never afraid of nurturing and selling, nurturing and selling. And they've always had a blueprint of how to develop a player.

Even the Manchester City people must have a blueprint on how to develop an Australian player. We need to document this, (and) put it on paper to understand the psyche of an Australian player and bring in Indigenous pathways, which I believe the game is missing. We should have a plan. It's not just about going up and doing a few camps. We as Australian football need a dedicated plan.

The plan should aim to have an Indigenous kid in the English Premier League by 2028.

On leaving the agent industry

It is a ruthless industry and that's maybe why I'm no longer in it. You don't want to have conflict in your day-to-day life.

You can be angry every other day as an agent (smiling). That's not good for your health, and particularly when you're fighting shadows; many of those illegal or fake (unlicensed) agents were shadows during my time. I didn't have their numbers.

I think I'm now more geared in my thinking to help the game. Whatever I was doing, whether it was player management or putting an event on, I was always thinking of the good of the Australian game.

We haven't produced that many great commentators. We haven't produced that many great journalists and don't always have a lot of dedicated journalists in the newspapers. Ray Gatt has sadly retired. If you don't have a voice in the media, you're doomed. Now, we have some media voices that are constantly condemning us. And the other thing we don't have is enough clout with government (until recently maybe).

There are too many things not spoken about that need addressing in the game and there isn't always enough intellect in the game here. From my observations, some of the youth coaching can be very mundane — just my opinion. I've heard from colleagues that the influence of all the Dutch coaches possibly destroyed a lot of the Australia youth development DNA. They didn't bring the success we wanted.

I think the difference between me and anybody else that's been a player, club consultant/academy manager or agent is that I've actually been all three. I have been the true professional with an education in the game. I'm one of the youngest players that's ever played for Australia.

I've never coached. It's the only thing I've never done. But I believe I know a lot about the game. I don't think I've got many antagonists around in the game. I don't know of anyone within the game that has any animosity towards me, because I've never done anything wrong as one of the first in the agent business.

Chapter 3:
The Youngest FIFA Agent
– Miro Gladovic

All Australian football fans talk about the 'Golden Generation' of Australian players of the late 1990s and 2000s, many who were playing with significant clubs in Europe. Who was looking after their affairs? Who were their agents? Were Australian agents involved or had the players linked up with European agents or football advisers?

I was then advised by a mutual agent colleague to speak to Miro Gladovic. I recall his name being on the Australian FIFA agent list back in 2006, but I had never met him. He was a frequent flyer to Europe and has lived in the United States for the past 15 years. Miro is now working under the umbrella of his Marasava media and consulting business, which is named after his mother Mara and father Sava.

Miro left his mark on the Australian football agent space. In 1997, he became one of the youngest agents in the world to be accredited by FIFA. At the peak of his activity in Europe, in addition to scouting international talent and consulting, Miro represented 30 professional players from all over the world. Many of his clients were national team players from Croatia, Australia and Germany who played in the FIFA World Cups of 1998, 2002, 2006 and 2010. Having been based for significant periods of time in Europe, Miro understood what type of players were in demand in the top European leagues. Miro has said that "football is such a subjective sport, and while there is data which helps evaluate performance, most nations and clubs base their evaluations on the style of play."[41] He made a great living as a FIFA agent and was always realistic about the waters he navigated as an Australian in the European club landscape. Miro played in the Victorian Premier League in his early twenties and ended up at Heidelberg United under coach Michael Urukalo.

Background

Miro was a risk-taker in his efforts to become a leading Australian (and even European) agent. He put his family's home on the line to obtain funding to take on the European markets and invest time and work for his players. His hard-working father invested in him by covering his FIFA agent bank guarantee and insurance in the late 1990s. Miro's father was a silent financial partner in Miro's successful sports management agency, Mondial Sports Australia Ltd. As one of the significant early Australian agents, Miro would see the high point of players being in demand around the time that Australia's national team qualified for the 2006 World Cup. During that period, Miro had also dealings with the English Premier League and German Bundesliga scene, which included representing three members of the winning 2001 European Champions League team, Bayer Leverkusen.

Additionally, Miro was working in Australia at a time where there were hundreds of talented NSL players coming through the ranks and just two FIFA agents, George Christopoulos and Miro himself. It's ironic that Miro became Australia's second Australian FIFA agent on the weekend of the infamous 2–2 World Cup qualifying draw with Iran at the Melbourne Cricket Ground (MCG) in 1997. Miro's focus as an agent was on representing very good Australian players at their peak and getting them into good European clubs to build their careers. He represented many Australian players including Josip Simunic, Frank Juric, Ivan Ergic, Ljubo Milicevic, Goran Lozanovski, Peter Buljan, Mark Silic, Fausto De Amicis, Dean Anastasiadis and Anthony Magnacca.

In his own words

On opening doors for Australian players

I was indirectly involved with many Australian players being exported and moving clubs, including Mark Viduka, Brett Emerton and Jason Culina. When I started marketing Aussie players in 1996 to European clubs, I was ridiculed, dismissed and berated for wasting people's time. One major European club scout told me on day one, "Miro, when you talk about Australian players to teams in Europe, you must understand you may as well be talking about a player from Luxembourg." That was 1997 and Australia had not qualified for the World Cup since West Germany in 1974. We were considered a joke to European teams. Ironic, since the next ten-year period would yield the best ever stable of Aussie talent. I was the one that opened the door to Mark Viduka at Celtic via my involvement with him at Dinamo Zagreb, and I was scouting for Manchester City who were a second-tier Championship team at that time. They had a scouting association with Glasgow Celtic and that is how the club found out about Mark, via my work and a videotape (that) I spent $2,000 editing.

On Miro's relationship with Ange Postecoglou and South Melbourne FC

I worked closely with Ange Postecoglou for many years when he was coach of South Melbourne. When South Melbourne Hellas/Lakers won their back-to-back NSL Championships and went to the FIFA Club World Championship, I represented 8 of their starting 11 players. On my watch, South Melbourne never lost a player during contract negotiations between Ange and I, including when Steve Iosifides was offered a lucrative contract to go to Perth Glory and he opted to stay with South Melbourne. A funny footnote to my link with Ange is that when he first became assistant coach to Frank Arok, I was still playing with Heidelberg United. I attended an open tryout at South Melbourne Hellas conducted by Frank and Ange, and I killed it, made some incredible saves and Ange came up to me after the session and got my details. Frank was brutal at culling candidates and yelled out to me "How old are you?"

I replied, "23". He barked back, "Too bad, you are 5 years too old," and that was the end of that.

Ange thanked me for my effort afterwards and apologised for Frank's somewhat ruthless handling of the situation (but this is the reality of trials).

On entering the agent business and the use of (VHS) videotapes at the time

I was best friends with Frank Juric who was the goalkeeper for Melbourne Knights and he was going to the Atlanta 1996 Olympics. After I stopped playing, I wanted to be in marketing. I wanted to be in soccer. I took it upon myself to start ordering video cassettes from *SBS* in Sydney and putting together highlight reels. I told Frank that by the time he got to the Olympics, I wanted everyone in Europe to know about him.

The Olympic team didn't do so well. They had a great squad, they had Mark Viduka there. Viduka did that back heel against Saudi Arabia, but they didn't make it to the second round. Frank didn't get any offers but I did arrange a tryout at St Pauli in Hamburg, Germany and Frank said, "You're coming with me." I think by then he was playing for Collingwood Warriors Soccer Club.

So, we've got a trial in St. Pauli and Frank and I flew there. It was 1996 and the film *Jerry Maguire* had just been released. I hadn't even thought about being a FIFA agent. I remember we took the Qantas flight from Melbourne to Singapore together. And back in the day, there was only one in-flight movie. It was *Jerry Maguire*. When we arrived in Hamburg, I discovered that the agent, Jurgen Milewski, who had set all this up, actually he may have had an ulterior (but cheeky) motive. He wanted Joe Simunic.

By then I was helping out Joe and making these videotapes for him. Jurgen basically said, "Look, if you give me Joe Simunic, I'll get Frank Juric on a team." Frank was still not ready for Germany at the time. I went back to Australia and Joe is laid up with a fractured foot. It was like a soap opera. It took six to nine months before Frank signed his deal. He ended up going to Fortuna Dusseldorf. I basically took over as Joe's agent and he signed with Carlton Soccer Club. The general manager of Hamburg SV flew to Melbourne. There were many meetings behind closed doors and then Joe Simunic got his wish. He was transferred after we forfeited the Carlton deal.

He hadn't even kicked a ball for Carlton and then he was off to Hamburg. I got him the deal at Hamburg. I made some decent money on both transfers and I wasn't even an agent. Jurgen Milewski paid me for bringing the players and I thought, "Yeah, I'm going to do this," and I applied for my FIFA licence.

I sat my exam with the late Peter Russell who was the technical director of Soccer Australia and two other board members. I was approved that weekend. However, I didn't receive my accreditation for another seven months because nobody at several banks knew how to set up a bank guarantee for 250,000 Swiss francs with FIFA.

On presenting Australian players to European clubs

Once accredited, I went and lived with Frank Juric in Dusseldorf, Germany, and expanded my roster of players, promoting Australian players in Europe. It was the most difficult thing you could ever undertake.

As soon as they found out that players were from Australia, we were treated like an anecdote. I presented Goran Lozanovski and to this day I think he's a better crosser of the ball than David Beckham, but negotiations always stalled based on where he was from. Goran could pinpoint a guy 30 or 40 metres away and deliver the ball onto his forehead. But the fact that he was Australian played against him. That was the biggest challenge.

I'll never forget one of my first meetings with a scout in Borussia Monchengladbach. He said, "Miro, I love your players. They look great on tape. But you have got to understand that when you present a player in Germany or in Europe, we're going to look at these players like players from small leagues.

I said, "I'll fly them in, give them a place to stay, and I'll prove you wrong." I started paying for airfares, which was ludicrous and unsustainable.

For the players I represented in Australia, I never took a commission. At one stage I had about 25 Australian players for whom I did all their domestic contracts. I never took a cent off any of them.

*On how (in the past) Australian clubs did not know how to deal
with the emerging agent profession*

I got to know Branko Culina and he said, "Miro, you've got to get my son (Jason Culina) overseas. He doesn't belong in Australia." Jason was young, 17 and by then I had contacts in every country and partnerships with agencies. After I'd done the deals for Joe and Frank, I had some money and some credibility.

I worked with a Dutch agency and they knew about Jason. We started going back and forth and there was interest there from Ajax. And so, it looked like there's going to be an invite going for him. I told Branko, "I'd like to get something in place with Sydney Olympic to get my percentage." He said, "Miro, they're not going to go for that. You know how (some) people are, you really don't want to deal with those guys. They're very stubborn. They're (maybe) not going to want to pay an agent." I managed to convince Sydney Olympic.

Eventually, the transfer went through. The Dutch guys paid me 13,000 Dutch guilders which is about $10,000 Australian. It was my first lesson in terms of playing poker with club officials to get a deal done.

On there being no precedent to undertake the agent business

I remember going to Europe in my first year or two, with the videos of about a dozen players. My pitch was, "Listen, I don't want anything from you. I want to sell players. So, it was easy to get them on board, but it was not like I ever made money off those guys. They were a drain. By the time I had 15 players, they were costing me tens of thousands of dollars to fly them, to promote them, to spend nights calling coaches and negotiating. But it was the clients that were already established overseas, like Joe (Simunic) and Frank (Juric), that were paying six figures. I used them as a tax write-off and increased my stable. It was hard getting players because I was often their similar age and I was not a former player that had made it big in the NSL. It was harder in that regard, but I had almost no competition.

On Miro's dealings with Mark Viduka

I knew Mark Viduka from Australia, but reconnected with him in Zagreb and asked him if he would think about playing in Europe. He was very guarded. I spent two months working on a video showing every single one of his goals and pumped that out all over Europe. One of the places I sent it was Manchester City, who called saying, "Listen, we don't think he is ready for England, but we have a sister club agreement with Celtic." I believe that Bernie Mandic and his agent team negotiated the deal of Mark signing at Celtic.

On talent identification and recruitment of players to Miro's agency portfolio

Two things really forged my Mondial Sports Australia agency. The first was access to the Melbourne Knights and South Melbourne FC Hellas teams. The other was my cousin Vilson Knezevic (an ex-goalkeeper) who became my scout in Australia. He connected me with so many players. I would send him to the AIS in Canberra and he'd come back and say this guy, this guy, this guy, and then I'd watch them. He had a great eye for talent.

The first two players that he sent my way were Ivan Ergic and Ljubo Miličević. He actually came to my house and said, "Give me two contracts. I'm going to give you their signatures." I'd never even seen them play. I gave him two contracts. He gave me two signatures. I went to Canberra and I sat down with both of them when they were 16 and had a great rapport with both.

On a promising player career and helping to get a deal for Ivan Ergic [42] (rated as Australia's potential Zinedine Zidane at the time)

By the time both players left the academy, I took Ivan Ergic when he was 17 to Perth Glory. I got him ballpark $95,000 a year. I got Ljubo to the same club because they were best friends and that was actually the start of one of the most incredible sagas that I've experienced as an agent.

In 2001, I flew to Berlin to renegotiate Joe Simunic's contract extension. By then, Ergic was just killing it in Perth. In my suitcase was a videotape of Ergic and I'd already sent it to the scouts. I was very tight with Jurgen Rober, the head coach of Hertha Berlin and Dieter Hoenes, Hertha's CEO at the time.

After arriving, I literally went from the airport to the Hertha Berlin boardroom. They watched his video and they said, "Miro, we want him."

Ergic had one more year with Perth Glory and I got to know his father. By April, the Germans came to Australia to do the deal. Two months before the end of my representation of him, Ivan started pushing back a little from me. Ivan was quite shy. I was like his best friend, his mentor. I spent time with him at the Institute and I noticed he just pulled back. Then he stopped really talking to me and I finally called him to ask what was going on.

He said, "Miro, I'm sorry, but my father he's taken over my management (this happens a lot in player agency with successful players). So, the last two months of our contract is going to be the last two months you're representing me." I said, "Ivan, I don't agree with that. I've got your best interests at heart. I begged him to stay in contact."

I recall that Ivan also had a new agent from Germany. The interesting thing about Hertha Berlin was that shortly after the fall of the Berlin Wall, a lot of East German players, agents and officials gained access to West German soccer. One of those agents represented multiple players at Hertha Berlin at the time and got wind of the talent of Ivan Ergic. I knew at the time that he flew to Australia to sit down with the East German coach of Perth Glory. I recall that I was told by one of my Perth contacts, they went to Ivan's house, and had dinner with his parents and I believe (from anecdotes that came back to me) the agent said something to the effect of, "You may need to change agents." That's exactly what happened. My contract with Ivan was not renewed.

There is a footnote to the story because when Ivan played in a game at Subiaco Oval, Perth, in front of 40,000 people, he lit it up. He took the ball from end one to the other, dribbled past everyone and scored. Hertha coach Jurgen Rober had flown in, resigned to the fact that I was not doing the deal.

We sat down in Perth and he said to me, "Miro, I'm going to look you in the face and tell you one thing. I'm here to sign the player. It's not my responsibility to pick the agent. I'm not going to do the deal. I'm not going to negotiate. I'm here to say yay or nay."

I said, "Jurgen, I respect you for that."

I'd told Ivan that I would work as his agent until the last day. I contacted a Swiss agent, who I won't name, who was connected with Juventus. He said, "We'll get him a deal in Serie A."

I said to Ivan, "Will you at least explore other options that I will facilitate for you?"

Those options were used as leverage (players who have several clubs interested in them get better club contract).

The Swiss agent was coming to Perth with another key scout from Africa, I believe. I met with them in Perth. I stayed there for the week on my own dollar and I went to the game. Jurgen said, "We're signing him. I'm sorry Miro. You're not under commission, not because of me."

They didn't know that I was there with the Swiss-African agent/scout contingent and I have the Serie A connection. We went to the game because they wanted to see if Ivan was good enough to go to Serie A or the Swiss league. He tears it up. Man of the match. They win and then the African scout says, "Miro, we need to speak to him."

I said, "His father is in control or the new agent and I don't have access to the father."

I recall that it as maybe Ljubo Milicevic who told me that Ivan would be at this nightclub in Subiaco, Perth. So, I went there with the African scout and Ivan was there. Monday morning, the whole family were on a business class flight to Europe.

I was told that the Swiss-African agent/scout contingent had turned up to the family house with four business-class tickets and an invitation from the general manager of Juventus. If they went to Germany first, the offer was rescinded. I had Hertha Berlin calling me the next day, the CEO saying, "Miro, I'm sorry, where is Ivan? Bring me Ivan. The commission's yours."

I said, "Ivan's gone, there is no Ivan."

Ivan signed the contract with new management. His father and maybe another agent took over his management. I recall (that) Ivan gave me one call after that. He said, "Miro, I just want to thank you and apologise for the way this has turned out. I can't pay you now. But you know, down the line, how about we talk? Is that okay?" I never really heard from Ivan again (I always respect Ivan as he was a rare prodigious playing talent).

I went to see the agent, the Swiss agent, six months later when I was in Europe. We had lunch at a nice restaurant in his hometown in Switzerland. He said, "We're going to give you a commission Miro, how's 10,000 Swiss francs?" I said, "You've got to be kidding me, that was a $4 million transfer." He said, "Take it or leave it." I left it.

On the Australian Institute of Sport's (AIS) football program

I hope someone does a book on the AIS, because it was absolutely one of the most incredible developmental factories of talent that I've ever seen. Just look at those classes of Viduka and Ergic. I think they were a generation ahead of their time. I don't know why they closed it down. That was one of the greatest production talent lines and I think it's a reflection of why Australia is really struggling to mirror that era. Why would they even tamper with something that was so successful?

On the reality of the day-in, day-out, 24/7 international agent business

When I first moved here, people would ask me if my life was like *Jerry Maguire*. I was one of the first. I started with one client and the film is just like my years between 1996 and 2006 when I was primarily based in Germany. I'd fly all over Europe and I've calculated that I have spent over 320 days in a year on Qantas aircraft. I did the kangaroo route from Melbourne to London or Melbourne to

Frankfurt about 150 times.

The question that people always ask is why would you get out of a job like that? Simply, I ran out of areas for stab wounds in my back. The problem with the international transfer system is that you're selling invisible real estate. You have two real estate brokers on each side that set the fee and then distribute the funds any way they want.

On getting out of the agent business and moving to the United States

I always knew that life as a FIFA agent was limited. I got to the stage where I started interacting with a lot of the big clubs and doing some major deals. I was sick of flying from Australia to Europe and needed to move there and immerse myself in not only the location but also the culture.

I funnelled a big deal that I did into property in Australia and was able to shrink the stable of my players down. I still planned to do the agency, but just two or three clients like George Christopoulos. I had gotten to the stage where I was financially secure.

I wanted to be connected. I wanted to have my businesses, but not for it to be my sole focus. I ended up getting divorced and I happened to be in the United States while it happened. I always wanted to explore consulting, marketing and media. I came to Los Angeles, lived there for 10 years and I now work with a number of European teams as a consultant. The United States is a melting pot of different sports and European teams are all clamouring to get in. They think that the United States is like China and that they have open arms, but it's not. Real Madrid came in the late '90s, opened an office and then packed up shop and went back to Europe. The USA is a showcase when it comes to sports and people were asking, "Real who?"

I created a niche where I worked with Bayern Munich for a couple of years. I helped them set up their office (in the United States), I also worked with FC Barcelona and a couple of other teams.

I am obsessed with internationalisation and because I have the global perspective of having been born and raised in Australia, lived in Europe, partly raised in Croatia and lived in the United States, the concept is easy for me.

Chapter 4:
Crafting the Deal –
Paddy Dominguez

Every Australian football fan and pundit had an opinion on Aaron Mooy — which club was he going to transfer to from Melbourne City? Was it the English Premier League, was it the Dutch Eredivisie or Belgium Pro League? What about Italy's Serie A? The agent who had carriage of the Mooy move was Paddy Dominguez; Irish, Spanish and Australian. Understated, problem-solver, silent achiever, he was best placed to direct Mooy's next move.

With 31 years' experience in the United Kingdom, Europe and American sports scenes, and having completed 15 English Premier League deals, Paddy is his own man and an agent influencer who prefers to stay under the radar. In Paddy's view, Australia is an export market where most young Australian players want to go to Europe and a lot of good international players want to come to Australia for the lifestyle, good schools and quality city and regional environments.

Not afraid to take on the big agents in Europe nor the club chairperson or executives who can be quite assertive, Paddy does not accept interference or disloyalty. He also ensures that no value is left on the negotiating table for his clients in a market where many player salaries have grown in the big 5 leagues in the world (i.e., from 5,000 pounds a week to some players getting 600,000 pounds a week). Paddy believes that a good agent determines a base salary to start a negotiation for their player — as no agent on the planet will determine or lock in a ceiling for the player.

He is always willing to provide colleagues and new agents with advice and mentorship. Paddy was pivotal in setting up the new Professional Football Agents

Association (PROFAA) because he wants to lift standards, professionalise the industry and improve its reputation.

Background

Paddy is disciplined and humble. He is not press-hungry; however he can open doors that most agents cannot. In an interview with Aidan Ormond in June 2020, he summarised the hard work that agents must undertake. "Transfers represent the culmination of all the work that intermediaries/agents do during the other nine months of the year, which largely goes unseen. Agents live through the ups and downs that their clients experience, and this takes a toll on the intermediaries/agents too, as they are the first people blamed."

The requirements of agency mean that agents "are traveling, maintaining and building networks/contacts, spending weekends away from family at football games, scouting and tackling any ongoing issues that their clients may have, either personal or professional, on a daily, weekly or monthly basis."[43]

On any given day, Paddy would deal with emails and then invariably track his mobile phone, as a pile of messages come in from overseas overnight. Those long hours are worth it, as every time Paddy sees a client realise their ambition and dream, it is a special moment for him. Paddy says "That is why I do what I do. Nothing else in my book can replace that feeling."[44]

In relation to the Mooy deal, Dominguez revealed that the initial reaction he got from many people when he orchestrated the star midfielder's contract with Huddersfield Town was that he had done him a massive disservice,[45] and he was met with some criticism in Australia at the time. Mooy signed a three-year deal with Manchester City in June 2016 but was loaned out to Huddersfield in July, where he thrived. Paddy balanced the deal by considering that Huddersfield coach David Wagner had success in producing teams which were full of amazing, very high-quality midfielders. Brian Marwood, football director of Manchester City, held a private view at the time that Huddersfield would be a good place for Mooy.[46]

The move to Huddersfield exemplified Paddy's experience, planning and strategising, as there are a lot of moving parts in a football transfer.

In an interview with Adam Peacock of the *Fox Football* podcast,[47] Paddy explained that good agents work within windows — both the proactive transfer window (European summer or Australian winter) and the reactive transfer window (the month of January) where clubs have a chance to reset loan deals or sign a few new impact players. For Paddy, agency is about working within different transfer window constellations to plan and shape things to your player's favour.

In his own words

On starting in football player agency

It started out in the early '90s. As a kid, I was always massively involved in sports. I played pretty much every single sport I could. People of my era grew up in a time when there weren't any computer games, so everything really revolved around (the) outdoors. We were often driven out to play football, tennis, basketball, (and) anything that we could do to fill our time. So, the love of sport has always been there, whether it's just by default. But in my case, it just was a passion. When I left school, my intention was to get my coaching badges. In those days, coaching badges were designed for former players that played professionally or got to a high level. So, it was very strange, I think, for the governing bodies, when a young 20-year-old walked in wanting to become a coach and get the top qualifications. I think they fully anticipated that I would try, but I wouldn't get too far. However, I moved through the levels very, very quickly to the point where when it came to the absolute top qualifications, I felt like they were trying to find reasons to not allow me to gain them. I don't think they could have a 22-year-old with a UEFA licence qualified the same as an international coach. However, they were very fair, so I managed to get those qualifications.

My aim was to go into coaching and that was how I intended to marry my passion for sports with a future. I continued to do football coaching badges and also got into rugby union, which at that time was an amateur sport. I realised looking around that there were stadiums with 75,000 people in them and (I) felt like 'the sport they play in heaven' (rugby union's slogan) must turn professional.

There was no way It could continue to be amateur with that level of interest, the numbers, the commercial aspects of it. So, I decided to set up an agency. I didn't know anything about it and a US-based player, which is not the strongest country in rugby union, contacted me. He asked me if I would manage him. I told him I was thinking about it at the time, but I didn't know anything about management. He basically said, "just give it a go."

He sent me his physical statistics, which were off the charts. There wasn't a rugby union player on the planet that had the same stats as him. I rang him back in the United States and told him that they had better be correct because they will ask him to bench press the same weight. He became the very first professional rugby player and signed for a club in England. He was a superstar. There weren't any other agents, so when everybody saw the result, I got loads of phone calls from rugby union players.

I signed up hundreds of players very quickly because there just wasn't anybody else. That was the start of my sports management career. From there, after a couple of years, rugby union did become professional and then I got to know many other people in many other sports. Football was a passion of mine as a kid growing up. That's what we played on the streets. Soon after, I got to know a lot of people in football.

I applied some of the things occurring in rugby union, a sort of cross-pollination from a management perspective. It was a bit Wild West in the '90s in terms of football because money was starting to flood in with the advent of the English Premier League. Suddenly, guys started to earn huge amounts of money and that brought loads of people out of the wardrobe. I was very fortunate. If that very first player had turned out to be no good or had lied on his CV, I might not be here today doing what I'm doing.

On the early years in the agent industry

As an industry, sports management is fairly new. It's not even close to most of the other industries that people go into or study at university. So, it's probably still evolving. The very first visual that people had of a football agent was probably not the best representation of what a modern professional football agent looks like. The big fur coat, the big cigar sitting in the back of a Bentley, talking about millions of dollars that you've made and how you control the football world. Things have changed in the modern world and that is very far from accurate these days.

On moving to Australia (a sporting utopia)

Until I arrived in Australia in 2000, my work was European based. I moved here because I was intrigued about Australia. I'd managed Wallabies (Australian national team players in rugby union) and seen the interaction of Australian footballers in Europe. I'd learned a lot about Australia from a sporting perspective. It's a very sporting nation. So, it wasn't really a challenge to come here.

It was quite exciting because it was a sporting utopia and I was keen to learn a lot about it. I wasn't disappointed when I arrived. I didn't think the actual football league was doing well, particularly after I went down to watch a game featuring the old Parramatta Power of the NSL.

I think they were playing the team coming last at the time. I came away thinking, "Oh my God, this is the top level of football here?" That really inspired me to maintain my European connections.

The 2003 Crawford Report[48] gave a lot of optimism. People in football hoped that something bigger and better was going to come, which it obviously did in turn with the creation of the A-League.

With all the talk about the A-League, it was an exciting time to wait and see how that would evolve as the new top level of professional football. It often gets criticised, but when you're creating something brand new, sometimes there are certain elements of it that are going to be challenging and other things you are going to discover on the way to building something special. We're here now,15 years later, with a league that's visible on TV and a high-definition broadcast that's visible around the world. It's played in good stadiums.

Is it perfect? No, but again, it's only 15 plus years' young. It's still evolving.

On Paddy's day-to-day work in agency with its characteristic international dimension

I'm very fortunate that I don't actually sleep a lot, so that allows me to deal in multiple territories. I get up early, (and the) first thing I do is check my emails. I prioritise them and put a list together, then I'll check my mobile phone. There's a whole pile of messages that will come in from overseas and it virtually takes until lunch time before you've even spoken to somebody in Australia and done anything.

In the afternoon, I generally tend to focus on everything in Australia. Returning phone calls, speaking to clients and anything that's Australia related will take up most of the afternoon. By the time it gets to early evening, a lot of the Europeans are up and about.

Up until about 2 a.m.–3 a.m., it is phone calls to Europe, Asia and the USA. America is normally last because timewise, that's when they're getting up, I can give them an hour or two of their morning and that's it.

It's pretty full on.

On talent identification

When I look at a player, my criteria is whether I believe he can play for Australia, for the men's senior team. That's what I'm looking for.

What I look for when I scout a young player is football intelligence. It's an area where I differ from a lot of the coaches. A kid who has a football brain and understands space and movements etc., has been hard wired that way. If he also has the right attitude and the right work ethic, then that's the complete set for me.

I'm not looking for the things in a footballer that we can add. I'm looking for the stuff that he or she has naturally.

When Aaron Mooy was playing for youth teams, you would see him roll the ball into space for a winger to run onto, but the winger actually wouldn't make the run. The ball would just roll into space and the full-back would take possession as people on the sideline screamed bloody murder. And I'm looking at it, thinking, no, he's actually doing what we want him to do.

It's the winger who has checked his run that made it look like Mooy has just turned the ball over casually. But actually, he has put the ball in exactly the spot that an English, French, Spanish or Italian coach would instruct him to.

So, he's not actually wrong. It's the other guy that's wrong. That's part of my frustration.

On Lucas Neill and other players

Lucas was always a fantastic footballer. Very clever. One of the best passing centre-backs in the English Premier League. And that's actually statistically, (it's) not an opinion, at one point during the South Africa World Cup, he had completed more passes than any other defender in previous tournaments.

He was right and left-footed and his accuracy was amazing. When you see guys captaining their country at a FIFA World Cup, just the fact that you're associated with that person and helping them to achieve their goals is amazing.

Of course, you take great pride. It's almost like reflected glory. The glory is theirs. I mean, they're the ones on the pitch having to do the work, and they're the ones day-in, day-out training. But you also take a great sense of pride.

When you have to support them the most is during those dark, cloudy days. And that's the time when you have to constantly try and talk to them, try and build up their confidence, their optimism. You live that journey with them through the ups and downs.

When they have issues, they'll come and speak to you. I was chatting earlier today to Brett Holman. Every time I speak to Brett, I can only picture that goal in South Africa that he scored. A lad who started at the Parramatta Power (of the NSL), (was now) in South Africa and scoring a great goal in the World Cup.

It's a privilege that the players give to you as an agent. A part of that journey with them. Their success just means you can breathe a big sigh of relief and say, "Job done." That's actually a huge part of being an agent. If I was an accountant and went to work Monday to Friday, nine to five, I may make more money, but I would never get that sense of satisfaction of being involved in a player's journey and seeing him step onto a pitch in front of 1 billion people viewing on TV worldwide.

On dealing with European clubs, including in the English Premier League

I live in Sydney, Australia, but in a normal year, (I) would spend up to five months in Europe traveling. I get to meet the European club representatives and agents face to face, not just as the voice on the phone or on the end of an email. I get to meet a lot of them frequently. I don't know if they regard me purely as an Australian agent.

It may sound clichéd, but I deal with everybody the same whether it's a Premier League club or an A-League club. I deal respectfully and honestly with them. Sometimes they don't appreciate the honesty. Sometimes they do. But my goal when I speak to a club is to represent my clients and to represent them well, to be professional, articulate on their behalf and to debate when it's needed.

You can rationalise with them very well. They basically know what they want so it's easy for them to decide quite quickly. Budgets are not normally an issue for them. So, generally speaking, the budget conversation is eradicated when you're dealing with a Premier League team.

It just comes down to trying to get them to offer your client a contract. What that looks like is down to the agents. Only eleven players will start every weekend for each of those teams. You just have to be careful that your player doesn't become a sidebar to the whole show.

You have to pick the right places for your player. So strategically. Huddersfield was very much part of our strategy for Aaron, the same with Mile Jedinak when we got him to Crystal Palace. Crystal Palace were one of the favourites to become an English Premier League team at the time, so a bit like Aaron, Mile could learn the English game there. It's a very tough league (the Championship) and you can grow into the English Premier League and be battle ready that way.

Strategically, you're not best off to go directly to the English Premier League. Riley McGree is in the English Championship, so that will do him very well and he'll probably be ready (in due course) for the Premier League in the future.

The English Football Association is extremely professional and the framework that surrounds a transfer into the Premier League is very, very well built. There are nuances as an agent, and some visibility certainly helps when creating a Premier League contract.

Essentially, you understand what you're dealing with, where the slightly flexible parts of a contract are because, again, they operate with a relatively standard contract space, like most leagues around the world do now. But in terms of the player and his bonuses and the entitlements, that's all negotiable.

So, if you don't have experience in what you can and can't negotiate, that's the sort of grey area in which some agents fall down.

On the cultural nuances or strategies in representing
players in various countries

I don't want to mention any particular country, but some football associations are not as well run as the English FA and the framework around the clubs is not quite solid. That has a trickle-down effect. The clubs are not so professional. Some territories don't have a standardised contract.

There are a lot of horror stories and agents don't get paid or contracts are not respected. So, everybody ends up having to go to the dispute resolution chamber at FIFA. That rarely happens in the Premier League, it doesn't even get passed to FIFA because it's so well structured. Dealing with countries outside the top five leagues where it's very, very professional, you just have to be cautious.

There are still some territories that are a little bit frontier town-like in the way they deal with transfers. There's not much respect. Sometimes it comes down to constitutional law. They kind of just know that their courts will back them no matter what, so they don't need to respect the legitimacy of a contract. Sometimes it's just salubrious in how they behave because they know a player won't go to a court in a certain country and spend two years chasing a situation.

On the recent trend where it's become harder to get Australian players
into the bigger European leagues

People often refer to the past and the Golden Generation and how many Australians were playing in top leagues in Europe, and there's two factors involved. One of those is that that period produced very good, high-quality players.

Denmark has seen the same, Greece won the European Championship in 2004, but it doesn't mean that is always going to continue (developing 'golden generations' or a talented, one-off group of players).

The trick is to learn what we've done with those players and try to implement that, but it won't guarantee you that you will produce more Tim Cahills, Lucas Neills, Mark Vidukas etc. I think in general terms, certainly in European leagues, the A-League is somewhat respected, but it's not at the top of the food chain. So, I think it's particularly difficult for Australian players because the perception is that they're still building the A-League. It's not totally disregarded, but it's not yet at the forefront in terms of reputation.

That impacts Australian players. Back when the Golden Generation was being developed in 2000, we didn't have things like Hudl or Wyscout, we didn't have the technology that we have 20 years later. It's very, very easy now for

THE STORIES OF AUSTRALIAN FOOTBALL AGENTS

scouting departments in Europe to look at a player from anywhere. They can now sit there without sending a scout or talking to anyone on the phone and watch a player in say, Angola.

They can watch a kid improve, like in Australia. So, you're up against a far bigger market now. Now everyone's on the radar because we have all the tools to be able to watch them from anywhere in the world and see footage of them and be able to make a decision. They can even talk to them on Zoom. That builds networks and relationships now as well. And the scouting networks are vast, and they have relationships with people in every country.

It's just an organically built competition level that is far more challenging numerically for Australian players compared to what they faced 20 years ago. One of the bonuses for Australian players is their English language.

There's a lack of patience among some young Australian players that want to play in Europe before they're ready. They don't understand the damage it can do to you if you are not prepared for it.

People remind me that Lucas Neill went at 17 to England and Tim Cahill the same age, John Aloisi at 16, and even Aaron Mooy and Jamie Maclaren at 16 and 15. But nowadays, it's a little bit different and there's a lot more competition. And when you actually arrive there, you have to be prepared to make it happen. You don't get a second chance at a first impression.

So, I prefer to make sure players are fully prepared before they go there to make sure they stay.

On dealing with difficult players and coaches

Generally speaking, if you find that you can't work together, you should probably try and find an amicable solution, shake hands and part ways in a harmonious manner. That's the only advice I can give anybody. There are unfortunate times when these things end up in the courts.

If you feel you can't work with someone, then don't get into it just for the sake of money, don't just do it for the sake of it. Because if it doesn't work out, you'll regret it. Working with likeminded people in agency usually produces a good outcome.

On dealing with difficult agents

I always take a collaborative approach to things. I have no problem working with other agents. It's like any industry in the world, any profession. You get to learn the types of people or signals that tell you that an agent might not be somebody that you should work with. But I work collaboratively with many agents. We can have two parties, sometimes three parties in a deal. And over time, you build strong relationships.

You get to know each other. You get to know how you're going to work and organically build a network that you trust. But dealing with those agents that are not reputable can be very challenging.

It's a sensible business approach, if nothing else. I don't think being an individual and adopting a siege mentality is going to grow your business. Dealing with other people is representing your client's best interests. And I frequently speak to agents about my clients in doing deals that benefit them. It's part of your job to deal with other agents. What you have to do though is work with the agents that you know can get the job done and who are reputable.

On the future of the player agent industry in Australia and overseas

I think obviously it will come back into a much more regulated format. I hope it will be a sensible regulatory framework that we'll be working in. What I hope is that it will professionalise our industry a lot more. Secondly, the reputational capital of agents is important, and I hope it will seriously improve because I don't know that we benefit from a good image and a good reputation all the time.

I hope that through a more transparent and regulated professional framework, we'll be able to address those issues and people will see us as proper professionals who operate correctly.

The Wild West approach is gone. We need to adhere to regulations, otherwise it will prevent us from being proper footballing stakeholders.

On what keeps Paddy up at night

Everything keeps me up at night.

There's always something. There's always a player who's got a situation going on. It can be an issue between him and his club, (or) an issue between the player and his coach that maybe you can feel is starting to come to a head.

Sometimes it can even be domestic issues for players. There's just a constant raft. I have four children of my own, but sometimes it feels like I have 400 children on any one given night.

Will that player go in tomorrow and say something that's going to upset someone? (If they do) Then I'm going to get a phone call and I'm going to have to mediate a situation. In nearly 30 years, I could count on two hands the number of completely peaceful nights of sleep I've had.

That's why, again, these are the things that people don't see in agents. They have a picture of agents showing up in a transfer window. They do a deal; they get paid an awful lot of money and then they just sit by a pool and drink as many mai tais (rum/orange curaçao beverage) as they humanly can. That's absolutely not the case. In fact, the vast majority of an agent's work is done between transfer windows. It's quite stressful. I don't know many agents that don't experience stress because you're managing people's livelihoods, and that's a very serious thing.

You're managing multiple personalities. You're not just managing your clients; you're managing the people. On the other side of that relationship, there are coaches, clubs and various sponsors.

I've missed plenty of school plays, graduations and birthdays. I don't think in another lifetime I'd be able to make up for the amount of time I've missed with my family. Those are the things I think the public doesn't see in regard to the agent business.

To anyone thinking about becoming an agent. I'd say, "it is hard work. It is stressful. There is a lot of work involved." It's rarely Disneyland, and every night is not Christmas Eve, nice and peaceful. In fact, Christmas Eve is probably one of the only nights that I do get to sleep, that's one of my magical days of the year.

On Australian agents

Obviously, I work in many territories, but I have to say that one of the territories where I find that agents do tend to work collaboratively is in Australia. The camaraderie, the friendship between agents here is fantastic. I think it's a great template for other territories. Some of the other territories are just dog eat dog.

I think the agents here in Australia are very professional in how they go about their business, and they're knowledgeable. They almost always act in their client's best interests, which is fundamentally the job. I think we're very fortunate, as the A-League grows, to have good people in place in terms of agents in Australia.

We've got good leadership at Football Australia now, so I feel very positive about the outlook for Australian football. If we can get the production line happening again, talent wise, the future does look bright.

I think the only real impediment to agents here working internationally is time zones, it's difficult. That's just a natural impediment. The main impediment is just time. But if you're willing to put in the hours and if you get your network built, that kind of addresses the issue. Because while you're asleep, if you have good partners on a good network, they're working and vice versa. It's about building a system that works around your business model. Most of the biggest agents don't even live in the countries they operate in. I think Mino Raiola (RIP) lived in Florida, United States most of the time whilst Jonathan Barnett spends a lot of his time in Spain. So, even a lot of the big agents operate by phone and by computer.

Australia is a hugely expensive place for an agent to work from in terms of business expenses. When I travel to Europe for five months a year, it costs a lot of money. It's hotel to hotel, planes, trains, taxis and meals. My phone bill goes through the roof when I come back, it's just crazy.

It's one of the most expensive countries for a football agent to operate from. And yes, revenue wise, it's one of the lowest for an agent. The tyranny of distance to, I suppose, the biggest purchasing market in the world. (Our distance from) Europe is a huge impediment for us in terms of business. But the guys have overcome it well through networking, and they'll continue to do so.

Many agents in England, with a home office and little travel, have virtually no costs. Most of their three or five per cent commission is pure profit. So, it's a tough market here. If A-League clubs could transfer players between clubs, agents here would prosper. We currently have to operate in effectively what is a transfer drought in our domestic market. Most of the guys have made their money in deals to South Korea, Japan and the Middle East.

On players getting paid in gross salary amounts in Australia

It's the harshest environment here. In the A-League salary-cap system, if there isn't enough money, the agency fee will just be reduced. If an agent was entitled to ten per cent, but there's only five per cent available, that's all they will get. It'll all be gross, and all be taxed. It is possibly the harshest market in the world.

Australian players have very high expectations, but some of them have very high opinions of themselves. You get guys who play three or four A-League games and already want to move to Europe. I'm sorry, mate, I'm good, but I am not that good. I am not David Copperfield (world famous magician). You can only do what you can do with what you are working with.

On Australian players going to MLS
(Major League Soccer in USA or overseas)

Before Aaron Mooy signed for Manchester City, he had a lot of MLS interest for really big money. Jamie Maclaren has had a lot of interest from the MLS and I've sat down with the players and we've looked at it thoroughly and, depending on what your goals and ambitions are, it's not a bad option, certainly for our A-League players. I don't know if it's a mental block but I think we have to change the culture of this whole "going to Europe at a young age thing." What I find with young players, when they get to 18–19 years of age, is that if they're not already on a plane to Europe, they start to panic. I have to keep on reminding them that at 23, Mile Jedinak was mixing cement in Melbourne. At 27, he was stepping foot on an English Premier League pitch. Aaron Mooy, at 26, finally made the English Premier League. So why are you in this rush?

This panic attack about the need to get to Europe before we're 20 needs to change. The last two outfield players to debut in the Premier League from Australia were closer to 30 than they were to 20-years-old.

Chapter 5:
Compelling and Elusive – Bernie Mandic and Nikola Mandic

Bernie Mandic

Bernie Mandic is based in Paris, France; suave, evocative, well-spoken, fashionable and not afraid of speaking his mind. His story has fascinated many in Australian football for a long period of time. I am a great admirer of Mandic's style and followed his pathway as one of the first Australian agents to really shake up the competitive European market. Mandic is someone I would now call an agent influencer. He follows the trends from both club and player sides, and understands the market dynamics and player values, whether it is in Australia, England, France or elsewhere. Mandic is there not to always be liked but to deliver for his client.

Mandic was one of the agents I approached who did not want to give me a direct interview for this book. However, no book on the Australian agent scene can leave Bernie Mandic out. I researched his player deals and agent philosophy in the form of views or quotes he has publicly stated over the years.

On becoming a player manager

Mandic was coaching at the former National Soccer League club Sydney Olympic FC before transitioning to the agency business. His motivation to become a player manager in 1997 was that "too many Australian players were being looked after by agents that made more money from the respective deals than the player was earning in a year. I thought that was an outrageous rip off."[49] This view was mainly based on operations of the slick agents in Europe at the time, who were more interested in getting deals done and not looking at the careers of their players. Bernie Mandic became a player manager while his brother Nikola Mandic (who successfully sat the FIFA exam) became a Football Australia and FIFA-licensed agent. Therefore, the regulatory side of the agent's business was met by Nikola, while Bernie acted as players' commercial manager, similar to what happens in the worldwide entertainment and media industry. Both Bernie and Nikola worked for the same company, Max Sport, which would also retain lawyers when required to advise on the legalities of player deals.

On the journey with Harry Kewell as a client

The Mandic and Harry Kewell story is one that fascinates most Australian football fans. Mandic advised Kewell, one of the most elite players Australia has ever produced, for close to two decades. Generally, it is well recognised in the agent's business that talented professional players who stay with one or two agents in their career tend to succeed. Mandic first crossed paths with Kewell when he was playing for Marconi under-13s, aged eleven. Mandic, in an interview with *FTBL* stated that, "My mate Frank Arok, who was then the national team coach, alerted me to Harry and a few of the other stars there like Brett Emerton and Paul Reid. When we played Marconi, Paul Reid was the best out of all of them. I made the point on how good Reid was and Arok said, 'No, no, no — that little *bastard* over there,' pointing at Harry Kewell."[50]

Mandic formalised this relationship as Kewell's agent around 1998 when Harry was due to renegotiate his Leeds United contract. Leeds was known as a club at that time with one of the United Kingdom's best youth development and academy programs. During a successful career at Leeds, where at one point Inter Milan were prepared to pay £25 million for a transfer, Kewell was ready for a move. Mandic, as any capable agent would, worked in the background on possible deals, including a Liverpool one which had been in the pipeline for several months.

In the football article, "The Men who made Harry," Mandic outlined how the Liverpool transfer materialised. "So, we went through everything, picked some numbers. AC Milan and Liverpool were his two favourite boyhood clubs. He said he would like to go to one of those clubs, preferably Liverpool. However, these are the parameters and whoever meets those first, we have got a deal. Before inking a deal with Liverpool, a host of other top European clubs launched bids to land Harry's services in 2003. Liverpool was the second worst offer. The best was naturally Chelsea and that was about 30 per cent above what Liverpool were willing to pay. Then it was Manchester United and Barcelona equal second, then AC Milan, before Liverpool and then Arsenal who had the worst offer. All great clubs, all great managers and Harry could have gone to any of them."[51]

Curiously, on the day of Harry's medical at Liverpool, Mandic received a call from Manchester United — "Whatever it takes, we will do the deal, right now." Manchester United ended up signing Ronaldo.

Mandic advised Kewell to consider all those offers and that "you have to do what your heart tells you to do."[52] At the end of the day, it is the player's decision — an agent can only advise on the merits of any deal.

The reason for opting for Liverpool was Kewell's in-person meetings with their coach Gerard Houllier instead of just talking to club football directors. As Mandic explained, "your client's best interests have to come first, and for all the supposed bad stuff I did with Harry Kewell, at the end of the day, he had better offers from other clubs and he was the one who chose Liverpool rather than going to Chelsea, for example, or at that time Arsenal or Barcelona, because one, he loved the club, secondly, he felt that he had the best connection with Gerard Houllier compared with anyone else."[53] Further, Mandic conceded that Harry's Liverpool career "didn't turn out how we wanted it," but as his agent and close personal friend, he was on hand to provide the help and support Harry needed at the time of his injury-plagued Liverpool stint.

Further, Mandic was in a position that all agents aspire to be when they have a genuine star player in their portfolio. The best agents have the clubs come to them for players and can dictate terms.

Mandic intimated at the time of the Liverpool transfer that Harry Kewell was such hot property that clubs were clamouring to buy him. "I didn't have to find a buyer. There were plenty of them out there. I just sat back and let them call."[54] This also occurred in 2008 when Kewell had interest from Premier League sides Portsmouth, Aston Villa, Fulham and Tottenham, Roma and AC Milan from Italy. Spanish side Valencia were also interested in his services.[55]

Mandic's approach on advising and deciding on the next move was to "walk through the scenarios with the player. In terms of options for top players there are always three or four and sometimes ten very good ones and often three great options and then it's really up to the player to make that call."[56]

Interestingly, Kewell did not pay Mandic for the Liverpool transfer. It was Leeds who paid Mandic's fees. Many critiqued Mandic's tactics on the 2003 transfer from Leeds to Liverpool where it was alleged that he received £2m of the £5m transfer fee. That is an unconfirmed figure, but the British press relentlessly attacked Mandic for the deal. However, Mandic is about getting the best deal, based on a balance of factors including where the player will play, the coach, the team's tactical style, whether the family wants to live in that city or country, the pay, the bonuses, the access to European competitions, etc. In dispelling the effect on Leeds of the Kewell transfer, Mandic stated: "They (Leeds) invested $2,750 into Harry. That's what they paid to Soccer New South Wales. Nine years later they received about 7 million pounds. If you ask any normal human being whether that's a good return on your money, I would suggest they'd say yes."[57]

When Kewell was injured at Liverpool, Mandic delivered a tough assessment of the Liverpool medical team. "Kewell lost three-and-a-half years of his career at Liverpool because the guys over there in England had, quite literally, no idea what they were talking about, it was worrying the way Harry was treated."[58]

When Kewell signed at Turkish giants Galatasaray in 2008, Mandic knew he was going to a more exotic and culturally different football market. Therefore, during the negotiation of the transfer, he referred Kewell's playing contract to the PFA Chief Executive and General Counsel Brendan Schwab as they were more "plugged into the legalities and commercial environment of every major football market."[59]

When Kewell was negotiating with Melbourne Victory, Mandic was innovative with commercial arrangements to make a deal work and requested additional staff to support Kewell. Abel Balbo (ex-Argentinian striker and international) had the brief to get Kewell fit and ready for the 2014 World Cup. Balbo was represented by Mandic. Melbourne Victory confirmed that Balbo was set to become involved in Kewell's personal training regime, however the option of Balbo working full-time with Melbourne Victory was ultimately rejected by the club's board.[60] As part of the Victory deal, Mandic requested that Kewell be entitled to a "significant share in any boost in club revenue and a cut of home and away gate takings, involving a 30-70 split of additional gate revenue from away games going to Kewell."[61]

Bernie Mandic on the A-League

In the first few years of the A-League, Mandic was not a supporter of the recruiting policies of clubs and noted that some were overpaying players. In a passionate plea, he stated that "With all due respect to the Aussie players playing abroad, none of them would be rated in the top 100 in Europe, nor would they have the capacity to attract crowds. The expectation given to players by agents is unrealistic about the new league. I honestly believe anybody who is going to pay any player over $150,000 per year is being financially negligent for the long-term future of a club. I don't see that as a slight on the A-League."[62] Interestingly, for a long time, the A-League's minimum wage was higher than that in American Major League Soccer.

This initial critique of the A-League by Mandic softened over the years as the competition developed. Seven years later, he was much more positive when Kewell made his move to Australia. On the A-League's attraction, Mandic revealed "the deciding factor in his next move would be about which city could afford his family the best lifestyle, with Kewell often saying he wants to give his young family a taste of Australian life. The key to any deal for Kewell is the environment for his family and not the club offering the best financial offer."[63] Kewell signed a three-year contract with A-League club Melbourne Victory in 2011, scoring eight times in 25 league matches. Unfortunately for the A-League, Kewell was forced to return to England after one year in Australia due to personal obligations.

On building a profile in Europe and dealing with clubs

The Harry Kewell deal from Leeds to Liverpool brought Mandic to the European agency business limelight. Once there, he saw the manoeuvrings of football agents and became cynical about most agents' loyalty. Mandic would seek to tread his own path and not allow the supposed controversy of his deal-making cloud the picture of brand "Bernie". In a 2003 interview, he stated that the transfer market and the agent business had regulations, but some clubs push their own agendas. "But the regulations are meant to work where a player is consulted in all aspects of the process of being sold. It doesn't happen. Clubs are constantly forcing agents upon the player and his representative. That's precisely what set this whole thing in motion. The whole thing can be best summed up as a total package in that there's a lot of people in the esteemed establishment of British hierarchy, whether it's politics or football, who are mightily miffed that two blokes from Australia have basically showed them that they're going to do it their way and not what's forced upon them."[64]

Continuing, Mandic would observe: "But the thing is, with Harry Kewell and me, we've done it our way and on our terms. And if we've offended people, so be it. But I know one thing, I've got a happy client and I know that my boss is happy as well. So that's it, that's my job done. Liverpool, by the way, has no complaints about anything. So, we've got one party who isn't happy. It's inevitable."[65]

This rebuttal aimed at his detractors indicates that Mandic, as a proud Australian, had the tenacity and confidence to tackle the competitive and cutthroat English market. Interestingly, as it was all over the English papers, the Football Association sent a dossier to FIFA to investigate the role of Bernie Mandic in the move of Harry Kewell from Leeds to Liverpool. FIFA's Players' Status Committee ruled that FIFA "does not have jurisdiction to pass a decision because Harry Kewell's transfer was not an international one." This decision irked the establishment. However, Mandic was working with his brother Nikola, who was a licensed agent and under those arrangements they could work in Europe or any other market.

On managing other Australian players and coaches

Mandic's influence in the Australian market is significant due to his longevity and experience as a player's commercial and talent manager.

He has also represented other top Australian players at various times such as Mark Viduka, Nathan Burns, Michael Thwaite, John Aloisi and Tomi Juric, as well as Tony Popovic as a coach. Just like with Kewell, Mandic had the expertise to deal with a plethora of coaching and commercial offers for Popovic at the time Western Sydney Wanderers had their Asian Champions League victory. As a well-informed agent, Mandic would be working behind the scenes advising Popovic on pending contract negotiations with the Wanderers and other clubs.

Further, as any good agent would do, he would be at the big games watching the players and coaches that he represented. Mandic was a visible presence in Riyadh, Saudi Arabia, to watch four of his playing clients in the Asian Champions League Final return leg; Tomi Juric, Ante Covic, Brendan Hamill and Matthew Spiranovic, as well as coach Popovic, as they competed (and won with Wanderers) in the biggest game of their careers.[66]

Mandic was big on the attitude of the player. It was Mandic who took Australian player Jacob Burns from a small NSL club, Parramatta Power, to Leeds United. In Jacob's third game, he was playing at Old Trafford against Manchester United. Burns may have not been one of the well-known, elite Australian players, however his determination was unbelievable. He had to go to Leeds on trial and won a contract because he "took on Lee Bowyer and actually smashed him into the hoardings during training and then faced off with him, which no one has ever done."[67]

In conclusion, over the years Mandic's thinking and agent philosophy, has been articulated through his various public observations. When taking on a new client, Mandic emphasised that he is big on a player's attitude, ability and the players' immediate support circle, including the parents. If all of the three criteria do not align with his values, he declines the opportunity to represent. Further loyalty is important to Mandic, as he observes that if (a player) has got 20 people looking for a deal, what incentive has he (as an agent) got to actually be working that hard for the player. Finally, Mandic reiterates, it "is the clients that are your judge and jury. And if they're happy with what you've done, that's it. Everything else is irrelevant and you don't stay in the game for as long and continue to do these incredible deals"[68]. Mandic was always inspired to turn a challenge into an opportunity in the agent's world. One of his favourite quotes is from the English fashion designer, Mr Paul Smith - and it goes something to the effect of "you can find inspiration in everything and if you can't, look again"[69].

Nikola Mandic

At nearly every Australian football agents' workshop or seminar hosted by the Professional Footballers Australia (PFA), I would see him there. Well-dressed, confident with a cool and relaxed aura, friendly and poised. Nikola (Nick) Mandic. Brother of Bernie Mandic. As an agent and player manager duo, it was Nick who has held a FIFA agent's licence since at least 2003. With the longevity of a more than 20-year career and experienced insights, Nick can never be underestimated in an industry where many agents give up or cannot do business. Whether it was on the theme of transfer fees, resolving an A-League salary cap query or what clauses should be included in player contracts and deals, Nick would always ask the insightful questions at PFA workshops and always seek solutions and information that were in players' interests.

The Nick Mandic I know has always been his own individual even though he had a well-known brother in the agent industry in Bernie Mandic. In fact, Nick would never talk up his achievements nor his journey in the player agent's industry (interestingly, as a player Nick Mandic used to car pool to club training with top players Joel Griffiths and Tim Cahill). Nick has always had a dose of realism. Like his brother Bernie, Nick wanted to remain private and not do an interview. Nevertheless, the endurance and work ethic of Nick is an appealing story to explore within the Australian football agent's context.

Background

Nick Mandic became Harry Kewell's official agent in July 2003 during the time he transferred from Liverpool. Nick was embroiled in the controversy of the Kewell transfer (as was his brother Bernie) that was completed by Kewell's English lawyer Chris Farnell. The critique that Nick received at the time would have damaged any agent's motivation and shaken their confidence. Both the English and Australian press focused on the transfer for a prolonged period of time. This scenario would have hardened Nick for the brutal agency environment and paved the way for him to become one of the more effective agents within the A-League environment. He grasps the ongoing challenges and has seen it all, whether it is how to deal with one-sided clauses put in player contracts by clubs that affect future transfer deals or how to deal with players who seek to go solo in their negotiations after the agent has done all the groundwork.

Nick is also an agent who understands the demand for Australian players and their value. Whether the market was Croatia or South Korea or A-League, he was always well informed, and he knew what those markets wanted, something not all agents can sense. The A-League context provides a lot of uncertainty for players as many contract deals were no longer than one season. Within this uncertain transfer landscape, Nikola is one of the few Australian agents who has managed to open doors to all A-League clubs and established a strong portfolio of players over the years. They include Rhyan Grant, Luke DeVere, Tomislav Mrcela, Ante Covic, Nathan Burns, Alex Cisak, Joe Gauci and Eugene Galekovic.

Nick did not just have a profile in Australia, he was also involved in many overseas player deals. Interestingly, he was chosen by Croatian World Cup star Marcelo Brozovic to negotiate his contract extension with Italian giants Inter Milan in 2022. The family lawyer of Brozovic who had been representing the midfielder throughout the negotiations is not officially registered as an agent with the Italian FA, meaning that the club were unable to officially finalise the new extension deal. Consequently, Brozovic "chose Australian-Croatian agent Nick Mandic as his representative for the official agreement."[70]

The agent philosophy of Nikola Mandic

In 2013, Nick gave an all-encompassing overview of why the South Korean K-League was a good launching pad for Australian players in order to challenge (or disagree with) some assertions made by former Australia midfielder and football analyst Craig Foster. At the time, Foster asserted that by Australian talent opting for Asian leagues, it was harmful to the national team. Foster stated that "seeing our best young talent head to the United Arab Emirates, South Korea and China is extremely worrying."[71]

In 2013, there were at least 20 South Koreans in the European leagues and this included clubs in the English Premier League, Spain's La Liga, France's Bordeaux, and three teenagers at Barcelona.

Nick, who brokered the transfers of Luke DeVere from Brisbane Roar and Brendan Hamill from Melbourne Heart to the K-League, pointed out that the K-League cannot be overlooked as a pathway for Asian players, including Australians. He opined that the "K-League has consistently and repeatedly produced players, and in particular young players, that are wanted by the world's best leagues and clubs. No one that knows football would argue the point that transferring to a good European club is what is ideal for all players in order to reach their peak. But there is more than one way to get there and when an Asian country is able to produce this number of young players playing in outstanding European leagues, it is logical that Australian young players are going to be influenced by it." Further, Nick stated that "transferring to South Korea for these players was a football decision made with reaching the top in mind and a decision that was supported by former Socceroos who were consulted by the players on their transfers."[72]

Nick's knowledge of the intricacies of the South Korean K-League and market indicates that he is a thinking agent and has done his research. Further, he has other important qualities as an agent. He ensures his players leave on good terms from former clubs, deflects media speculation when necessary and works behind the scenes to keep pushing so his players get further opportunities.

Chapter 6:
Marquees – Lou Sticca

Liverpool, Juventus, Alessandro Del Piero, Los Angeles Galaxy, David Beckham, Arsenal, Shinji Ono, Glasgow Celtic, AC Milan v AS Roma. I walked into Lou Sticca's office near the iconic Lygon Street, Carlton in inner Melbourne and knew that I had entered a place where significant international club tours and player deals within Australian football had been fashioned. Lou was the Australian version of a super-agent who could move effectively between being a club agent, player agent and match agent.

Passionate for both Australia and Italy, Lou's career in player agency and the football club business resulted in him having the most extensive black book of contacts in the Australian game; the who's who in football decision-making. With his commercial focus and acumen, Lou was all about starting the conversation and then bringing the deals together, whether it was new marquee players into the A-League, Australian tours by powerhouse European clubs or A-League club squad assembling and roster structuring.

Background

If there is one agent who has left his mark on Australian fields it is Lou, who operates Tribal Sports Management. He is adamant that working on behalf of clubs makes it easier to be commercially viable in the agent business. However, it is rare to be a club agent in Australia. Sticca knew way back as a Brunswick Juventus junior that he wouldn't make it as a professional footballer, but the motivation he received from the team camaraderie in football during those days made him into an Australian football game-changer.

In an interview in 2007 during the early days of the A-League,[73] Lou explained that being an agent "is about relationships and you need good contacts worldwide. A good agent is no different to any other professional. Ultimately, his client has expectations and you're there to assist in their career. It's about listening to your client. The reality is that there is an infinite supply of players, but a small number of jobs. Every agent will have their own speciality — Asia, Europe or Scandinavia for instance — but I think your speciality is your last deal. For me, my speciality is probably the UK."

Lou articulated why Australian players were so prevalent in the United Kingdom in the 1990s and 2000s. "The roots of the steady influx of Australian players into British football came from the influence of one man: Terry Venables gave Australian players a respect that was taken up by many other British managers. When he took over the Socceroos in 1996, he was very quick to appreciate the qualities of Australian players, the obvious physical attributes and the single-minded approach to winning. When he returned to the UK in 1998, I think he helped to spread the word. His spell in charge of the Socceroos put Australian football into the limelight and agents who were used to effectively cold-calling UK clubs found them willing, if slightly bemused, audiences. There has been a steady stream of players ever since, leaving a troubled National Soccer League behind them."[74]

Sticca further expressed that "two logistical factors also favoured Australian football imports to the United Kingdom up until Brexit. The first is the fact that the vast majority can head for the green channel at immigration. With Australia a nation of immigrants, young players are likely to have a British, Italian or Greek heritage that can gain them a European Union passport and an immediate advantage over African or South American youth players." The second area of advantage is the ease with which they assimilate into British life, something that Sticca has encountered with his UK based players. "They get there, and everyone is speaking the same lingo, driving on the same side of the road and eating the same food, basic lifestyle aspects that make it easy for players to fit in immediately and get on with improving their talent."[75]

In 2006, Australian players were also well paid in England's lower leagues. As Sticca observed, "one of my clients, Patrick Kisnorbo, was being paid $30,000 by South Melbourne three years ago. Now he is at Leicester City and he signed an improved contract last season that pays him seven figures annually. If he was here in Australia, he could maybe get $100,000 at an A-League club. It is a much, much bigger stage in Europe."[76]

Sticca also has a compelling influence in the marquee player market in Australia. He brought both Alessandro Del Piero and Shinji Ono as marquees to the A-League. In an interview with Tom Smithies in 2016, Sticca shared his view of what a marquee player in the A-League should be. "A marquee has to go beyond improving the team on the park. To me the KPIs for a marquee are that they drive crowds and drive TV ratings. But the thing that will drive the growth of the league is bums on seats and eyeballs watching on TV. If we can't improve those, it impacts directly on the club's ability to earn and spend money and becomes a self-fulfilling prophecy. That's the thinking that should inform the choice of marquees. Fans aren't stupid — they know who is and isn't a good player, and who they're prepared to pay to watch."[77]

The Del Piero factor was an example of this TV and fan boost, in that "The league had its best opening round ever: audience ratings up by more than 35% on the previous season and about 93,000 streaming through the gates to watch games live."[78] In simple terms, Del Piero was the quintessential marquee player for the A-League, as "Alessandro brings certain factors that very few players in the world can bring. The fact that he's played the bulk of his career for one club, the fact that he's won a World Cup, the fact that he's voted the most loved sportsman in his own country, even at 37 years of age."[79]

Sticca's impact on Australian football is momentous. His hard work, ideas for improving the game and entrepreneurial spirit in bringing big names to Australia has generated a better football industry going forward. Lou is all about building and scaling the Australian football economy and architecture.

In his own words

On becoming a player agent

I was the CEO of the Carlton Soccer Club in the latter years of the NSL from 1997 to 2000. When I left Carlton in 2000, I started getting phone calls from some of the players that used to play there. I was actually the national manager for a large company and within a couple of months, I started getting phone calls from players telling me they needed help with their contracts. One call became two, became three, became four. I spoke to my accountant and got his opinion. He said, "Lou, you're well-known, this is something that you know, you love football, and this is a way of you staying involved in the sport that you love. The only thing I would say to you is that if you're going to do it, you need to do it right."

And at that time, it was sitting an exam to become what was then called a FIFA licensed player agent. I sat that exam in 2000, and that's where it all started.

On the early days of the Australian agent's business

Prior to my agent career, there was another licensing system that involved putting up 200,000 Swiss francs as a bond. And I think at that time, the only agents that I was aware of that were qualified under that system were George Christopoulos and Alan McGrouther (McGrouther was one of the earliest licensed agents operating from 1998 under the AMG Sports Consultants entity). I was one of the first graduates of the first examination intake, and in those days, it was a pretty small bunch of registered or licensed agents. There'd always been another group of middlemen who didn't get accreditation and just continued to operate regardless.

My first batch of players that I looked after were predominantly players from Carlton Soccer Club, guys like Lubo Lapsansky and a few others. I started investing in the business and by investing, I mean getting on the plane and going for long trips overseas to meet players, (and) to meet clubs. That's probably one of the things that I would be saying to any aspiring agent under whatever the new system is going to be; you can't do this part-time and you can't do it just based on the Australian market because it's too small. I was very fascinated with the international scene. That was an area in which I was very keen to progress, again through contacts. In my days as CEO at Carlton, I established a pretty decent international network; guys like David McPherson, who came to play at Carlton before he went back to live in Scotland and played at Rangers and Hearts. We started working together and I was quickly introduced to a number of Scottish clubs. I had players like Andy Vlahos, who had gone to Panathinaikos. Vince Grella and Mark Bresciano that had gone to Empoli and that enabled me to make some contacts in Italy. By the time I started as an agent, I had enough clientele locally and contacts overseas. The aim at that stage for Australian players, if you wanted to get anywhere, was to go overseas.

Scott McDonald, had gone over to Southampton at 16 years of age, started off on a high and then hit a bit of a roadblock. We played a part in helping him start that climb back up the mountain. It was so pleasing to see a young Australian kid start off at the bottom, work at a small club like Motherwell in Scotland and then progress up to the peak of his career at Glasgow Celtic. I was fortunate to do the contracts at that stage, so again made contacts at these clubs that then came in handy throughout my career as an agent.

We brought an assistant coach into our agency that used to work with me at Carlton, a guy called Fabio Incantalupo, an Australian under-23 international and a star of the NSL in the '80s. Fabian took Patrick Kisnorbo for six to eight weeks, three or four sessions a week at La Trobe University. Just working on fitness. We told Patrick we were going to send him overseas to Scotland, but we needed him in tip top condition. We got him into Hearts and at the time in Scotland, centre-backs were usually six-foot-four, six-foot-five, solid men. Patrick isn't that tall, but when it comes to courage and fearlessness, he's up there with the best. He went and trialled, stood out, signed a contract, played at Hearts and became very, very well-liked by the fans because of his courage in the shirt.

It's been so pleasing to follow his career and Patrick winning the A-League grand final was no surprise to me. His work ethic is unmatched. There's a bunch of other Australian boys that we also sent overseas, players like the McGowan brothers, Ryan and Dylan McGowan went to Hearts in Scotland. The overseas path was a path that was starting to become well-worn.

On being a club agent for Sydney FC

In 2005, I was contacted by the chairman of Sydney FC (Walter Bugno), who asked if I was interested in helping build the team. That was a very unique experience for me because what it meant was that I had to recruit coaches and all the players. I literally built their football department and I remember calling other agents whilst recruiting. I decided to suspend my licence so that I could act on behalf of the club. When I dealt with agents, they needed to be sure that I wasn't going to be sharing their agent fees. We recruited a team that went on and won the inaugural A-League. It was probably the most pleasing and exciting twelve months and enabled me to go overseas and talk to coaches like Pierre Littbarski, Arie Haan, Roy Hodgson, Paulo Di Canio and Harry Redknapp. As history shows, we went with Pierre Littbarski. Ian Crook was the only appointment that was already in place, and I worked really closely with him. It was actually Ian Crook's friendship with Steve Bruce, who was at the time coaching Birmingham City, that brought Dwight Yorke to Sydney.

I spoke to his agent, Simon Bayliff, who was a senior partner at SFX and to cut a long story short, it took us a little bit of time, but we negotiated a deal, and recruited the biggest name ever to come out to play in Australia. No footballer at the time, or probably since, has put Australian football on the back page of the sport section so often and he had us on the front page of the socials whenever Dwight went to a bar or a nightclub, it was plastered all over the papers with his nickname of "all night Dwight." He loved to party. He was likeable to many and what he did for Sydney FC in the A-League to this day is quite remarkable.

In football, there are many selfish people and we all care about what's in it for us. I've never been given a gift in all my years of working in football. But when Dwight Yorke and Simon Bayliff got in the limousine from Sydney Airport to take him to Sydney FC to sign the contract and start his career here, they had one for me. They gave me a Montblanc pen with my name engraved on it. That pen still holds pride of place in my study because it's just a very, very touching example of exactly what Dwight Yorke is about. Financially, for him, that would be petty cash. But it's beside the point. It was the gesture.

We had players coming in from all corners of the world and after the second year, I went back to my agency role. At the same time, I decided to apply for, and was granted, my FIFA match agent licence accreditation, which enabled me to facilitate the hosting of international games.

On being the only Australian agent having a
FIFA match agent licence

At that time, I was one of the few people in the world that actually had both licences. People who are usually going to do matches do matches only, but I was attempting to do both. I got my match agent's licence and I ran that concurrently with my player business and it worked very, very well. I was able to access clubs and players that perhaps otherwise I wouldn't have been able to.

In 2007, two years after the A-League started, we brought LA Galaxy out with David Beckham. Then in 2014, I brought out Juventus to play the A-League All-Stars, which to be frank, I hated as a concept.

In 2013, the same year that I brought Alessandro Del Piero to Sydney, I negotiated Liverpool to come out and play in Melbourne at the MCG in front of 96,000 people. Between Del Piero and Liverpool, I was able to use that momentum to then negotiate to bring Juventus out in 2014, followed by Celtic, Tottenham Hotspur, Chelsea and Arsenal. We also had Leeds and Manchester United come out. In the last couple of years, I helped build Western United in the expansion of the A-League and again put together most of the inaugural playing roster at that club.

On giving a reference on behalf of Tom Rogic for the deal
at Glasgow Celtic to happen

When Tommy Rogic was playing in Australia, I didn't represent him, but what I did do was contact the CEO at Glasgow Celtic, Peter Law. I said, "Look, there's an Australian player running around at the moment. He's not my player, but I really urge you guys to take a look at this player because I think he's a little bit special."

I can say that I've played a part in getting him to Celtic, but without ever actually meeting Tommy or having anything to do with him as an agent. Sometimes you play an ancillary role because of the relationship built up with clubs and CEOs and people in the game. Now I can't even see myself as an agent, I just see myself as a person that's got relationships in football.

On Kazu and Benito Carbone

I was very fortunate to bring an Italian player to Sydney FC as a guest. And that was Benito Carbone. Benito made the biggest impact in such a short amount of time. He only played three games for Sydney. He came out as a guest player, which is one spot on the roster that has been rarely used since the creation of the A-League.

He was just an incredible footballer, an incredible personality. I've never seen a person dominate a game of football like he did when Sydney FC played in Adelaide. Even though it was for four weeks, I've built a relationship with him that has now helped me get into other player deals that I would not have otherwise.

We signed a Japanese player called Kazuyoshi Miura. Kazu, as he was known, is today about 56 years of age, and was still playing professional football. He is the David Beckham of Japanese football. He was the first big Japanese player to go overseas and he played in a number of countries. All the time that he was at Sydney FC, I'd converse with him in Italian. I never conversed with him in English. He didn't speak English, I didn't speak Japanese, but he played in Italy, so it was fantastic to be able to converse with him in another language. He was an absolute legend. We were once in a train station in Tokyo, and we were catching the bullet train to Nagoya. There were thousands of people at the station and Kazu walks in with Sydney FC on his tracksuit. When they realized it was Kazu, it was like Moses opening the Red Sea. Everyone just parted, they bowed, they took photos. There was no pushing, no screaming. I've never seen anything like that. It was a very unique experience.

On the Alessandro Del Piero deal

In 2013, I attempted something which I didn't think was going to come off, but I thought I'd have a crack anyway. As a keen, passionate follower of Italian football, I noticed that Alessandro Del Piero could have been in his last season with Juventus. I was in Turin, about to watch the last game of the season at their new stadium. Juventus had been through a lean period, they had been relegated to Serie B. They'd signed Antonio Conte as their manager and the team was improving.

It was a huge game.

I saw Alessandra Del Piero score, get substituted around the 70th minute and then conduct a 360-degree circumference of the stadium while the game was on. It was the most bizarre experience I've seen in my life; a guy doing a parade around the ground while the game kept going. The fans were going berserk and people were crying. I asked to speak to Del Piero and the guy that I was dealing with at the time gave me Stefano's Del Piero's mobile number. Stefano is his brother and he's also his agent. We had a coffee and did all the niceties and then I launched into my pitch. I said, "Look, Stefano, I hear that Alessandro is going to be leaving Juventus. I'm not sure whether you're going overseas, whether you're going to go play for another club, but I want to put forward an opportunity to come to Australia." I'll never forget the look on his face. He was trying very hard not to laugh. He was being very respectful. I may as well have said, "Would you like to come and play on the Moon?"

We kept in touch. Every couple of weeks I would drop Stefano an email. I heard Del Piero might be going to America. I offered them contacts in Los Angeles, just doing anything to remain relevant. 2 months went past.

I told Sydney FC CEO Tony Pignata that I was making a play for Alessandro Del Piero. He asked if I was serious and then spoke to Scott Barlow and David Traktovenko, the owners of Sydney FC. And he came back and said, "Look, we really want to have a red-hot go." All of a sudden, out of the blue, I get an email. Stefano Del Piero and another gentleman that was Alessandro's financial manager would like to talk.

In the space of 24 hours, the whole thing went to another level. Stefano and Dario (cannot recall the surname) from Italy requested a Skype call.

The call went extremely well to the point where we closed it by saying, "Okay, you guys get yourselves here to Turin. Let's do this deal." We couldn't believe it. We left the next day.

On the plane we're like two little excitable girls, just laughing and wondering if we were wasting our time.

If there was no one at the airport to meet us, as they promised, we would be gutted. So, we've whipped ourselves into this frenzy of negativity. When we come through the doors at the exit, lo and behold, there's a driver there. So, we looked at each other and thought, 'okay, step one, we've passed step one.'

We then checked into our hotel, we were told to be at the offices for a meeting as soon as possible.

The owners of Juventus historically have been the Agnelli family, something like the Kennedys in the USA. The Agnelli's own, Fiat, Ferrari, Maserati, Iveco, and a raft of other luxury brands. They are based in Turin (Torino).

So, we sat there, and we negotiated. We're on the phone to Scott Barlow, toing and froing and to cut a long story short, we had an intense set of negotiations that went for quite a while, and got to the point where we were told, "Okay, just give us a couple of minutes." Out of the blue, Alessandro appears. We're sitting in a boardroom, Stefano, Alessandro, Tony Pignata and myself, we agree to terms and the rest is history. Alessandro signed the contract.

At this point, I must really underline what Australian football owes to particular people. David Traktovenko and Scott Barlow particularly, because the investment that those two gentlemen made in bringing Alessandro Del Piero to Australia and the impact that it would have on the A-League and on Australian football would be immense.

We then had press conferences the next day. Things just went berserk at the time. Daniel Garb, a football journalist, was working in London. His TV crew flew over to Turin to do interviews. The press conference was something that I've never experienced.

But the biggest buzz was when we finally got him on a plane and he arrived at Sydney Airport. The response of the fans that came out for the Alessandro arrival made back page of *The Daily Telegraph* and *The Sydney Morning Herald*. TV crews were everywhere and it was not too dissimilar to Dwight Yorke, but very special in another way, because Alessandro had won the World Cup in Italy and only played for one club. The second club in this guy's CV was Sydney FC. What a huge statement. What a huge affirmation for Australian football that our little footballing country could be so bold to bring Alessandro. The Del Piero deal without doubt was one of the pinnacles of my career.

On other marquee players

Apart from recruiting all the Aussie boys and all the quality foreigners, bringing marquees is something I really always enjoyed dealing with. I suppose if I had to pick one area of expertise, I just seem to be able to do the marquees well. I had other great experiences with Panagiotis Kone, a Greek international, and Italian international Alessandro Diamante. Obviously, COVID interrupted everything — Kone went back to Greece and is now a football director at AEK Athens. Diamante went on to win the Johnny Warren Medal and has become an absolutely incredible personality on and off the park in Australian sport.

On being an Australian agent and dealing with the European market

There's no question that being able to speak a European language (Italian) was very helpful. And it's probably not even so much the language as it is the mentality and understanding cultures. In fact, I felt right at home.

Dealing with United Kingdom clubs is straight up and down. Black and white. There's no funny business. It is what it is. Dealing with continental clubs is more of a challenge. Some of them. Not all of them, but some of them. They are a little bit more difficult to deal with.

On the Asian football market

And not only in Europe. I started dealing in Asia for Australian players. The first player I took over was Brendon Santalab after he left North Queensland Fury. I took him over to China and he signed with a club called Chengdu.

We got Rostyn Griffiths over to China, he was coming out of contract at the Mariners, and he had two months to go. We were able to get the Mariners a substantial transfer fee where otherwise he would have walked for nothing. The other one was Ryan McGowan. We took him out of Scotland and put him into Shandong and South Korea and all three of them were a great example for Australian football. All three Australian boys were sensational, typical Australians, easy going, not pretentious. They were very well respected by the locals, and the relationship worked really, really well.

And then there's the Asian clubs, the Chinese clubs, the ones that I dealt with. Dealing in China is actually quite a different experience, they just have a different way of doing things. Chinese football has been through some pretty tumultuous developments over the last 10–15 years. It's gone from a sport that the locals had no real interest in to one that President Xi Jinping wanted to promote and make super successful. He's a big fan of football and Chinese clubs were spending ridiculous amounts of money.

Dealing with the Chinese had its challenges. We saw what they did with Marcelo Lippi (coach) and with Carlos Tevez (Argentinian international) and a lot of big-name players, they spent ridiculous amounts of money. We all thought at the time that it was going to be difficult to sustain. And it's been proven as a lot of those clubs have now gone out of existence. They would change their name every year, as soon as a new owner would buy them.

On talent identification and selecting clients

Scouting wasn't my forte. There's guys that I really admire like agent John Grimaud, who tends to identify players very, very young, and then follow it through. I was more of a listener. I would listen to people in the game, talk about players and their attitude. If I hear a guy being mentioned by a particular coach that I respect, my ears would prick up. I was more of a listener and probably went for more of the established player rather than the young, up-and-coming star.

My skill set wasn't scouting, mine was more doing deals for established players. That's what I really enjoy. I love doing deals. I love the negotiation process. I love the travel that goes with it. I love all the key parts in closing the deal. I think we really need to understand the environment and the ecosystem required to produce a footballer that's going to go on and play in the English Premier League, LaLiga or Bundesliga. There are certain characteristics, and I've always looked for a certain hardness, and I look at the family background. Streetwise and street-smart young men like Brendon Santalab, Dylan McGowan, Scott McDonald and Patrick Kisnorbo.

These are Aussie boys that come from working-class families. In Patrick's case, he lost a parent at a very young stage of his life. These are people that have had to do it hard, working-class. Vince Grella, Mark Bresciano — both from working-class families from the suburbs who worked hard. Guys like Simon Colosimo, probably the most talented footballer that I've ever had anything to do with.

On the most difficult aspects of the agency business

I think Australia's now got a real problem. I think some kids that are playing have parents that are too domineering. They do all the talking and I would say, "Look, I don't really want to talk to you. I really want to hear what the young player has to say." The parents would get their back up. Some parents wanted to hear big stories. In other words, they wanted me to say that their son is going to go to Liverpool or to Juventus, or to Arsenal, but they didn't want to hear things like, "Look, I think Scotland's a good launching pad or Italy's Serie B."

Australian players going to an environment to get game time as quickly as possible is the key. I just see that too many Aussies have gone to some of the big clubs, and even EPL clubs, and then they get lost in the system and you never see them again.

It just goes to the calibre of the people you're speaking to; some parents and some kids are just more realistic. They're happy to further their careers and take time to do so. A lot of people want to hear what they want to hear. I've never been the sort of person that will just say what needs to be said. I'll just say what I believe to be right. And that has generally worked. All the players I have worked with, none of them have had an easy ride. I don't think any Australian players (ever) have. If you are an Argentinian or a Brazilian or an Englishman, you've got pedigree. Coming from Australia, without offending anyone, you are seen sometimes as B-grade. Those times may change now, although we don't have a lot of good Australian players (until recently) playing overseas like we did in the Golden Generation. But what we do have now is guys like Ange Postecoglou doing it in another sphere, which is coaching. So, that will increase the respect factor for us. Qualifying for World Cups certainly helps with respect as well.

On young Australian football talent coming through and the challenges faced

We are a very unique country in that we have so many other sports that take the best athletes. NBA basketball now takes all our big six-foot plus players. And they're earning mega-money. We've got Australian Rules Football and National Rugby League. We have a real issue in that our small population, 26 million people, has all these sports tugging away at our Australian athletes. I also think we've lost our edge as a country. I think we're becoming somewhat of a spoilt, and a little lazier, middle-class country where some of the youth of today may have a bit too much privilege. They want $400 pairs of Nike boots every two months. They want the latest of whatever the fashions are. We may not always have the hunger due to the comfort zone. If you look at the greatest exporters of talent in the world, countries like Argentina and Brazil, there isn't much of a middle class (although its growing in Brazil now) and the kids come from the neighbourhoods. They kick the ball on the road, like my generation did as kids, from morning to night. These kids have the desire to find their way out of poverty to help their families. In Australia, I don't see that. Some of our kids and maybe get too much too early.

We've become a jack of all trades and a master of none.

We talk about Harry Kewell and Mark Viduka and the Golden Generation and Paddy Kisnorbo, Scott McDonald and Matty Ryan and all the boys that have made it. But what about the hundreds and hundreds of players, boys, and girls now, that get sent overseas?

I sometimes label them 'Contiki tours' where people promise them trials and that they'll get looked at by decent clubs. You talk about what's wrong with the game? Well, there's one thing that's drastically wrong. We've got an industry of some people taking money out of the game through private initiatives or academies (with no pathway at the end), but yes, there are some good ones. I look at a few and see good people like Diego Ferreira, who played at Melbourne Victory, doing the right things.

However, there are some other overseas academies that sometimes have ripped off families by getting them overseas, asking them to pay for flights and accommodation at clubs or academies. People would ring me up and tell me their son has been offered a contract with a particular club, but then have to pay €2,000 a month. That is not an offer. I think the parents need to wake up and become more discerning.

Parents are sometimes (not the majority) the biggest impediment to the game improving in this country. Especially if their kids are somewhat entitled, just have stars in their eyes, and they're not prepared to do the hard yards. On the flip side of that, we've seen horrific stories of some of our kids ending up in far-flung countries with no money, basically left in the middle of the road. I urge parents, don't be gullible.

The kids that are doing really well at the moment in the A-League and potentially playing for Australia are many of the boys of African-Australia descent. Why? Because maybe they don't have the wealth and they see football as a way of improving their families and futures. Another criticism that I do have of Australian players is that they tend to listen to the last person that they spoke to, and again, this sometimes could be the parent's fault. They tend to change agents every six months, (or) every twelve months. If they don't like what they hear, they change.

They blame the agents, yet most successful players have been stable in their management across their careers. Like the workforce, if people see your CV and you've been at a place for three months and then another place for two months and then another place for three months, that doesn't inspire confidence. I think the same thing applies in representation. Whether you get a lawyer to help you with legal affairs or an accountant to do your financials, do your research and find someone that you're comfortable with. Then trust them. At the end of the day, if you're successful in business or you're successful on the football pitch, it's up to the individual and what they do on the park that ultimately matters.

Agents don't build your career. They help you monetise what you're doing on the park.

On being invited to the 1st FIFA agents' roundtable meeting in 2018 with the super-agents

I'm going to be honest with you. I absolutely loved it. Agents like Pini Zahavi, Mino Raiola, Giovanni Branchini, really established agents, (they are) global names and we read in the media how they take so much money out of the game. There might be elements of truth there but what people have to understand is the players' thoughts. Ask Erling Haaland if he was happy with Raiola's agency. Ask him how much money he has made. And that's one of the things the fans need to be a little bit more understanding of. I think agents don't really care whether they're liked it or not. Their job is to look after their players.

On the park, if the player does the job, it makes his agent's job a lot easier because the player is getting all the rave reviews.

As the agent, you walk into a meeting representing Erling Haaland or Paul Scholes or David Beckham or Roy Keane, and you have a lot of power. Agents use that power to get the best deals. And if that means they're making a big agent's fee out of it, well, that's a by-product.

On losing players to other agents

I've never really made money the major issue and I've got to be honest with you, I've actually lost a lot of money on players.

A lot of players leave you at the drop of a hat. I've had players leave me after I've given them good service. There is another agent at a bar who says, "Why don't you come with me? Oh, geez, you're better than that. You should be at a bigger club."

Sometimes it has been heartbreaking because I've invested tens of thousands of dollars in flights to visit them and be there for them, and then at the first chance, they leave. The interesting thing is, no player that's ever left me has really gone on to anything greater than what I'd already achieved for them. So that's my point, for young and up-and-coming players and parents — find a good agent, trust them, hold them to account.

Question if you're not happy, have a meeting and put everything on the table. But ultimately, the agent doesn't get you to Liverpool or to Manchester United. It's the player's work on the ground. The cream rises to the top.

So, if you're in Second Division and you're in the top three, week-in, week-out, you'll get noticed. Players like Mark Bresciano and Vince Grella are two prime examples of players that worked hard, and Aaron Mooy in the current generation. He was wallowing in the Scottish Premier League, not doing anything great. Came back to Australia, catapulted himself back into the headlines and look at him today.

On negotiating and structuring player deals

The calibre of the players I've had, depending on the market that they've been in, put the onus on me to research what clubs traditionally paid.

For instance, some have a ceiling, they have an imposed salary cap. What I used to do was research where they were going, what the typical pay was and then do the best for my player. I think of them all as my sons, and I love them dearly.

If I was a Mino Raiola and I had a Zlatan Ibrahimović, or other agents like him, they could be doing exactly what Raiola does, which is ask for telephone numbers in terms of pay. Some clubs will pay it because that player is elite. At any given time, there's probably a handful of players in the world that are in that stratosphere.

Australia has had probably a handful of players that I would say at any given time were elite. Mark Viduka, Harry Kewell, Timmy Cahill, no doubt Mark Bresciano and Vinnie Grella, and you just have to look at the moves that they made and the clubs that they played for.

Mark Viduka started at Celtic and probably could have moved around a lot more and moved to bigger clubs. But some players find an environment that they're content with and when you're getting paid really good money, you're respected and happy in that environment, why do you need to move?

There is no one answer. Everyone does what they think is right at the time.

On marketing and sponsorship of Australian players

I've always stuck to player contracts; I've never delved into giving them financial advice. I've never promised marketing deals. That's an area that is a very unique one, and probably only a handful of Australian players have capitalised on that. The greatest example is Tim Cahill, who I think conducted himself in such a way that sponsors were falling over him. But I can't think of anyone else other than perhaps Sam Kerr at the moment.

The boots and apparel companies have changed. I remember 20 to 25 years ago, companies were giving boots and apparel and some cash to anyone that was playing at a professional level. (But) If you look at their global strategy now, Adidas, Puma, Nike, New Balance, Umbro and Mizuno don't saturate. They just go for the biggest athlete that they can sign. Adidas has got Messi and Ronaldo's got Nike, and they'll just put all their eggs in one basket.

On FIFA's deregulation of the agent industry in 2015

It's an absolute dog's breakfast. FIFA completely stuffed it up. In the A-League, you've got 12 teams with 23 players on their roster. So that's about 280–290 professional contracts. And there's probably about 100–150 intermediaries floating around. Player agents or intermediaries who have one player are stuck. What the hell are they going to do for those players? How much money are they going to take off that player to survive? If they're doing it part-time, then what can they actually offer to improve their players' careers?

It's crazy. It should go back to licencing. If you want to sell a house, you have to have a real estate licence. If you want to be giving people legal advice, you have to do a legal degree. If you want to give people financial advice, you've got to be a licensed financial adviser. If you want to be an accountant, you've got to study it and get the education. If we look at football globally, you need people that are full-time who have an understanding of contracts and are serious.

Intermediaries with no education all think that the next player is going to be their Harry Kewell or their Mark Viduka. I'd like them to ask someone like Bernie Mandic, who engineered Mark Viduka and Harry Kewell's careers, what toll it's taken on their life. How many months of the year are they away from their families and children, their wives, traveling around Europe, living out of a suitcase and going to meetings, often wasting time. It's an expensive industry to be serious in.

And fans don't see that. We've got a glut of kids now going to university doing sports management degrees. What for I ask myself sometimes? There're not enough top jobs. They aim for the AFL but move to soccer because that's supposedly really easy. Anyone can do it! But can they?

On being so far away from European leagues and the effect on Australian players

We're always under threat here in Australia because of the tyranny of distance. Many times, I've lost a player because I've got on the plane to come home and the next day someone else is in his ear.

It is tough for some of the players abroad. Living in one-bedroom flats in the cold, you almost want to say to them, "Come home, come back to Australia. Go live with your parents, go back to university, go get a job." But these kids are so hungry they want to do it.

On negotiating with foreign players

When you're talking to foreign players, you have to go straight for the jugular. I actually convert any offer into net and into their currency. If an Australian club is offering a $200,000 gross package, I'll quickly convert that to euros or pounds or US dollars, depending on where they come from. Then I'll work out what the tax on that would be. So, I'll say to someone, I've got a contract for you here in Australia for $60,000 US net. Then they can get their head around it.

Chapter 7:
One Good Partner –
John Grimaud

There he is again. At nearly every National Youth League game (was known as A-League Youth or Y-League) that I attended between Melbourne Victory and Melbourne City (formerly Melbourne Heart), there was John Grimaud in the crowd scouting for talent or watching the young players he represented. A hard-working, strong-willed, realistic, opinionated and level-headed agent who is ardent about the players he represents. It is widely recognised within the Australian football ecosystem that Grimaud is passionate about Australian youth development and has one of the strongest understandings of where many Australian players are at in their football and what decisions need to be made. Grimaud can spot Australian talent and understands that international youth tournaments are a showcase for players. Not many agents travel to watch Australian national youth teams internationally like Grimaud.

In his 25 years in the agent industry, Grimaud has his own unique model in terms of what type of players he will take on as an agent. John is big on values and the mentality of the players, as well as holding the firm view that they need to play. In one of his most compelling quotes, he sums it up. "Do they want to be footballers, or do they just talk about being footballers?" This approach is why he has made millionaires of some Australian players. For John, negotiating a player's deal has two aspects — the financial package and the playing package. His track record is impressive. He has instigated the transfers of players such as Mitch Langerak (Borussia Dortmund), Robbie Kruse (Fortuna Dusseldorf) and Josh Kennedy (Nagoya Grampus), and recently consulted on the Nestory "Nestor" Irankunda deal to Bayern Munich. He has also represented in club deals a plethora of players like Michael

Zullo, Ben Halloran, Kwame Yeboah, Brandon Borello, Connor Pain, Jason Geria and Chris Harold.

Background

Grimaud has provided a 20-plus year support network around Australian youth players that incorporates his passion for player pathways. He was the agent for young tyros (at the time) including Thomas Deng, Christian Theoharous, Birkan Kirdar, Gianluca Iannucci and Jacob Italiano. In an all-encompassing interview with Louise Taffa on the *Next Gen* program on *Football Nation Radio (FNR)* in 2018, Grimaud outlined how he caps the number of players he takes on to about 20 and that he is totally committed to each player he signs. John's template for signing players is that he looks for points of difference and the ability to decide games. In an agency business where agents have different specialties, Grimaud sees Germany as his market and has sometimes expressed that he wished the AIS still existed.

Keen to see improvements in the local scene, he is not afraid to give his feedback or recommend hard-hitting improvement ideas to decision-makers. For example, he suggested that the Socceroo coaching staff should include some younger project players in the national team. Similarly, he raised his past concerns over the lack of Victorians picked for the U/17 Australian national team (the Joeys) due to the lack of a proper scouting system and possibly a little Sydney-centric bias.

Grimaud's ability to identify young Australian talent is highly regarded, and his relationship with Borussia Monchengladbach chief scout Mario Vossen has created key pathways for Australian players. Matthew Leckie was the first player identified by Vossen when he was playing at Adelaide United. Leckie, who was represented by Grimaud for all of his career, ended up being the second-highest rated player in the Bundesliga when it came to 50-50 duels, second for his one-on-one duels in the opposition half and third for his defensive work tracking back.[80] Vossen observed that Grimaud and his Dutch partner (Jan Van Baal, who is based in Germany) are "two agents, in my view, excellent at identifying young players who can go on to make big progressions."[81]

As a promoter of young Australian talent, Grimaud is vocal on seeing the A-League salary cap done away with, as he sees it as a form of complacency and not mimicking the world league benchmark. "Let the clubs pay what they want, what I'd prefer to see is incentives for players to play well. If you perform and the team wins, then you should be rewarded. This isn't reinventing the wheel. That's how it is around the world. If the bigger clubs want to go and spend more to keep up with the rest of Asia, the smaller clubs have to do things smarter. Adelaide United has proved that you can do it, you can bring in kids at 18-years-old and they can make a difference."[82] Grimaud is adamant that when these exciting younger players are injected into the game, they can be catalysts in shifting and transforming it. He also favours fast-tracking players from Australia's national youth squads who are capable of successful careers in Europe. Grimaud has a huge track record of consistently completing player representation deals and between 1 April 2019 to 31 March 2020 he made 20 A-League player club deals alone.

John Grimaud has seen all the challenges and successes with Australian players. His client Joshua Hope walked away from the professional game due to his experiences with online social media abuse. Conversely, he opened doors for Alou Kuol, another one of his former clients who lit up the A-League with Central Coast Mariners with his exuberance and ability to take on and pressure defences, obtained the opportunity of a lifetime in Germany. Enigmatically, Grimaud has one of the most thought-provoking, insightful, attention-grabbing and must-follow X (Twitter) accounts for a football agent.

In his own words

On becoming a player agent

Frank Farina and David Mitchell were on a coaching course with me. It felt like it was going to be hard to get to the top as a coach in Australia because these guys had bigger names football-wise, and they'd had better careers. So, then I toyed with the idea of becoming a player agent. I spoke to my cousin, Joe Spiteri, he was playing in Belgium at the time, and I went to see George Christopoulos at his hotel in Port Melbourne. I've got good eyes for talent now, which I didn't really have in those days. But I just talked a good story to him and said, "Let me work with you." He said it was tough and was right in telling me that, but I had the opportunity to go through Joe Spiteri's agent to take a player to Europe. I took Tommy Pondeljak from the Melbourne Knights. Through Tommy, I met my business partner, who I'm still business partners with 23 years down the track, Jan Van Baal. He's very intelligent and the clubs respect him highly.

On his early player deals

Ajax wanted a goalkeeper, and Joey Didulica was with Bernie Mandic at the time. He was trialling at Charlton Athletic, but couldn't go to England, he's a Croatian/

Australian, so he simply couldn't play in England. I got a DVD of him playing and I sent that to Jan Van Baal in Amsterdam. They were impressed. Joey flew from London to Amsterdam and spent a week trialling. He killed it. And that's how the story started. Joey Didulica ended up getting a deal at Ajax, that was my first one. Then Jan Van Baal and I set out to find a young striker for Wolfsburg in Germany.

Josh Kennedy. He'd already played a handful of games in the old National League. I paid for his flights and he went over there for a trial. Three days later, John's getting a call from Wolfsburg to drive from Amsterdam, just three days into a two-week trial. I had two out of two.

The next one was Archie Thompson. I took him from Morwell Falcons to Carlton Soccer Club and he had a chance to trial at Anderlecht in Belgium. He wasn't signed by Anderlecht, but we had ten clubs watching him play and Lierse was the club that took him. They offered him the deal and he ended up in Belgium before he came back to Melbourne Victory as a marquee. I was three for three. I had a lot of misses after that. But people were thinking, who is this guy? And I built up a relationship with them. They trusted me.

When you're dealing with European player agents, to be successful you have to either control the player or control the club. There're so many player agents that are now middlemen. If you don't control the club and you're just the middleman, you have to force your way into deals. It doesn't work that way.

On the saturated agent market

They've saturated the market. It's created a lot more middlemen trying to get involved in deals. There are so many intermediaries. I look at the list of intermediaries from Australia, and I don't know how many there are, but there's probably about 80.

They all think it's easy. The misconception is that it's an easy way to make money, but I'd love to know how many of them are successful at what they do. I look at the A-League and think to myself, how many players in this league could you seriously generate some revenue from?

It's fairly minimal at the moment although that is changing. If you look at young talent coming through, the saturation means we are limited. I'd love to see that exponentially grow, because it would be great for my business, and I'd be able to employ people. But at the moment, I look at the A-League and it is a handful of players that you want to have on your list that you don't have, and that's it. The rest, all those other agents can have. I made those mistakes 20 years ago, just trying to sign as many as I could. The problem is trying to look after them, the expectations.

On losing clients to other agents

Managing expectations is the most difficult part of the job because players always think that they're better than they are. I don't even concern myself with that anymore. I have lost some clients. I lost Mark Birighitti and I lost James Holland before getting him back. I did a lot for Matthew Spiranovic because we got him to Nurnberg, he played in the Bundesliga. We got him a super deal with Urawa Reds. He had a chance to go back to Germany through Hertha Berlin, but he chose to leave me at the time. That's football agency, but admittingly it is disappointing (as agents we get used to losing players – but it's hard to fathom for us).

I think we're as good as anybody maximising opportunities for these players. If they're doing what they have to do on the pitch, we'll maximise the opportunities for them. That's the difficult aspect of our role that we play.

On having a European-based partner

I don't have to deal with anyone else but Jan Van Baal, so it makes my job a little bit easier. I trust him with everything. He has helped build the success that we've had over the journey. I don't have to do phone calls; I don't have to ring up an agent who I don't even know. These are the problems for Australian agents. How do his parents know who they're dealing with, who that agent's dealing with overseas to try and get him a deal? This is crucial in terms of having a successful career and comfort; knowing that your son's going to be well taken care of when he's overseas and not just sending him over.

On his day to day as an agent

It's definitely not nine-to-five. If you look at my phone list yesterday, it was ridiculous. I probably would have fielded 20 to 30 phone calls. It's not the same every day. But my life revolves around watching football and watching young gun players. There's no one in Melbourne that I don't know about that I think I should. I'm watching them live and I don't see too many other agents watching live games of football.

When a parent wants to tell me that their kid is this and that, I'll tell them how it is. It's black and white. There's no real grey.

On young talented players

I believe there's a big void in understanding where these talents need to be at certain levels throughout their career. I always tell parents that to go to Spain or Italy with one of these tours for ten grand is a mistake. They are better off investing in a personal trainer, even a dietician. Have a look at the English national team and have a look at the size of them. They're beasts physically, and that's where the game is heading.

If you don't have that, then you don't have the total package. I don't just blame the clubs. I blame the players, because they should take responsibility for their conditioning. The clubs don't know what to do with these talents, (and) how hard they need to work them. They don't have enough conditioning coaches with any experience or understanding. We have the understanding because we travel. I see the French national team at under-17 level, (and) under-20 level. Some guys have no idea. They don't invest in themselves. The good ones do. And that's why you've seen Melbourne City improve. They've gone head and shoulders above everyone else because they've got the best conditioning staff. They've got the best coaches, they've got the best of everything.

And that's where clubs, even NPL clubs, need to take it to another level if we're going to produce better talent.

I think technology has hurt us a lot because we've got it too good in Australia and there's too many young people. I speak to German scouts and they say the same thing. It's happening around the world. We had a curriculum that went away from what we were good at and tried to develop more technical players. I'm seeing a lot more technically proficient players than what we had back in our day, but they don't have the total package. It's not just about how good you are technically, that's (just) one part of it. It's the mentality, it's the physical attributes. It's the game sense and awareness that will determine where you end up as a footballer. So even if you're technically decent, it doesn't necessarily guarantee that you're going to have a career because you see a lot of technically good players.

We are creating better technical players in Australia but we're still a long way away from those guys that are coming from Africa, South America, (and) parts of Europe where they don't have much and they're fighting for everything. The whole football structure in Australia, I call the A-League Complacency League. No relegation, clubs get complacent. A salary cap, we're competing equally with everybody else. Young players come in, earn $60,000–$70,000 minimum salary and don't have any incentives (bonuses) to get better.

In my opinion, drop that minimum salary a little and if you play and start in a game, you get a thousand dollars. You get $500 every time you win. Bonuses, incentives. So, what are you (players) going to do then? You're probably going to do an extra training session or extras on shooting, finishing, all those things. There's more incentive.

On which player deal John is most proud of

It was about 2010 I reckon, maybe earlier. But I can remember Mathew Leckie playing in the summer league. The kid was everywhere, scoring goals, creating goals, jumping, (and) headers, he was unbelievable. I organised a meeting with his dad and at the end of the meeting, he asked for a contract. He said, "I want to sign with you but just make sure you look after my son." I didn't even have my contract agreements with me at the time.

I wrote emails to every single club in the A-League, saying that Leckie is not trialling. If you want Mathew Leckie, you have to sign him. The only one that believed me was Lawrie McKinna. He came down to Melbourne. I picked him up, put him in the hotel and then we went to watch a game. Bulleen played against Frankston Pines, out at Bulleen, and he (Leckie) scored two and he made two and they won 4–2. He was outstanding.

I think it was about five or six weeks later that he made his A-League debut for Adelaide. And then 16 games after that, the Reds had an offer of $500,000 from Borussia Monchengladbach, which they said no to. They'd paid him $16,000 in salary, and they said no to half a million after he played 16 games for Adelaide. They (Borussia Monchengladbach) followed him for another year and got him as a training compensation at the end of the second year.

That's when he was at Ingolstadt in Germany. He went to Borussia Monchengladbach in January, and I can remember they were in a relegation battle. Lucien Fabre was the coach, and he was training with the first team. He impressed them significantly and the team started to turn their fortunes around. They were even taking him on the trips away as a lucky charm. He was adapting to life in Germany.

They ended up avoiding relegation and a year after, he was registered and made ten appearances for Borussia Monchengladbach. He would have been 19 or 20-years-old at that stage but for other reasons, he didn't make it at the club. He was well-respected. He needed to turn that experience around, which he obviously had. He's had a wonderful career, but that's where it started. Mathew is technically proficient, but you look at the total package, he's got so much more than other players, and that's why he's been able to carve out a successful career in Europe.

A lot of our Australian players, good players, don't understand what their roles and responsibilities are without the ball. Matthew understands what he needs to do.

When Robbie Kruse learned what to do without the ball over there, he also became a much more complete footballer and also had a successful career.

On guiding Australian players

I'm always trying to guide players and get them to understand that if you don't work harder in these areas, especially running all day, then it's going to be very difficult for you to have a career.

With younger players, I am always honest with the parent and say, "If you want me to lie to you, I'll lie to you, no problem, but if you want me to tell you the truth, I'll tell you the truth. Your son either doesn't run or can't run, or chooses not to run. Both are going to cause him a lot of problems in his career."

These things are so important. If you're never physically fit, it's very, very difficult to make it at the top level. It's near impossible. Name me someone who we've sent over that's been successful in Europe in the last 10 and 15 years that physically wasn't elite.

On why there are not many Australians currently in the elite European leagues

I've got Liberato Cacace over there now. He's got a chance. Alou Kuol was over there.

I've got Jacob Italiano over there, physically he's a beast of a player.

It's going to be even more challenging now than ever. But I also believe that there could be more opportunities. Our point of difference as an agency has been value for money. For example, Liberato Cacace, if he was South American or Brazilian, he would have cost a hell of a lot more for Sint-Truidense (a Belgian Pro League club) and they wouldn't have been able to afford him.

Clubs will continue to look to these markets like Australia and Japan for good quality, but at a cheaper cost. We need a success, we need a Jacob Italiano at 19 or 20 years of age to play in the Bundesliga, score a couple of goals and then all of a sudden people ask where he came from. Just like when we had Mark Viduka, Harry Kewell, Tim Cahill, Lucas Neill, Brett Emerton, Jason Culina, John Aloisi and Craig Moore. All of these guys were playing at the top level and all of a sudden, we had credibility. Which we don't necessarily have now.

On dealing with international clubs

I've dealt with a couple of people in Japan but I haven't done any deals in South

Korea or Thailand. Japan need to see you face to face, and then you've got that credibility and respect and they know you take your vocation seriously. I found it similar to dealing with clubs in Europe and even with the agents. If you have an agreement with a club in Japan, then you can guarantee that your fees are going to be there on time when they're due.

And obviously, their care and hospitality for clients we've sent over has been nothing short of first-class. They do everything possible to ensure that the player is well looked after. I've never had any issues dealing with Japanese clubs.

On talent identification

All players have a point of difference. What takes you from being just a good player to being a successful professional footballer? That's what I look for, and we don't have too many that have it unfortunately. I know why that is. There's not enough people here that understand what the level is. Not enough people who travel. I invest in what I do. I don't think there's a lot of agents in Australia that invest as much as we do in terms of going to see world tournaments, and going to see what they're doing in Europe.

I took Ben Kantarovski, from winning the best player in Newcastle Jets when he was 17, to Bayern Munich on a ten-day trial. I spent the whole time there with him and he was training with the under-19 youth team. He looked as good as them, not better, but he looked very good. He looked comfortable playing with them. But then it came to any of the real sharp drills — shooting, crossing, even passing — he was not totally standing out. Game sense, no problem. But in those areas, he needed some more development. And that's the difference sometimes.

That's why Liberato Cacace is going to make it — because his power and running is elite. If you look at his data — high speed metres and all these statistics, which is how they assess players now — he's elite in Europe, already at the age of 20, and he scores goals.

He hasn't scored much yet for Sint-Truidense, but in Wellington in his last season, I think he scored four goals. For a wing-back, for a left-back, that's gold. When you find those ones and his mentality, it's second to none.

When he got there, he was told he had to get a little leaner. He got there within three or four weeks and even with Kevin Muscat leaving, he still played. It says a lot about him, and he plays 90 minutes every week.

(In) The last under-17 World Cup, I had Birkan Kirdar, Luke Duzel and Ryan Teague. Teague was captain — a very talented player, the other two started on the bench. They came on in one game and both made a difference coming off the bench.

The trick for those two is to be able to have that same impact for 90 minutes, not just 20–40 minutes. Christian Theoharis, Gianluca Iannucci and Daniel Arzani were always alight for 25–30 minutes when they were coming on in games in their younger days. But clubs don't want players to play for 30 minutes, they want players that can play for 90 minutes. I am sure all three have now moved up to 90-minute players now. Mathew Leckie. Robbie Kruse in his prime, Brett Emerton, Jason Culina; these guys could run all day long. That's why they were successful.

It all comes down to the understanding of coaches as to the requirements. How do you transition from being a junior player to a senior player? If you don't understand those requirements, it's very difficult to make that transition.

People don't understand that it doesn't matter how good you are, it takes a lot to transition and agents, analysts and coaches will all have a different opinion. Football is a game of opinion and an agent I have a different view on player types.

On understanding the level required to make it internationally

I speak to Cacace about his club, Sint-Truidense, which just avoided relegation last season. How would they go in the A-League? They're a team that's just avoided relegation, so you can imagine the top teams, like the Club Brugges' level. Understanding the level is a big problem in Australian football.

On the most difficult part of the player agent business

I'm happy to make a difficult phone call. It's never been something that I find a difficult challenge or a challenge I'm not up for. Obviously, different regulations in different countries makes things tricky, as does having to register as an agent in Japan. I'm lucky I've got Jan Van Baal.

If we could all come together under one umbrella and have one registration, things would be better. I'm happy to pay a fee, but to have to register and understand the differences in the regulations in each different country is a challenging aspect.

On the best type of player deals

Generally, the best deals are the win-wins, when the club is happy and we are pleased with what we've got. For example, Central Coast Mariners with Alou Kuol. I put Kuol basically on their doorstep because they wouldn't have had a clue who he was. He had to go there and trial and they didn't just offer him a contract, he was playing for a youth salary. Now we've sold him to Stuttgart where they're making money.

Cacace was the same. Deals where the clubs are happy to release the player and you're happy with the situation are the ideal ones. Then, no one feels like they've had the wool pulled over their eyes. The deals I like to do, (I hope) everybody feels like they win.

On the former AIS football program

It comes down to the grassroots and youth development. Do we have enough people like Ron Smith that understand what's required to make us competitive with the top nations? I don't think we have.

It's proven, you can see the talent that has gone through — Mark Viduka, Craig Moore, Lucas Neill — all these guys went through the AIS. We don't have that now. So, we are relying on clubs. It's not adequate. It's not at a level where we can produce the kind of talent that we want to produce. And that's a big problem for Australian football. The clubs have taken ownership responsibility for preparing players but are they producing the same level of players that Ron Smith was producing at the AIS? I'd say not really, clearly not yet.

Chapter 8:
Marketing and Management
– Leo Karis

When it came to structuring a high-profile player contract or understanding the practicalities of an endorsement and sports marketing deal, there was one agent you would go to. Leo Karis was not just an agent licensed by Football Australia but a manager of big-name sport and media personalities. Karis would look at the total management of a player, not just his or her football contract. Whether it was at his office in the Sydney CBD or at a café in the vibrant Sydney suburb of Woollahra, Leo would always make the time for a coffee and chat. His expertise in the commercial value of player deals, marketing and sponsorship opportunities was well-known in the industry. His advice was sought after and if you can get a coffee with him during his busy schedule, you must take it (as I did).

As a manager-type agent, Leo would always ask the questions that you would never have considered or (on) the issues you hadn't identified. Our conversations often turned to cutting- edge themes like incorporating strategies, the viability of player moves or 360-degree overviews of player deals which were all new concepts to the player agent industry at the time. Leo also understood the media cycle, public relations and what risk management issues needed to be addressed by agents and player managers. His sophisticated thinking and savvy approach to agency was world-leading in the early 2000s and ahead of its time. Many of his strategies, his reading of market trends and his methodology for player negotiations have now been adopted by bigger European player agencies. Karis brought best-practice endorsement methods from other sports and product segments where he was operating to football player management. Top and marketable players have now become content creators — something Karis (again ahead of his time) was cognisant of when promoting a player's value.

Background

No one understands player values from a promotion perspective like Karis. Always a sound decision-maker, he understands the value of players to clubs. Strategy and planning are at the forefront of his agent philosophy to enhance the commercial scope for his players. Karis approached the industry as a talent manager with brand management and commercial expertise. It is well-known that in the USA, athletes do nothing for free on the marketing front and Leo would seek the same arrangement for his players to maximise their value. For Karis, agents need to understand that every branding deal is unique and that there is no agreed rate for endorsements. Therefore, good agents need to understand the maths, player value and their alignment with brands.

When Karis was negotiating an endorsement deal, he would aim to layer something a little more complex into the contract. Karis has stated that endorsement deals in Australian football first came with artistic players like Harry Kewell who was seen as very attractive during the World Cup 2006 period. Kewell had deals with Adidas, which used him as the cornerstone of its soccer marketing in Australia, and with BT Funds Management, Qantas and the Nine Network, while Tim Cahill and Lucas Neill featured in an advertisement for Sanitarium that appeared before, during and just after the 2006 World Cup.[83]

Karis also managed and worked with Brazilian star Juninho for his endorsements. Like many international football stars, Juninho had a separate endorsement company set up overseas to deal with his marketing rights.

In terms of his agent business, Karis' football clients included Paul Okon, Mark Bosnich, Ante Milicic, Naum Sekulovski and Michael Beauchamp, who he transferred from Central Coast Mariners to Nurnberg in the German Bundesliga. Karis always kept a low profile, however he had "a real passion for the job, particularly when he saw a player's career grow." He saw his job as a strategic one, playing a "significant" role in a player's development. He observed that "it's about developing a plan for the player's career as well as looking out for his potential outside of football in, for example, coaching or in the media." Karis preferred clients with "attitude and character as the first thing, followed by their potential as a player to move either into the A-League or beyond that league."[84] He is also very selective with clients and has been quoted as saying, "I want to do a handful of, you know, quality pieces of business."

In his own words

On becoming a player agent and manager

I started in the talent management industry in 1992, working for an entrepreneur named Harry Miller who was the guru of talent management back then. But he wasn't interested in sport. It was only when I left and set up my own business in the mid-'90s that I kind of looked at my passion, which was football, and how I could get involved in talent management in the football space. At that time, the old National Soccer League was running. It was struggling. I knew a lot of the elite players in the NSL, but in my opinion, they didn't require representation at the time. Being a semi-professional league, what I focused on was trying to do some business with some of our international stars who were playing abroad. I was building a talent management business across other sports — rugby league and cricket — but not focusing on my passion domestically.

Mark Bosnich and the Socceroos were assembling in Sydney in 1997, and they were staying at a hotel, which was about five kilometres from my house. I remember being in my office on a Friday afternoon and sending Mark Bosnich a fax at the Novotel Brighton Beach, Sydney, asking if he wanted to have a meeting whilst he was in town playing a friendly game for the Socceroos. What piqued his interest was that I was looking after one of the top cricketers at the time, and I still look after him, Mark Waugh. He was one of the stars of the Australian team and I later found out that Mark Bosnich was a huge cricket fan. So, we met the following day. Bosnich was, in a sporting sense, probably after Greg Norman, the highest profile Australian sporting export. He was a huge name at the time, so we had lunch. Bosnich basically said to me, if you're good enough for Mark Waugh, then you're good enough for me, so let's start working. It was as casual as that over a seafood lunch at Brighton Beach, Sydney.

Very quickly, in the space of a couple of weeks, I facilitated his contract with Channel Nine and News Corporation. Just a whole lot of media deals. He was doing a weekly report with *2UE* and *3AW* radio stations, and my pitch was that even though you are in the United Kingdom, you're very far away, you need to be kind of visible. People need to hear from you on a weekly basis. So, he wrote a column for the Australian, which was ghosted, he did two interviews on 2UE and 3AW every week, and then later on picked up a Channel Nine TV contract around the Iran v Australia World Cup qualifier game as a special reporter. Our relationship started way back in 1997 and continued through the period when he came back to Australia. We still maintain a very close friendship over 20 years later.

On the introduction to Paul Okon

I thought I'd reach out to one of my favourite players of all time, Paul Okon. Mark Waugh basically introduced me to Paul, and I drove out to Marconi Stadium to meet up with him at a time when he'd sustained a bad knee injury.

He'd been told by a couple of doctors that his career was over. So, he listened to my spiel about what I could do to help him and he said, "There's nothing to manage, there's nothing to represent." He quickly changed his mind. "I'm going to ignore that medical advice and I'm going to prove them wrong."

I ended up representing Paul in all his transfers out of Italy to the English Premier League and then full circle, returning back to Australia to play for the Newcastle Jets.

On his early representation of players

I was ignoring the NSL, and that sort of lasted until around 2004 when they were talking about the emergence of an A-League. What other sports had taught me, particularly in the National Rugby League (NRL), was the challenge of salary caps.

The elite players in salary cap structures normally get 10 to even 20 per cent of a salary cap. Back in those days, the salary cap was $1.5 million. I went out and reconnected with a whole lot of guys I got to know over the years — Ante Milicic, Simon Colosimo, Andre Gumprecht, (and) young guns like Danny Vukovic and Andrew Durante.

I told many of them that star players in the AFL would be on 10% to 15% of their team's salary cap, as would the equivalent star NRL player, and said, "Why would it be any different for you? If I was representing you, I'd sit down with every club owner and say, 'If it's good enough for that sport and that sport, then Ante Milicic, who was the player of the year in the final NSL season, should be on AUD250–300 grand.' All these guys basically signed up with me and finally, I found the opportunity to help the elite players domestically in a new A-League era, but also had to make things stack up commercially for them and for myself.

On the Juninho deal to Sydney FC

I guess the biggest opportunity was with Juninho Paulista signing for Sydney FC. I heard that Sydney were in the market for a big name and they had a pretty decent budget. So, as us agents do, we spread the word out through our network of partners internationally. Juninho was looking for an opportunity. He was pretty close to signing at Celtic and that fell through. So, he was available and my partner in Brazil said, "I'm going to approach Juninho, do you think there would be interest?" It all happened very, very quickly. He was super keen and with George Perry, the then CEO of Sydney FC, we worked hard to put forward an attractive proposition commercially. Juninho had a young family, so we needed to make sure he was comfortable, and the family was going to be comfortable in Sydney. That was one of the highlights of my career, and I got to be very, very friendly with Juninho. My family and his family would have barbecues weekly, and he was an absolutely fantastic footballer, but a better person.

It's a shame that we didn't see the best of him because he sustained a very serious shoulder injury. But to his credit, he just got jabbed and strapped up and tried to keep playing. Not many people who had achieved what he had achieved in the game would have done that. He was a very impressive character. Had he not sustained that injury, he would have had a serious impact on the park and probably would have signed the following season as well. There was certainly a real desire by Sydney FC to keep him, but maybe the coach at the time wasn't quite convinced that he would have an impact. It's a great shame that he sustained an injury but no doubt he opened some corporate doors.

On the challenges of bringing marquee players to the A-League

I think the big competition now is Major League Soccer (MLS) and its budgets. We've got a lot to offer these players. It's not easy but we should not give up. I think it's really crucial. It's almost as if we've seen a relaunch of the A-League recently and all stakeholders should be trying to reach out to networks internationally to try and secure big names that will bring value. That is the key. It's not just a case of bringing a name, they've got to do the business on the pitch, (and) do business in terms of marketing the league and not just marketing the league domestically. We need to market internationally as well. There are good people in the game at all levels. It's about clubs really opening the purse strings to be able to make these deals happen. But I'm confident (hopefully) given the relaunch of the A-League with a new broadcaster that has an appetite to grow the game.

On the challenges of being an Australian agent and manager

How do you build relationships with people? The person who I ended up doing business with for Okon in the English Premier League was the guy who was representing Bosnich at the time. And obviously, I was collaborating with that agent at the time. But it's just (that) it takes time to build these relationships. I remember being in the United Kingdom one year, and I reached out to the Stellar Group, as I was looking for an agency in the UK during an Ashes tour for someone on the ground to create commercial opportunities for Mark Waugh. They were obviously very, very keen to talk to me because of Mark, not because of me. And that's what I'm saying. You get the access simply because of the reputation of your client and any agent who doesn't understand that has got an ego that needs to be reined in.

On the big spending in the Chinese league when Australians had five years of great opportunities

In the early years, the A-League wrapped up around February and would recommence in August. So, it was a really long off-season. And when things opened in China, there was this opportunity for players to go for three to six-month stints. Mark Bridge played at Tianjin Teda. Bruce Djite was another one, as was Alex Wilkinson and they made more in six months than they were making in the A-League for the season. The last significant piece of business I did in China was with Adrian Mierzejewski after his fantastic season at Sydney FC; he won the Johnny Warren Medal. He's still in China, that was a good piece of business, a fantastic salary for him. Sydney FC got a great transfer fee and I'm all for clubs benefiting. They need to make money out of these transactions.

But I've had some recent conversations with my partner in China, and the culture there is challenging. I have a very, very strong partner that I've developed a relationship with over ten years. I've been to China half a dozen times and you know, my strength in the Chinese market is simply because of my partner. I'm told by my partner that (the Chinese) market will open again for Australian players. Budgets are shrinking there, which means they'll now reach out again to try and find the elite Asian players. I've really enjoyed sending Australian players there.

On Mark Bosnich promoting the FIFA All-Stars game in Sydney

I came across George Christopoulos as the promoter of that match in Sydney for the opening of the Olympic Stadium. There were some issues about the world team and who was coming. They were having problems promoting and selling tickets. I don't know why I was in Melbourne, but I was in this restaurant, George owned it, The European in Melbourne (central business district), I think it was. Bosnich was committed. He was playing the game, but they also wanted Mark Bosnich to take on a very active marketing role in the lead up to the game and promote ticket sales.

We were negotiating over a meal; an arrangement, a marketing agreement for

Mark Bosnich. It was a very friendly discussion. They put a proposition to me (but) the negotiations stalled. I went to the bathroom and told them, "I know what Mark wants, and I know what he's worth." I ducked off for five minutes, came back and we chinked glasses and did the deal, but they needed that five minutes on their own.

On the impact of Terry Venables in Australia

Paul Okon had played for Terry Venables (English coach) not only for the national team, but also at Middlesbrough. And they had formed this fantastic relationship. Paul was back in Sydney between clubs at that stage. Venables had joined Leeds United and they were in Melbourne playing pre-season friendly games. I kept harassing Paul to get in touch with Venables. Terry sort of sat back with his big personality and said, "Do you think you guys can jump on a plane and meet me in Leeds next week?" I looked at Paul and said, "Well I'm available." Terry simply said, "Look, I can't guarantee you that you're going to play every minute of every game, but you'll get your chances. You know what I think of you as a footballer. On that basis, you know, if you want to agree on that basis, we'll work out the money side, but you know, I can't guarantee you'll start the game." So, I looked to Paul and asked if he could live with those terms. We shook the great man's hand and said, "See you in Leeds next week." We jumped on a plane and went and finished the business. But what a wonderful man. Huge, huge personality and I really enjoyed dealing with Terry Venables. He was fantastic.

On representing Simon Hill — ex-Fox Sports and current Channel 10 commentator

I've always had an interest in media talent, (but) it was almost a fluke. I was over at *Fox Sports Australia* because I had talent that worked there, and I was meeting with one of the senior executives at the time, Tony Sinclair. Tony was responsible for production and the on-air talent. The season had just finished and he said to me that he wanted to create some new shows. He knew that I was a football nut and said that he wanted to add a new sort of commentator. I said that I knew of the perfect guy at *SBS TV.* Tony said, "Well, go and get him for me."

I cold-called Simon to catch up and have a coffee with him. It was a pretty modest contract at *SBS*, but he'd been loving the work and he had another year to run. Simon wanted to go to the World Cup in 2006 and couldn't break his contract and miss out on that opportunity.

(But) We convinced *SBS* to release him immediately so he could join *Fox Sports.*

In return, Fox would allow him to fulfil his obligations for the World Cup, which was very important for *SBS* to have their lead caller. Simon started his journey, which lasted 15 years at *Fox Sports*, over a casual conversation between Tony Sinclair and me.

On how relationships create football opportunities

This is a relationship business. There's no doubt about it. And through those relationships, opportunities arise. I've been very, very careful about building relationships. I have seen on too many occasions, where you walk into a meeting and you're with a key executive and the key executive brings in a junior. They do a lot of listening and that junior in three or four-years' time is sitting in the executive position. I've been super mindful that you need to be a calm and friendly operator.

In 2016, I was in Athens, watching the Greek national team play Finland in a European Championship qualifier (Euros). Greece lost the match 1-nil, which mathematically meant that they couldn't make the Euros. I was sitting with some pretty senior, experienced Greek football people, consultants, agents, etc., and the final whistle blows and everyone's devastated. I looked across and said, "Can Greece come to Australia and play some friendly games next year if they're not in the Euros?" You've obviously got to consider the opportunity. In a month, I'm presenting that opportunity to Ange Postecoglou and Football Federation Australia. Because I was on the ground, because I'd invested time to get to Greece for business, I just happened to be in the right place at the right time. And that's where the opportunity and the relationship-building intersect.

On how football agency and commercial marketing opportunities work

I've done a lot at that level, with the Brett Emertons and the Mark Brescianos, guys I hadn't represented previously, (it's) just that the brands reached out to me wanting to align with certain players for a tournament.

There's been good opportunities around tournaments, and the main brands that want to invest are those that are involved in the game, like Hyundai over the years and National Australia Bank, but there hasn't been a lot of activity lately. I hope that changes with a new free-to-air broadcaster.

I believe free-to-air certainly will help to build some brands, (and) some personalities of the players. But you can't just rely on the broadcasters, the clubs have to do their bit, the agents have to do their bit, and I'm hoping there will be a time where domestic players have profiles and brands see value and alignment with those players, but it will take time. The biggest stars we've had historically have been Tim Cahill, Mark Schwarzer and Harry Kewell. But those guys have now moved on. We need the next generation coming through (now the Matildas have been a game-changer for recent brand sponsorship interest).

On identifying talent

I'm not an active player agent these days, I don't have a roster of talent, but I still get approached by parents and players, and what I look for, first and foremost, is the character of the individual. Sure, you've still got to be able to play football but there isn't a sequential set of steps to becoming an elite footballer. There will be hurdles and setbacks. And first and foremost, if a player doesn't have the mental capacity to deal with challenges, they are not going to make it. Tim Cahill was told at 15 that he was too small and not going to make it. That was the message he was getting domestically, which forced him to go abroad.

Had he not had the mental strength to keep going and to reject all the negative noise, he wouldn't have made it, so that's the first thing I look at. I like technical footballers, I like speed and you need to be a worker. Good attitude is the first thing I look at beyond talent.

On the day-to-day business activities and the most rewarding aspect of the business

Matt McKay serves as a good example, alongside Paul Okon (of the most rewarding aspect). Supporting him (Matt) when he expressed his determination to work tirelessly to regain fitness for professional football. I played a small role, and I take pride in contributing. (Also) Simon Hill—where would his life be today? As for Juninho, I'm genuinely proud. While I wake up each morning mindful of my role as a commercial professional running a business, my primary objective isn't solely financial. With over 20 years in the field, I find myself at this stage (being) primarily as a consultant in football and sports. My goal is to engage in a select number of high-quality business endeavours. And, in terms of football, a handful of quality pieces of football business. And I think I'm doing that and I think I've done that. I haven't focused just on players and having a roster of 50 players, but that's what the industry tends to do with the exception of one or two players (agencies) in the industry. I prefer to have a broader approach. Some player business, some commercial business, some match-procurement business, (and) some media business. I just enjoy the variety that brings.

On how the agency business has changed over the last 20 years

It's always been cutthroat, no doubt about it. The biggest change I've seen domestically is the reluctance of players to commit to one agent long term. I've looked after Paul Okon since 1997, and we've never had a contract. But Paul Okon will never do anything commercially until he puts it to me because he's convinced that I will get the best outcome for him. Ante Milicic, since 2004, will not do anything in terms of business without me being involved because he sees value in it (me). They are very rare arrangements, very rare. You don't need four agents to represent you with only twelve buyers (A-League clubs). That's the biggest change and I don't know whether it's that players feel like they have been misled, I don't know what's led to this, but it certainly is there. It's not the preferred model. Players need to understand that the right agent and building a long-term relationship is a better approach for their careers. There seems to be this reluctance to commit and that doesn't serve them well.

On the challenges in the Australian agency business

The market is so small (here). A nation would really need to have a large market share if they're (agents) focusing on domestic deals, predominantly. I know there are some exemptions outside the salary cap, yet let's say every club can spend $5 million a year. Twelve clubs is $60 million. That ballpark $3 million (less now) in fees or commissions to be shared among the whole industry is pretty skinny.

Chapter 9:
From the NPL to England –
Gary Williams and Richard Rudzki

Gary Williams

Generally, and footballing-wise, Perth in Western Australia seems so far away for those of us based in the eastern States of Australia. Yet I kept hearing that there was one agent in Perth who was consistently sending Australian players to the United Kingdom to join professional clubs and academies. It is well-known that Perth has a lot of expatriate British migrants, however it could not only be the availability of young players with a UK passport that opened that pathway. It must have been more than that; the ability to recognise talent, have an instinct, an understanding of the player and the ability to open doors to club opportunities. This is Gary 'Bongo' Williams, an agent who is somewhat mysterious to many in the Sydney and Melbourne football markets, yet one who has been involved with many Australian players who obtained deals in England's top 5 football league tiers.

Gary and his agency team understood what type of players to scout for the British market and what league level a player could play coming from the NSL, A-League or even the National Premier League (NPL) competitions. Having a variety of networks in England, Gary has provided the launching pad for many Australian players, especially Western Australians, with subsequent access to opportunities in the United Kingdom. He has also utilised one unique NPL club and academy as the platform and driver of that talent.

Background

The player development at NPL club ECU Joondalup (now known as Perth Redstar after a merger) has been a major achievement in Australian football. It helped developed players like Chris Herd, (Aston Villa), Brad Jones (Liverpool), Rhys

Williams (Middlesbrough), Shane Lowry (Leyton Orient), Jordan Lyden (Aston Villa), Alex Grant (Stoke City) and others like Adam Taggart and Josh Risdon. Gary, who shares his residence between England and Perth, is quoted as saying that "I am not sure if there's something in the Joondalup water, but it has been a breeding ground for some excellent players over the years and it's a work in progress, still under the good development coaching of John Brown (originally from Scotland)."[85]

This form of talent development where an agent works with a development coach is a growing model used by agents. Nowadays, scouts, coaches and mentors all help agents succeed in their craft. Within the ultra-competitive environment that exists in the United Kingdom where around 1400 professional players are off-contract at any time, it must be recognised that Gary has forged an effective pipeline of talent from Perth to the UK.

In 2016, former English Premier League club Burnley recognised ECU Joondalup's outrageous production line of talent by entering an official sister-club arrangement which focused on a three-year technical and coach exchange deal. Burnley academy coach Lee Waddington, who has conducted sessions at ECU Joondalup, said that "one of the things I've seen is a really good attitude, character, physical attributes and players technically astute."[86] Basically, ECU's record was extraordinary in that "the production line is right and, pound for pound, it's probably one of the best in the world."[87]

Gary is also well-connected in the England club scene and monitors all the professional or emerging Australian talent playing there at any one time.

In his own words

On his background and how he became a player agent

In 1973, I was released from Manchester City as a player. I was 19-years-old and had the opportunity to come and play in Perth for Ascot under gaffer Reg Davies, the former Newcastle and Wales international coach. I ended up playing all over the world: Hong Kong, Singapore, Belgium, France, and then when I got married, I came back to Perth in the early '90s. I was good mates with Dave Bassett who was manager of Sheffield United and we tried to organise a tour of Australia and Singapore. Soccer Australia, sadly, really gave us a hard time. I recall that they didn't want to do it. It was only Eddie Thompson (former Australian coach) who had some influence that stood by our proposal for the tour. So, I had to finance the tour all by myself. Sheffield United were relegated at the end of the season. I had Barry Greenwood traveling with them. Barry used to be a reporter in Western Australia. He said, "Well, we're all in, we're all on the plane, but they're all on a downer."

I met the team at the airport the following day at three o'clock in the morning. I said, "I'm taking control now. We're playing at the WACA ground against the Western Australian State team." I got all the lads on the bus, turned around and said, "It's two o'clock in the morning. I'm dropping you back at the hotel. You've got half an hour to get changed and get downstairs then we're going out. Anybody late is fined." So, they all came down, and I took them to Perth's Crown Casino and told them they didn't have to front up for 24 hours. And that started the tour absolutely brilliantly.

On the Sheffield United tour opening the market for him as an agent

I'm good mates with Stuart Munroe and Doug Hodgson (both coaches). If you want to get hold of Dougie, get hold of Stuart. So, Dougie came around, and the second game was at Adelaide. It was a Sunday night at Hindmarsh Stadium that holds 12,000, and I had people with me on the gate. I was taking the gate money.

People were queuing up outside. I pulled the lads off the gate and said, "Lads, don't worry, it's going to be 12,000, it's full," and it was and (it) was a great game. This positively impacted my organisational reputation both here and in the United Kingdom.

On the West Ham tour and its impact on Australian players

The next year we did the West Ham tour to Australia. Soccer Australia again did everything they could to possibly stop it. It was only Eddie Thompson (coach) agreeing to play the Australian Olympic qualifying squad at the time that got it done. He said, "Gaz, don't worry, I'll make sure I put a full Olympic side out. When they played Western Australia, Stan Lazaridis had a worldly (game). I ended up putting Stan into West Ham, and also Chris Coyne.

I put Chris Coyne over there on trial and also Richard Garcia, who was just 15. West Ham signed both of them. And they were the first club to open an overseas academy here in Australia. They opened one in Perth, which eventually became Joondalup. Then, we opened one at Blacktown City in Sydney with Kent Trembury. That's how we started sending the players over to England, through these academy tie-ups.

On Australian players having EU passports and UK passports

Many Australian players have European or United Kingdom passports. For me, getting them to the UK was the goal, but in the early days, Soccer Australia made it somewhat difficult for them getting transfers. They made it as difficult as possible (in my experience) to get an international clearance (international transfer certificate) which was required by FIFA for players to move and register abroad as players.

On the difficulty in retaining players and the chaotic agent market

It's chaotic, any man and his dog can go in there. With no regulation it's like the Wild West. And there's no trust. Because you've got agents going in there saying, "I can get you this, I can get you that." I've had players leave me because they've been promised something elsewhere. "I can do you better. I can do this." A lot of English agents are assertive, if not aggressive. And they also have the big companies (agencies) there which take a lot of the cream. It can sometimes be a nightmare business mate, it really is a nightmare (especially in the UK where there is huge competition in the player agency business).

On his negotiation strategy

It depends on what level players are at. We've got such a great reputation of success with Australian players that we've sent over and they ended up playing in the first team and they get them cheap on a transfer (compared to European players).

When I say 'cheap', I mean, we always make sure that the clubs get paid, but gone are the days where a club will pay ECU 50,000 pounds to sign a player at 16.

So, it's all down to reputation. The latest transfer we did, a lad called Matt Dench from ECU, we put him into Charlton Athletic on trial. We just rang Charlton up and said, "We've got a lad looking for this position." We pay the airfares over. And the club reimburses the airfare if they sign them.

We put Ashley Brewer there as well at Charlton. Ashley's in the reserves now, on the bench as reserve keeper for every game. So, you build up a reputation over time and that's what it's about to get the players in or on trial.

On the Kevin Muscat deal to England

Kevin Muscat (Musky) played in the Australian Olympic squad against West Ham. We got on well, and he was playing for South Melbourne. I said, "Perform well for a full six months, then give me a call." He did. Dave Bassett was still at Sheffield United and looking for a right-back. I got Musky over on trial. He loved Musky. He loved Musky's attitude and wanted to sign him at the start of the season. I've done the deal with South Melbourne, flew Musky over. (Then) Dave Bassett rings me up. He said, "Where's Muscat?" I said, "He's in my house now, we're going to be driving up in a minute." He said, "Don't come up, as I'll be leaving."

A week before the next season starts, Dave rings me up and he says, "My left-back's injured, I've got no left-back for next week against Birmingham." We got Musky over on the next plane. It's about ten days before the game, he's trained, he's played left for his first game and he'd never played left before. That's Musky, true story.

On why there are less Australians in the English Premier League now

We went (possibly) Dutch for too long, didn't we?

We got rid of the inside left and we thought we had a number 10. It all went to numbers. I used to say that up to the age of 17, Australian players could match anybody in the world. But then, you've got the academies everywhere in Europe and if you miss on that, then it's really hard to get back in.

On advising players to be patient

I love finding a kid at 15 and putting him overseas and then watching him run out for the first team, like Scott McDonald. I put him into West Ham and he didn't make it. He was very, very close. McDonald told me that Ian Wright went over to him and, and said, "Scotty, you've done well. But remember I got knocked back by seven clubs before I got signed." You can look back at what Ian Wright has done in his career. Then I put McDonald into Southampton. I love when you see them (like McDonald) doing the business.

On how he scouts players in Australia

I'm over in Australia a couple of times a year, I've got the coaches at ECU, (and) Kenny Lowe (ex-Perth Glory coach) now as Director of Football. There's a couple of lads there who I trust completely (their football player judgement), like John Brown and Mickey Quail who are both in their 70s now, but both can pick players capable of going to England. And then I've just got people around Australia who let me know what's going on at clubs and with potential players. All the A-League games are on *BT Sport* live over here in England as well (which I and many English — you will be surprised — watch).

On being a straight type of operator as an agent

Straight down the line (with clubs, players, coaches, football directors and other agents). If they're straight with me. I'm straight with them. We get on and we don't get on.

On the past foreigners he brought to Australia

I brought over epic players like George Best, Bobby Moore, Jeff Hurst, Alan Ball and Norman Whiteside (all legends of the English leagues and football). We did coaching clinics all around Australia. They all loved Australia as a country and lifestyle to bits. I could tell some stories about all of them, but the stories — they're not for printing!

Richard Rudzki

"It falls on me to provide honest, reasonable, fair and emphatic representation for the player." These words from Richard Rudzki encapsulate the essence of what it means to be an agent who works hard and transparently for his players.

Background

Raised in Nottingham, England during the time when Nottingham Forest were one of Europe's premier clubs, Richard Rudzki resided in the hotbed of stylish football. Add his Polish heritage; being known for hard work, organisation and solid technique, and it is no wonder Richard became an agent who shared his knowledge and insights with a tight portfolio of loyal players. Having known Richard for many years through the Australian Football Agents Association Inc., he is one of the few agents who knows the level, pace, power and intensity that players require to make it in the United Kingdom as a footballer. Richard is passionate in seeing NPL (National Premier League) players make it professionally and has an insider understanding of what is happening at the A-League club level.

In his own words

Richard's football background

I migrated to Australia in 1987, (I) was headhunted to come on a two-year contract and I'm still here. I love the place, so I never, ever wanted to go back.

I'm born and bred in Nottingham, but then worked all over the United Kingdom and in fact, quite a number of countries around the world. I've been very privileged to spend time in Brazil; getting involved with the football culture there.

Football has always been a kind of a predominant motivator for me wherever I went, whatever I did. (If) I wasn't watching football, watching Nottingham Forest, then I was playing or coaching. It's a huge, huge part of my life. And then, of course, the kids came along.

On how Richard got into player agency

I'm a professional business manager, trained and educated. I'm retired now, but football has always been my passion. From a very early age I'd played, but stopped when I was about 22 or 23. I got into coaching and did quite a lot of badges, I did some in England and some in Australia.

It was obvious that there was a lack of pathways and opportunities for youth football in Australia, particularly 14, 15, 16 and 17-year-olds.

There were very, very few agents around. It's funny how things work out in life. I had to go to Switzerland on business. My first appointment after I landed the day after was in a place called Frauenfeld, which is 20 kilometres outside of Zurich.

I got up in the morning and it had been snowing overnight and there was two or three feet of snow everywhere. And you couldn't move. I talked to the people at the hotel, and they said there's no chance of getting out to Frauenfeld.

I pottered around a bit and I suddenly thought, FIFA is in Zurich, I'll just go up to FIFA's offices and find out about this agent's nonsense. I caught a taxi, and boldly walked into reception. I said, "My name is Richard Rudzki, I'm from Australia and I'm in Zurich on business. I'm wondering if I could just take up 15 minutes of somebody's time and talk to them about agency, becoming an agent, because I don't really know very much about it."

A few minutes later, a well-dressed lady asked me into her office and spent two-and-a-half hours with me discussing agency. She said that later on that year the rules were to be changed and agents would have to be licensed by their national association. She suggested studying up on the right things and taking the exam, potentially becoming an accredited agent and licensed by the Football Federation Australia (FFA).

That's how I became an agent.

There was a lady (Anne Nichols) at FFA at the time who said the exam would take place in September. I studied the regulations. I still remember Bernie Mandic was there with me and I sat next to him.

The pass mark was 75%, and it was a lot of multiple-choice questions, but they weren't easy. I got 76%, so it was meant to happen!

On the ebb and flow of Australian
youth player development

What we thought was inefficient and inadequate (in Australian player development) now seems to be considerably worse today. We've not made any progress in that respect. In fact, looking back on it now, the structure we had has disappeared. We had Super League's youth football (best v best youngsters playing against each other). We had regional competitions, we had the State teams, we had the AIS, and we had the Victorian Institute of Sport (VIS).

The demise of the VIS/AIS is tragic, absolutely tragic, and I think you can relate that to the lack of development of Socceroo players that go on now to play in the good leagues in Europe. The Ron Smith and Steve (Rocky) O'Connor era, where we bred player after player after player, they were fed into the system, through the regionals, through the State teams, even through the Super Leagues. We were better off then than we are now, in my opinion.

On the genesis of his academy idea
with Derby County

We synthesised a plan of what we would do to try and educate, motivate and find a pathway for the younger youth players. And we came up with an academy structure plan, but it was very, very different to the way academies are currently run, because essentially, they're profit- making. Some are quite good, but mainly they're profit-making centres.

I was charged with costing and putting a long-term plan into place. What we came up with was a very far-fetched, almost ridiculous idea. But I wondered if a Premier League club in the UK might want to get involved.

We wrote a business plan, refined it and eventually caught a plane and went over to the United Kingdom.

Being very friendly with Terry Hennessy, who is still a name in the United Kingdom, opened a few doors for us. The main club we spoke to at the time was Derby County. Terry was an ex-player and a very well-thought-of player.

We presented to the CEO of Derby County, a guy called Keith Loring. And he thinks the idea has legs. We also had quite a bit of interest from Aston Villa.

We came back to Australia and a few weeks later, we received a fax which said that "Academy Director John Peacock will be landing in Melbourne on Friday afternoon. He will spend a week with you, please organise his accommodation. Please show him what you've got. How you go about things, the quality of your players, the quality of your facilities, etc. This will help us make decisions regarding the joint venture."

John arrived on the Friday. He spent the week with us and we went through a whole load of scenarios. We introduced him to Ange Postecoglou, (then) the under-17 coach of Australia. He went to a couple of games, met some aspiring players and had a great time. I dropped him off at the airport and he said to me, "Look, I've had a great week." Interestingly, and to go full circle to 2024, John Peacock is one of UEFA's technical instructors and a UEFA Jira Panel member for coach education. He would be one of the main assessors of Australian coaches who have applied to have their coaching credentials recognised in Europe to coach a First Division club.

He went back to Derby County. And then a few weeks after that, we got a letter saying, "We wish to discuss engaging in a strategic partnership with you that we will finance. Can you please come over here, here's a couple of airfares, come over in the next week or two?"

Dean Hennessy and I flew over, we did four or five days there. We had a three-hour meeting in the boardroom at Derby County where we nutted everything out before we left.

We had a strategy, (and) we spent time with the academy people to emulate what they did. We had a business plan regarding the coaches, the players, how we were going to recruit, the whole bit.

We based the academy at Box Hill, Melbourne. They paid us every three months on the dot. I won't disclose exactly how much, but let's say it was erring on the generous side. We had kit, we had balls, we had everything. We caused waves in Victoria at the time and I think maybe the people at the Victoria Institute of Sport were not entirely happy.

Everything was supplied and they (many talented players) were clamouring to get in. We had Terry Hennessy coaching, six international caps, Jeff Hopkins coaching, forty international caps and John Kennedy, Dean Hennessy and Shaun Lang (all good coaches). We had a goalkeeper coach, we had a physiotherapist. We had everything, all paid for by Derby County. We had facilities, we had pitches, and we'd train once or twice a week, but where we scored was during school holidays. We'd have them in every day, or three times a week. We were ahead of the game at the time, and we initiated it.

Out of that academy came six or seven career A-League players.

On the players he has managed

Terry McFlynn. I bought him over here. Jack Hingert. Dylan Fox, we just placed him recently into the Indian Super League. Picked him up as an 18-year-old.

I don't like the word 'agent', mainly because of its international connotations. But even if I did like the word, I still wouldn't use it. We look at ourselves as player managers.

We are not transactional people. Don't get me wrong, we do transactions. Obviously, every agent does transactions.

On setting up trials for players in England

We were that far in with Derby County that on my old business card, we were allowed to use their insignia, the Derby Ram. That's how we became agents and they signed up five or six players from our academy, which included James Meredith, Leigh Broxham and three or four others. Derby County gave Meredith a 2-year scholarship, then I flew over and did his first professional contract.

It was a joy ride for us, but very, very hard work. But I had to concentrate on my own printing business as the Derby County relationship ended. If we got a Messi along the way, then the rules (would have) change(d). But we never really seriously thought it would happen. The chances of getting a really good one was very slight. It's a numbers game. You have 100 players. You might get one, the chance of doing it with 10 is very, very slight.

It was never, ever a money-making situation. Don't get me wrong. There were times where we made a few quid. And if one came along, and we made a lot of money, we'd say, "Thank you very, very much."

On capping the number of players his agency manages to around 10

I would cap the number of players to ten, and we still do that. We were at a stable of six or seven players, and we became bona fide.

We've been doing this now since the year 2001, so coming on for 20 years. There were four of us involved. My brother, he was our man in the UK. Over here in Australia, there's myself, Dean Hennessy and Terry Hennessy. Terry's now backed out. He's in a residential nursing home and has early dementia. He can still hold conversations, but he's declining, and we put this down to the heading of the ball.

On developing overseas markets for players

I probably used to go over to the UK at least twice, maybe three times a year, not necessarily for football purposes. I was always attaching football to it, but my work took me to England quite a bit because all the Polish people are there. That's where all the main machine manufacturers are, which I needed for my business.

Day to day, with only having ten players to manage, I probably would spend anywhere between three or four hours a week, or on a heavy week maybe 20–25 when there's transfers going on.

What keeps Richard awake at night

Well, international phone calls keep you awake at night. Because they train during the day, you can only get them before training or after training, and you have to schedule your lifestyle to theirs. Weekends and two, three and four a.m. phone calls are the order of the day, which is not terribly pleasant.

On the unique experience of the John Hutchinson trial in England

We were looking after John Hutchinson (ex-Central Coast Mariners all-time most-capped player), who played in the National Soccer League and was desperate to go to the UK. One of the trials was at Derby County and I happened to be in England at that time. I went along to Moor Farm on the Monday morning, just as Terry Wesley, the academy director, was standing next to John Gregory, who was the manager at the time. Hutchinson was playing for Derby, number 7, I think. John Gregory absolutely (got) stuck into him in the first half. His language was ferocious.

Roy McFarland was the coach at Chesterfield and I knew Roy really well. He said, "Is he an Aussie?"

I stood with him throughout the second half. McFarland was encouraging, "Well done seven, get it across son, well done mate, well done."

As the match finished, John Gregory says, "Hey Rudzki, you can take your player with you today, if you ever send me anybody like that again, don't bother setting foot in this club."

Roy McFarland then said, "Send him to me on Monday, I like the look of him. I'll have a good look at him mate, you send him to me."

It really is a game of opinion.

On the differences between the game in England and Australia

The game is invariably quicker and more aggressive in England than in Australia, and players have to adapt to this as soon as possible, Some find that they can't. It can be a baptism of fire when they play their first few games over there. Also, in a nutshell, some Aussie youngsters are lagging behind in game intelligence, game awareness and game management. These three significant game factors must be seriously ironed out before most players can get a career in England.

On negotiating deals for players

Generally speaking, my negotiations are not at Premier League level, they're in the lower leagues of England. I've done some deals in Holland (Netherlands), I've done a deal in Belgium, one in India, one in Poland, one in Denmark.

I find a few people I deal with in the A-League have not (got) a lot of higher-level negotiating skills. My whole business life has been about negotiating, and I've become, in a business sense, quite a skilled negotiator. My starting point is to use my negotiating skills.

I try not to focus just on the salary side of things. You look at a much broader package and you try to be as creative as you possibly can. Where you don't succeed in reaching an objective, you try and weave it in somewhere else. The thing in negotiation is to have it fixed with your player before you go into negotiation, it's managing your player and his or her expectations.

Then it all comes down to how badly the club wants them, (and) how much they've got left in their salary cap. Who else is in the arena? They're going to try and get what they want as cheaply as they can. The most important thing is to manage a player's expectations. Otherwise, the club's deal is dead and your deal is dead.

On how he deals with difficult players, coaches and agents

Difficult agents, well, obviously I'd confront them. I try not to be nasty about it. But if anybody wants to pick a fight....... Not so much nowadays, but certainly, I was always up for a decent scrap. But I tend not to go in as too much of an attack dog, more from a point of view of holding my own and getting my points across and winning the battle. I'll never shirk the battle. I'll always take it head on.

The one thing I've always stuck to is I don't want to be one of these agents that's in the CEO or coach's ear all the time and trying to permeate things, saying

"You should be doing this, you should be doing that." At the end of the day, the club is the employer of the player, not me. They have their culture, and they have their way of doing things. So, on a day-by-day basis, you've got to give them the freedom to do that.

On the challenges of promoting young Australian players now

We have a lot of good young players in the NPL, which I'm 100% convinced could play in the A-League. The A-League's got itself a little stale and into an ad-hoc pattern recycling of players (a huge proportion of Australians fans would agree with this proposition) and coaches too. In my opinion, the product is now sometimes boring. It's hard to watch at times. It's gone downhill from, say, five years ago, six years ago when we had some good foreign players coming in and the league was on the up. It's now a bit repetitive and boring, and probably just as hard to get into for a youngster.

The intensity we once had in sport in this country was probably second to none around the world. The advent of the AIS about 25–30 years ago was a world leader. It was a development machine at every level, and we were the flavour of the month around the world. We had the raw material they could mould very quickly overseas. We'd be able to send them abroad even though they were a bit raw. They could cope technically, but they were superior in athletic ability, etc. We were able to get players through.

Now, they all are light years away. They don't know when to step up, they don't know how to transition, they don't know when to get in front of the player. The kids in England and Netherlands and Germany had that bred into them from the age of 10, (and) certainly by the time they get to 13 or 14.

We don't have enough good players to be able to put the best versus best together.

And it's even harder now because the English system, the foreign systems, they're on the ascendancy, whereas ours, no way. That gap is widening at a rapid rate. We don't have the coaches, (and) we don't have the facilities because they've all been diluted.

On the future of the football agent industry when FIFA brings in new regulations

We don't know the exact nature of them, but we've got a fairly good idea and basically all we're doing is resetting the clock. We had a reasonable system in place.

The system fell down before because it wasn't regulated. It wasn't policed. If it was, they would have stamped out a whole load of problems. Instead, they changed the rules, thinking that was going to solve the problems. By deregulating, all they did was invite every bloody wannabe. Go to the United Kingdom and go to an eighth or ninth-tier game on a cold Wednesday night and there'll be 10 agents on the touchline. There are people pretending to be agents.

There's a lot to being an agent now, especially an international agent, the rules, and regulations and what you can and cannot do in different countries. The networking, it's a proper, proper job. If they change all the rules, and police them and get it right and restore some pride and some respectability and some education into the system, then it would be a worthwhile career to pursue. They'd have to be very, very good and smart to make a good living out of it.

Chapter 10:
The Pitch – Ritchie Hinton
and Zeljko Susa

Ritchie Hinton

When it came to understanding the structure, rules and intricacies of the A-League salary cap, Ritchie Hinton's knowledge was second to none. He was aware of what was in, what was out and how deals were structured by clubs. In 2015, Hinton had bedded down an 'A-League Salary Cap Pyramid' worksheet table which detailed how the salary cap worked and the club requirements for each category of players; from marquees, senior players, key role players, squad players to back up players, and how developmental talent fitted into the cap.

Ritchie was always transparent with his players as well as candid in his views, even if players or clubs did not want to hear it. He was a realist in that opportunities can come and go very easily in the business. He said, "If the player is injured, out of form, there is nothing an agent can do for the player's career progression."[88] Conversely, according to Ritchie, agents have a dual role in the football industry. They bring in money from transfer fees to clubs for players and they also introduce the next generation of talent coming through. Ritchie would concur the agent industry is a ruthless business and only hard work and networking gets results. In a business where there is no real course and template, you have to find your own way and learn how to get results for players.

Background

Hinton did not just understand the Australian football market, but he had key insights on whether A-League players should play overseas or what step was best to take their career to the next level. This insight was showcased by Alex Wilkinson transferring to the South Korean K-League from the Central Coast Mariners. Wilkinson's successful transition was based on market insights from Ritchie, as

K-League teams tactically aim to always win the ball, are more direct and get it forward as quickly as possible, while the A-League at the time was more based on tactical build-up and keeping the ball.

Further, Hinton understood that players may only get one big club opportunity in their career. For example, he had to ensure that the Luke Brattan deal to Manchester City was completed. Brattan stated, "I'll meet up with my agent [Ritchie Hinton] when I get to England and he'll go over some things with me. City is a massive club, and this will be a once-in-a-lifetime chance."[89]

Hinton's ability to complete deals was also highlighted when he was asked to assist in transferring players out of Adelaide United in 2009. He was given the remit to look for clubs for Brazilian forward Cristiano and Ghanaian national Owasu.

In his own words

On his background and migrating from England to Australia

I was a pretty decent junior sportsman. I was lucky enough to represent school, district and county in a couple of different sports at schoolboy level. I was actually probably better at cricket to be absolutely honest. I'm from South Yorkshire, a place called Doncaster.

I think there were something like 20-odd professional football clubs in the area, whereas there was only one cricket club. Back then that was Yorkshire. I wasn't really good enough to play for Yorkshire cricket, and I ended up getting scouted to join a Doncaster schoolboys' game to go on and try out for Leeds United in their youth setup. I ended up spending a bit of time with them and to cut a long story short, didn't make the grade there. But it did open my eyes, obviously, to the possibility of what a career might look like. Luckily, I was still pretty good at school, so it wasn't an all-eggs-in-one-basket approach.

I ended up qualifying as a lawyer and working in London. Then I met my wife, who is Australian, and we made the decision to relocate to Melbourne. That was back in 2005. To be honest, my heart wasn't really in law, but I took a job with a pretty big Collins Street, Melbourne firm. To be fair, the work was good quality. My boss was great, but I still didn't like it. I really enjoyed the study of law and the intellectual side of it. But the actual practice of it, I didn't find stimulating. I made the decision pretty early to get out, and I'm happy I did that.

I'd always had this sort of inkling in the back of my mind that sports law might be a good thing for me. The agency side of things sort of crept into my mind, but not in a really serious sense, because I knew how difficult it was to get into that industry.

Nevertheless, I sent off a few letters and got a response from an organisation called Proactive Sports Management. They had a bloke involved named Jesper Olsen (ex-Denmark international). He was one of my heroes, he was actually on my wall. He played for Manchester United back in the '80s, and he was part of the discussions. I came into the firm to basically provide structure, a bit of a business plan. But that was only ever really going to be short term. I spent six months with those guys. The next bit of luck came via my wife. She shared an office with a guy called Peter Mann, an ex-AFL footballer from North Melbourne and Fremantle. He actually kind of built the AFL Players' Association after he stopped playing football and became a management consultant. He introduced me to Elite Sports Properties (ESP), who had been his management company when he was a player.

On moving into football agency

The ESP company was run by former Olympic swimmer Rob Woodhouse and Craig Kelly, the Collingwood Football Club premiership player from the '90s, and a Canadian guy called Scott Davidson, who was heavily involved in licensing. I met with those guys halfway through the first A-League season. They were interested in football, but frankly were a little bit dubious of its credentials and had been a bit scarred by what they'd seen in the collapse of the old NSL. They'd seen the ethnic divisions, yet they were sort of interested because they had seen the new era of professionalism that John O'Neill had brought in, with obviously Frank Lowy as chairman. They were really keen to stay away from old-style soccer. I think I had the right accent. I had the legal qualifications. Obviously, I knew what contracts look like, I'd had some sort of background in the sport, obviously, albeit pretty embryonic as a junior. And I was willing to take a pay cut and try something different.

It was a bit of a sliding-doors moment, really. But I don't think there's too many other people who have been paid to start working without really having any contacts at all. I worked really hard. There were a couple of established agents who I respected but within a couple of years, I had about a 10 per cent market share of the A-League.

We managed a lot of AFL players like Nathan Buckley, Mark Ricciuto, Garry Lyon and Olympic Games swimmers Eamonn O'Sullivan, Jodie Henry and Michael Klim. It was those relationships that helped us get a toe in the door with football parents in particular.

The first point of difference that we had was the introduction of a mainstream corporate agency model to football in Australia. It had obviously existed in AFL but had never really been tried or developed in football.

On working with Elite Sport Properties

They had established contacts and networks, so that was really useful. The more transactional nature of football management and the opportunities to move clubs more easily were challenging. It was an interesting couple of years. We were starting off and we got pretty big, pretty quick. So, I took on a 2IC — Zeljko Susa (former player) and we became business partners.

It became obvious that what we had was a really good niche business, but it didn't really work in that environment. So, we decided to carve out the football side of things and went out on our own.

That was after about five years and we became Pitch Management. I've still got close relationships with guys at ESP to this day. And I'll be forever grateful for the opportunity. I think it was a bit of a trajectory moment that enabled us to grow that quickly.

On early player deals and the development of the
Pitch Management business

Some of those early guys we brought in had success to different levels. We brought in Cristiano who was a Brazilian, we brought in Joe Keenan, also straight from the Eredivisie and into Melbourne Victory. He'd been a former England under-21 international and had played for Chelsea's first team. We brought in some guys and it wasn't always the high-profile guys that did really well. We brought in one of the first Asians into the league, Song Jin-Hyung; one of the first guys to take advantage of the Asian spot. He came in and won the premiership with Newcastle Jets in his first five or six games. That was a great story, and we also brought in another positive story, Michael McGlinchey. Michael had been this sort of wunderkind at Glasgow Celtic and not really made the grade and was, frankly, floating a little bit and looking at lower league Scottish football.

We managed to get him the opportunity to come over for Central Coast Mariners and he had this link to New Zealand through his dad. He was actually born in New Zealand to Scottish parents but had no connection with it (New Zealand) and hadn't gone back there since he was an infant. Michael did quite well and we explored the New Zealand heritage and he ended up getting a passport, played for the national team, went to a FIFA World Cup and had a decent career in the A-League with the Central Coast Mariners, then the Wellington Phoenix and back at the Mariners again. There are some really nice stories. Cristiano is still in Australia to this day, settled in Adelaide. Joe Keenan is still in Melbourne. You realise you've helped these guys' lives as well as their careers.

When the old National Soccer League had collapsed, it had been a bit of an exodus of the top end talent and I wanted to spend some time getting those guys back; those who had perhaps not made the bright lights of the Premier League but were solid professionals. They were probably going to be much better options for clubs that needed to fill domestic spots than just trying to get the best of the local Victoria Premier League players. I spent a lot of time in that space and had a lot of success. We brought back Paul Reid, who subsequently went on to get Socceroo caps and had a great career with Adelaide United and Sydney FC. He was playing at Brighton. Daniel McBreen was struggling in Scotland to find a new opportunity. We brought Daniel back as well. He ended up having a really great career and I knew that those guys would.

We brought Shane Huke back in, he was playing for Dagenham. We brought back Gareth Edds, he had a really strong career with Tranmere. I bought back Reece Crowther, who was a six-foot-five Australian goalkeeper in the youth team who had a few reserve games at Queens Park Rangers but did not quite make the grade.

On the export side of things, the highest-profile one in the early days of the A-League was Danny Allsopp. I'm pretty sure he was the first Australian to play in Qatar. I think Tony Popovic may have gone from Palace to Qatar at the end of his career, but that's quite different to moving from Australia. We were the first to export a player to Qatar.

Allsopp's transfer fee was in the mid-600s. That was a big transfer fee back in 2009 and a great move. Danny's a great guy and got a good price tag on his career. The money that Danny got by moving to Qatar was life-changing for him, and we subsequently gave him another great experience and moved him into the Major League Soccer on the back of Qatar, which I think again was probably the first time an Australian had gone to the MLS straight from the A-League (via Al-Rayyan Sports Club of Qatar).

He had a great couple of years overseas and I was really happy for him on a personal level, but really proud to have done that deal. They were difficult deals to do early on. You're dealing with sort of quasi royalty, really. You're dealing with sheikhs, and it's not a normal business environment to be dealing in, they're not normal transactions. I sat in rooms at 1 a.m. in the morning, waiting for government meetings to finish before talking football, which was mainly a plaything for some of them to a degree back then.

Another one that gave me a lot of pleasure was Michael Marrone. I managed Michael from his days as an AIS player. He was a South Australian boy, however he only just managed to sneak into the last roster spot at Adelaide as a Youth League player. He really did it the hard way.

No one was really talking about Michael Marrone. He was probably under the radar. To manage to move a player like Michael to Shanghai Shenxin in the Chinese Super League at the peak of (the) Chinese league was really, really satisfying.

On pushing players' careers to the next level

This was in the time when Australia hadn't really achieved much as a nation. When we made the Daniel McBreen deal in 2009 and the Marrone deal and Matt Simon's deal, it wasn't at a time when we had an amazing national team that was winning everything. Budgets weren't always that big either. I think there's this misconception that the Asian budgets were huge. In truth, the sale came down to your relationships with the local agents over there. We spent a lot of time and money traveling to South Korea, developing personal relationships.

I think another example of that would have been Kosta Barbarouses, who we moved after he had a breakout season in Brisbane. Ange Postecoglou had taken a chance on him as a foreign player and took him to Brisbane.

Barbarouses has a Greek background. The passport is complicated. We saw an opportunity to move into Russia, which was one of those European jurisdictions that was non-EU and had more flexibility with who they could bring in.

We thought it was an opportunity to get some genuine game time in and get promoted to the Premier League, but it didn't actually work out for him in Russia. The team had some financial difficulties, but we then subsequently managed to move him into his favourite boyhood club, Panathinaikos.

The first club might not have worked out super well, but then within six months, he's playing for his boyhood team in an Olympic stadium in Athens, in a derby against Olympiakos and you're thinking, you know what? That's great. I've played a massive part in that.

Alex Wilkinson is a really down to earth, straight down the middle, originally a blonde kid from Sydney, and he'd probably be the first to tell you, not necessarily the most technically gifted.

He was always your eight-out-of-ten player that never had a bad game. Mr. Reliable. Lawrie McKinna had made him captain at an early age and saw leadership qualities in him at Central Coast Mariners after working with him at the back end of the NSL at Northern Spirit. He'd gone under the radar and played a couple of hundred games but was nowhere near a Socceroo cap and no one ever talked about him. It seemed like everybody except Alex was getting a look in. We moved him in

2012 to Jeonbuk Hyundai. He spent three years there and won two Championships.

He became a star in that league. He went to the FIFA World Cup and played every group game. I couldn't have been happier for him and his family. That was a really pleasing deal for me.

On the Luke Brattan deal to Manchester City

Luke Brattan's father Gary was born in England and is from a place not too far from where I lived in northern England. We developed a relationship and I managed Luke.

Whilst a top A-League player at Brisbane, the club were going through some pretty serious financial problems. They weren't paying wages. They weren't paying superannuation. This was after Postecoglou had left, I think John Aloisi was the coach at the time and again it was a sliding-doors moment. We saw an opportunity. Luke had not been paid his superannuation for a long, long time. We went through all the proper processes with the FFA, the grievance procedures, etc., and got him released from his contract because they had technically breached it. That enabled Luke to take advantage of his UK citizenship.

The move was actually to Manchester City, it wasn't to Melbourne City. He signed a multi-year contract with Manchester City and spent some time with them for about six months. They were assessing his level playing with their development team, although it didn't work out. There're a million reasons why things don't work out. It's competitive.

(but) That relationship with Manchester City came through because of the relationship with Melbourne City, where he went when he came back.

I think Daniel Arzani has gone down that path since, I was pretty proud and excited to be part of it. Spending time at Melbourne City with Brian Marwood at City's training ground, seeing the level of professionalism after flying over there with Luke.

On the day in the life of Richie Hinton as an Australian player agent based in Melbourne

No two days were the same. Sometimes it would be player identification, things like looking at youth teams and looking for talent. I'd spend time speaking to coaches, Youth League coaches, Institute coaches — picking their brains.

Depending on where you were in the season, there could be contract negotiations. At different times of the year, you'd be busy with different things. The January window became the major Asian window. But then you'd come to the end of the normal season, and in the June-July period you're renegotiating for your A-League players or looking at Europe if that was appropriate. It was very dependent on where you were and on the players you were trying to find spots for. It was dealing with your Nikes and Puma, trying to get some bigger deals. I think ESP did a deal on the back of the 2006 World Cup for John Aloisi because he was the face of football at that time.

I think back to the amount of time I spent on the phone. All you've got is relationships. That's what you've got, you're selling yourself, and then once you sell yourself, your ability to deliver on what is promised purely comes down to your networks and your relationships. I spent a great deal of time on the phone. And to be honest, sometimes in Australia, depending on the time of year, I spent more time on the phone outside of normal business hours because I was dealing with Europe. I think that's probably one of the things that made me quite different in the early days. I had a corporate structure that forced me to plan out people to report to. But also because of my legal background, I probably had the structure. I had a plan.

On dealing with difficult players, clubs, parents and agents

I can think of a few examples actually and it's probably not appropriate to name names. Some parents thinking they've got the next Pelé.

I pretty much always took a 'no dickheads' approach to youth recruitment. I would never sign a player who I didn't feel was right. The players and the parents come as a package. I never wanted to sign a player and I don't think I ever did knowingly sign a player who I thought was a brat. Or whose parents were delusional and a pain in my arse, to be honest.

I would spend as much time as necessary, talking, reassuring, (and) explaining, and whether they bought my version of management versus somebody else's was up to them. If they didn't, I can live with that. Then again, I think there was some sort of integrity that came from my legal background.

I'm not a natural salesman, which sounds weird because I was a football agent, but I think that was almost a strength of mine. It was obvious to people that what I was saying was genuine. It's the Yorkshireman in me as well.

I remember one player. He'd been a junior captain all the way through his age group, played for the national team at junior level and just was struggling to make it. I remember getting phone calls from his dad asking what I was doing. Why I wasn't getting him deals.

At that point, we were at another A-League club, and their off-field problems had become quite serious. You try to help as much as you can. I tried really hard as an agent to help as much as I could. People were aware of the issues, the PFA, the club, and suffice to say, that relationship didn't last very long. But I could live with that, because I did the right thing and I think managing people's expectations and telling the truth is key. Sometimes I probably cost myself players that I could have signed by telling them how brilliant they were, and that it was all going to be okay, rather than giving them the reality of what it was like.

I did go through an experience with a marquee player in the A League who basically didn't deliver. They wanted him out. He had time left on his contract. I had to deal with the coach. You shouldn't really be dealing with a coach, you should be dealing with a football director.

Sometimes you get these sorts of veiled threats (especially at some overseas clubs) that you won't work with this club again if you can't help, but of course, your client is the player. We want the player to be valued. He wants to be happy. You don't just sign a player based on his form.

On talent identification and recruitment

I think there's a lot of rose-tinted glasses when we talk about players of the past and we sort of bunch the players from Eddie Krncevic and Frank Farina all the way through to Brett Emerton together. You're talking about a 20-year period there. It wasn't always like there was a steady stream, and I think there's a little bit of revisionism that's gone on. There were top players here that if this production line that theoretically existed (really) did, (they) would have gone and they didn't. So, I think there's a little bit of a reality check around that mythology. There maybe was never this never-ending export line of players going to Europe before the A-League.

I'm a firm believer that you learn to be a player in a club environment. You don't learn to be a player in a classroom or in a bubble in Canberra. Now I understand why the AIS existed originally, but when you talk about Melbourne Knights and that model of developing players, there was a lot more organic growth through their own academies and the Melbourne Knight's program at the time.

When you look at that model, it's not a model that exists globally. You are really looking at minority models when you look at places like Germany and Holland where they develop players through their own academies. The future of development is that alignment and that is the silver bullet that everyone is looking for in Australian football — the alignment of the local grassroots football and the elite domestic competition.

It can't continue to be the case where the richest or middle-class parents can pay for their kids to play in the youth teams of supposedly elite National Premier League teams at State level. It shouldn't be for the richest people, it should be the best players.

The realities of the A-League mean that not all the clubs can afford structured academies from 15's to 18's. Well, why not partner? Why not look at a healthier relationship with the local State league teams rather than viewing them as competitors? There's lots of politics and history behind all this and I don't pretend to have all the answers.

I guess in a roundabout way, talent identification is something that happens organically. Through time, I've seen, and I'm sure we all played with guys that were brilliant at 12 and rubbish at 15 years of age.

And equally, some guys are rubbish at 15 and brilliant at 18 years of age. Guys all develop at different times. You can tell he's an elite 14-year-old, but there'll be various other obstacles he has to overcome, emotional and physical, before he makes it. For me, you just need to make sure that the pyramid is as big as possible at the base and connected as you go up.

Let's be honest, we're not that close in development terms to the leading Asian teams in the world. Look at how Japan and South Korea develop their players and increasingly some of the Middle Eastern countries.

On dealing with international agents and clubs

In the early days, talking about Australian football was a bit like the film *Cool Runnings*. Talk to Europeans about how good you were at football and they laughed.

They thought we were good at cricket and could surf. At the end of the day, your credibility as a nation was based around the quality of your national team. The Golden Generation gave us some credibility on a global level, as did winning the Asian Cup and even Western Sydney Wanderers winning the Asian Champions League, (they) all gave us little spikes of credibility. My worry now is that I can't see where the next spike is (Central Coast Mariners did well in Asia recently).

I was fortunate in my time to benefit from those spikes, which to a certain extent minimise the perception of us being a backwater. But now I worry because when you look at our national team, we don't have that recognisability (Of course the Australian national women's team — the Matildas — have done very very well!).

It's difficult to see us achieving big things on a global scale. The gap between us and the top Asian leagues looks to be increasing. We're not always viewed favourably and the only way that really changes is through spikes that occur normally through international level and competitions. So, Asian Champions League, Asian Cup,

World Cup, Youth Championships.

And that helped us during my period as an agent at least.

*On any learnings and wisdom that applied throughout
Hinton's career as a player agent*

On a personal level, I always needed to know that I'd done the right thing by the player, ethically. I worked as hard as I could to provide an opportunity and presented all the facts in a transparent way. I acted in an ethical way with the clubs on the other side, with the agents, whoever it was that I dealt with, and felt satisfied in my job.

I think I added a level of objective professionalism to the industry that probably has not always been associated with it.

Sometimes that doesn't make you popular with clubs, or necessarily always popular with your players. But I always knew my contemporaries knew what they got with me.

Zeljko Susa

The players' player agent is something that feels right as a moniker for Zeljko Susa. This label fits with his philosophy. "The way that I work, it's a collective decision. You've got to sit down and look at what I call the circle of trust." Susa brought his previous experience at the Professional Footballers Australia (PFA) as a player relations officer and as a top-flight player and former Olyroo (Australian youth international) to the player agency game. Always available for a Melbourne CBD-based chat and coffee, Zeljko's approachability was unique in the cut and thrust of football agency.

Zeljko's sincerity, empathy and simpatico for a player's career was formulated through his own experience as a player where he retired aged 24 after a freak injury. Zeljko comprehends that many young talented Australians would love to be professional footballers, but simply don't always understand the dedication and the commitment that is required, as well as luck.

Background

To do well in the agents' business, you need to win by affiliation. In other words, you need to connect with people, form good relationships, have good players in your portfolio and have a solid reputation. Zeljko had these qualities in spades, particularly within Australia where everyone knows everyone within the A-League. The football world is small, and with reputation being everything, Zeljko's transparent approach ensures that his phone is still ringing and that's important in this business. Dealing with players like Craig Goodwin and Ivan Franjic over their careers ensured that he had a player portfolio that brought interest from leading clubs.

In his own words

On how Susa got involved in player agency

I stopped playing at the age of 23–24 due to injuries. I had eight operations while playing in the NSL and had a wall collapse on me outside a change room when I went to Wollongong Wolves on trial from the AIS. I studied a Bachelor of Commerce and majored in Sports Management and Marketing. I began working at the PFA and helped guide players through life after football.

On setting up the Pitch Management with Ritchie Hinton

I met Richie Hinton while working at the PFA, and he was at ESP. I basically just jumped across and started working with Richie and ESP back in 2010.

ESP was once a massive sports management company, now it's largely an AFL company. At the time, they didn't actually understand our game, the world game. In the AFL, they have 18 teams that follow the same process. We've got hundreds of different countries, different ways of doing the deal. They never got their head around how we worked in football, so we came to an agreement. I think it was five years after I started that we decided to part ways amicably. They were really great. We still have a great relationship, but that's when we started The Pitch Management.

We looked at the industry and saw there were a lot of brokers; people in the middle of the club that requires a player and the agent that has a player.

We wanted to take a holistic approach where we were representing players, (and) having relationships with clubs, but also helping them with other things. There were a lot of marketing opportunities at the time. There was obviously more money in the game. There were World Cups at the height of the Socceroos where our profile was the biggest of all the national (Australian) teams at the time.

We realised the value of life after football. Even to this day, I still push players to work outside of football and get an education as well.

On Susa's day to day as an agent

It seems from the outside that we're drinking a lot of coffee.

There's a lot of meetings. Our days are pretty flexible. Obviously, ad hoc at times. I tend to go to sleep pretty late at night, past midnight the majority of the time. The phone calls or messages tend to be the last things I do at night. I get up quite early and there's obviously a hell of a lot of messages overnight. (From) Players, clubs and agents.

I tend to pick up the things that have happened overnight and then later on in the day, the local stuff as well. I speak with clubs, players and others.

After lunch, it's a case of speaking to the players after training. There's a bit of catching up. And then I attend games at night. There's a lot of time spent working. Is it a nine-to-five job? Absolutely not. And it never will be. You've got guys that call late at night as well. That's just part of the industry.

On agency becoming a WhatsApp-driven industry

I would say that WhatsApp has made our industry very efficient. You can send documents to get instant replies. It's become probably the best tool for us, especially with the international guys.

The flip side is that you're always accessible. Every time there is a message sent, people think you're available on the internet and then you need to reply.

On his interesting experiences in negotiating player deals overseas

Robert Cornthwaite was my first international deal. It was to South Korea, Jeonnam Dragons. When we went over there, I was quite young in the game, very green if you like.

The agent that I was doing the deal with wasn't available, but his boss was there. We'd agreed on all the terms and everything in the contract before we got onto the flight. We sat down in the office with the president, the chairman, football director and eight other people. We sat down, they pulled out a contract and said, "Sign here."

I said, "Well, hang on. We haven't even looked over the contract. We need to send this back and then obviously send it to a lawyer to look it over." Robbie was right next to me. Suddenly, all these credit cards start flying across the table. They said, "You want more money, here's more money." It was an incredible experience which shows the rich texture of football in Asia and how culturally business negotiations can differ. It all worked out, Robbie made 90 successful appearances for Jeonnam Dragons.

The contract they put on the table was a cut and paste that had some residual name on it.

On not losing face in the industry when a player reneges on taking a club offer

I had another player, we agreed to terms. He was meant to sign in South Korea.

He was flying out to Europe. I'm on my way to South Korea and called the player to make sure everything was okay. Basically, with a flight booked, he told me he was not coming. I let my partner know in South Korea. We drove down to the club.

They weren't happy with it but fortunately, we were able to find a replacement within 48 hours.

On lessons learnt in the agent business

I think the most important thing in dealing with players is being transparent.
I think just being an open book and providing a lot of information actually helps with gaining trust and obviously getting deals over the line. One of the biggest things in our game is the lack of trust. From everyone. It doesn't matter who we are, we're always the fall guy. When you deal with clubs and they're not interested in the player that you provided, it's okay. But if they're interested in the player and you don't come to the party, it was our issue. They tend to lose trust quickly and create a bad reputation for a lot of us.

On the changes in the agency business

What I've seen with the deregulation of the agent's business is that everyone's an agent now. It's quite amazing. I think it's grown and to be honest, there's maybe only five to ten other agents that I know. Some young players are actually signing with agents that obviously don't have the skill sets to take them to the next level. That will cause a lot of grief and plenty of issues moving forward.

On the changing landscape for Australian players —
from the AIS to the current state of affairs

I don't think we play enough football here. We've obviously reassessed and evaluated our youth development and obviously we've got coaching licences and coaching education. I think we've got better coaches, which contradicts what a lot of people say. Some seem to think that the past was actually done a lot better than now.

I think it comes down to kids playing on the street or park. We've lost hours and hours of kids playing football and the unstructured environment. That's where you'll be touching the ball a thousand times. Some Australian players have not touched the ball anywhere near as much as the Europeans, and that's the biggest issue with us technically. We aren't as good as we were previously. But there's a reason for that. You haven't touched the ball enough.

I had a young player overseas in the Bundesliga. He was on trial as a 16-year-old. Football is their number one sport. Our best athletes go to an AFL, rugby league and other sports. It was funny. I was sitting down watching a training session with the coach and he said, "My right- back should be a marathon runner. My number nine could be a sprinter. But they love the game, so they all play football."

Unfortunately, we tend to lose some of our best athletes to other sports. We're in a highly competitive market when it comes to athletes.

(But) I think we're coming back now, and I think you see through a lot of the A-League clubs that we are closing that gap.

The Golden Generation played football every day growing up as kids. Guys like Mark Viduka, Joe Simunic, Josip Skoko, Hayden Foxe and Lucas Neill all had technical ability before they entered the AIS program.

Obviously, they were tweaked and developed further. Yes, you had the sports science there, but it wasn't as heavily utilised as it is now.

On agents being central to scouting and identifying talent in Australia

A-League Academies obviously need to identify players and a lot of players are coming through the system now, where previously clubs didn't have that and they didn't have the scouts. When the AIS was still alive, all it was a scouting network for all clubs. It was pretty simple.

There is always going to be one or two players that we miss and we have recently seen some players come from NPL that actually have the quality and can actually play at the A-League level when given an opportunity.

On international players who come to Australia

I actually am not a big believer in the five import slots, I think it should be reduced. I think if we're going to grow the game, we need to focus on the young players coming through. When a foreigner does come in, you might see him for a year or two and he ups and leaves. Have they got it right? I'm not quite sure. I think the foreign players should be experienced guys that obviously can develop our game and help our domestic players. Potentially, the foreign players could sit outside of the cap, or tweak the rules and regulations regarding the cap to bring in better high-quality players to help grow and develop the game.

On what is the most difficult part of the player
agent business in Australia

There are a hell of a lot of agents and it's scary. At a World Cup in Chile, the under-17's World Cup, I was there with just four other Australian agents. Now the numbers have increased and our game hasn't grown enough for the number of agents that are involved in it.

It's opened up completely. So, competition is enormous worldwide. The A-League is not seen as a scouting ground for foreign clubs. So, it's very, very difficult.

There are less opportunities for players and some key Asian markets are not scouting players here as often as they once did.

On his agent negotiation strategies

It is just communication. I don't use the media or anything like that.

I think it's important to keep things internal. Speak to the club directly and see if there is a way out of a difficult situation. The majority of the time, especially within Australia, you rely on the relationships that you've built over the years. If there is a compromise. If it can be found. It's got to work.

It's got to work for all parties. No one likes getting their pants pulled down. If it's all fair and reasonable, that is a good result. I think the majority of the time you are able to come to some sort of compromise. Obviously, the heart of our business is representing players and they are our clients.

On Australian players being underestimated

Australian players are underrated, unlike Australian coaches. We've developed a great crop of coaches coming through and obviously some of them have gone overseas. But in terms of players, if you speak to European agents, they sort of turn their noses up because you are from Australia.

On advising players to deal with the 24-hour media
cycle and social media

I do have all the platforms, but the only reason I follow is to see what the players are doing. I don't actually post anything. Social media is a tool and it can be a positive tool. But also, when it's not used correctly, it can be a real negative for players.

I worked at the Professional Footballer's Australia (PFA) previously, so I still take a lot of that knowledge and information with me. Education, on not just the social media platforms, but everything else as well, is key. I think the biggest thing for us now is wellness and mental health.

I think we're all trying to get better educated and now realise how difficult it is to be a footballer living in today's society.

On recruitment of players into his agent portfolio

It's a collective approach. You are never 100 per cent correct with recruiting. Obviously, you've got to back your judgment. You speak to various people regarding potential players you're recruiting.

You want to meet them and see the current atmosphere, see if they do have the desire to move abroad. The reality is that some of these young boys coming to the A-League simply don't want to move overseas to better their careers.

We see the A-League as a development league and I think 95 per cent of leagues are. It's difficult to hear that at times. I know the A-League don't want to hear that, but the reality is that the majority of the competitions (outside the big 10 leagues) are about development.

On the most rewarding aspect of the business

I think the most rewarding thing is seeing a young player gain an opportunity and then take that opportunity. You don't see all the hard work and dedication prior to that opportunity. Breaking down stereotypes, especially overseas attitudes to Australian players, is also satisfying.

On coaches

With coaches it's case by case. They have their own opinions on various things and they tend to do things for now. I think that's an area where we need to improve in Australia. The coaches and football directors need to have a long-term strategy within the Australian football climate.

Chapter 11:
On Base – Frank Trimboli
and Vince Grella

I approached both Frank Trimboli and Vince (Vincenzo) Grella for interviews for this book. Although understanding the motivation of the book and wishing me well, both declined an in-depth interview. Nevertheless, not to include Trimboli and Grella would be a disservice to the story of the Australian agents, with Trimboli regarded as one of the more formidable agent dealmakers in the world.

Frank Trimboli

It was a cold morning in London and I decided to simply turn up to the Base Soccer offices to randomly ask for work experience. Just a week. I was told I would meet Frank Trimboli, managing director and another Australian. Frank, an Australian agent based in the big pond of England, came into the office and said words to the following effect: "You have one hour to ask any questions about the agency business and that's it. We get asked for work experience and internships all the time, however, as you would know Peter, football agency is the most competitive business in the world, and we must protect our IP (intellectual property) and player portfolio."

Frank was candid and fair. I understood his reasons for not giving enthusiastic new agents work experience. Established agents must protect their hard work, networks, access to players and hard-earned industry trade secrets.

After the meeting, I realised why *Forbes* magazine rated Base Soccer at number 21 in a list of the world's top sports agencies (and ninth in football) in 2018, estimating that its managed USD $325 million worth of contracts.

Trimboli was responsible for brokering some of the biggest transfers taking place between the main European leagues, notably England, Italy and Spain. A review of the Transfermarkt platform will show that Trimboli and Base Soccer represent more than 200 clients, including Raphael Varane, James Maddison, Dele Alli, Kyle Walker, Son Heung-min and even Carlos Ancelotti.

In July 2019, American entity Creative Artists Agency (CAA) bought out Base Soccer. They look after the commercial interests of players such as Cristiano Ronaldo and Harry Kane.

Background

In the compelling yet competitive and ruthless world of player agency that encompasses the English Premier League and British football in general, Frank Trimboli sits close to the summit. He is an Australian who has made the top echelons of agency and he wheels and deals with the biggest clubs and decision-makers. Astute, tactful and a true negotiator, Frank can sit at the table with top CEOs, presidents and football directors to negotiate from a position of power and purpose. In fact, according to Vince Grella who was previously also part of Base Soccer, "Frank Trimboli makes a football directors' job easier as he is a noted fixer and provides strategic options. Clubs' football director's call Trimboli for resolutions, and he has a lot of influence — that is the mark of a top agent."

Although Trimboli rarely gets involved in Australian players' A-League deals, he did assist Grella with the signing of Daniel Arzani at Glasgow Celtic. Trimboli also led the coaching placement of Ange Postecoglou at Glasgow Celtic and recently to Tottenham Hotspur.

Trimboli also helped facilitate Harry Kewell's first senior managerial job with English fourth-tier side Crawley Town and Yokohama F. Marinos. He also put together the previous coaching deal for Kevin Muscat at Yokohama F. Marinos. It is not easy to promote Australian coaches worldwide, however Trimboli is confident that they should get those opportunities. Trimboli will "always assess potential markets for his clients and push away old age-old perceptions and prejudices over the bona fides of Australian coaches looking to push beyond the glass ceiling of the A-League (which still runs deep)."[90]

After focusing on Europe, Trimboli's return to the Australian market coincided with Grella joining the agency in 2013. "He was persistent and wanted to help Australians. We moved a few boys and now we're involved with Ange." Grella, who prepared meticulously for games, says it's been eye-opening following Trimboli to meetings. "We visited a few clubs in Italy in 48 hours. It was like spending three weeks with another agent, it was that intense — you learn so much. Their calmness in pressure situations makes you feel more comfortable when you're responsible for players' careers. It's not buying a pair of shoes; get it wrong, buy another pair."[91]

When Grella accompanied Trimboli to Japan on a three-day negotiation regarding Ange Postecoglou to shadow and learn the negotiation ropes, he stated that Trimboli as a negotiator was in another stratosphere.[92]

Another important observation of Trimboli is that he does not interfere technically with coaches. Many agents who are ex-players are not liked by football directors as they interfere on the football side. Thus, some football directors prefer more commercial, solution-type agents who don't interfere in the technical side of the club strategy.

Trimboli knows that especially during the mid-season January transfer window when time is limited and nerves are frayed, too much can still go wrong with a deal. It can be a last-minute change of heart by a player, a squabble over money, an injury or a better offer out of the blue that dictates strategy even to the most tenacious agent.

The Frank Trimboli effect

Leon Angel, as chairperson of Base Soccer, and Trimboli are recognised as intermediation specialists within the English and Italian markets.

To keep at the forefront of deals and remain a leader in the industry, Trimboli attends dozens of lunches, coffees and dinners with sports directors and club presidents. It is a customary rule for the biggest agents to receive thousands of phone calls, take hundreds of trips, have extensive meetings at odd hours and sometimes be in the most unexpected places in the world.[93] Trimboli is a very private person who rarely gives interviews. However, in one of the few articles where Trimboli contributed, journalist David Davutovic compiled a compelling insight into his agent story when few local Australian football aficionados knew of his standing in the game.

Ange Postecoglou reflections on Trimboli

Trimboli and Base brokered the coaching deal which saw former Socceroos coach Ange Postecoglou take charge successfully at J-League club Yokohama F. Marinos.

Postecoglou reflected insightfully that "I remember going to a Premier League game and driving with (Frank) and Vinnie (Grella). In the two-hour journey he was on the phone the whole time. By the end he'd spoken to five Premier League clubs, three different managers, two Serie A (Italy) and LaLiga (Spain) clubs. Frank was confident that an opportunity would come up should I decide to leave the Socceroos. Sitting in his office you see people coming through who are among the most important in the game."[94]

Trimboli stated that Postecoglou had the potential to make a mark in Europe. "I wouldn't be working with him unless that was the case. His attention to detail is unbelievable." A bigger deal in Celtic was yet to come and it was Charlie Nicholas, Scottish former professional footballer who played for the club who revealed that Celtic's secret recruitment tool was Frank Trimboli.[95] Trimboli's impact on Postecoglou's career did not stop there and continues to evolve. With his behind the scenes influence, strategic mindset and work ethic, Trimboli is (considered) close to David Levy, Tottenham Hotspur FC chairperson, and worked on a move to Spurs for months before it was announced: "Ange Postecoglou — Australia's first English Premier League Manager."

Entering the agency business

Trimboli was raised in Karrinyup, Perth, and was a Western Australian 100m and 200m (athletics) State champion. He has Italian heritage and speaks the language fluently. He was in finance (qualified accountant) with no skin in the soccer industry when a switch flicked after reading about Italian Christian Vieri's €25 million transfer from Atletico Madrid to Lazio. "I was on the train from Bank to Mansion House and the lights go out, 20 seconds later they came back on. It was literally a light-bulb moment. I had to make a decision. Stay in London or go back and work in the family business in Australia. That afternoon I walked into a bookstore and asked one of the staff, 'Can you show me a book on how to become a football agent?' After realising no such book existed, I thought, 'What do I do here?'"[96]

"Leaning on Western Australian contacts, Trimboli's dad introduced him to Gary Marocchi, who in turn introduced him to local product Chris Coyne. Trimboli was still working in a bank when he completed his first deal, ducking out to meet as many people as possible during a one-hour lunch break. Coyne recalls, "I got a call from Frank (in 2000), he said there was a club in Scotland keen and asked if I was interested? I flew there, met Steve Archibald (a budding Trimboli contact), jumped in a car, and it was done in 24 hours. It was surreal. Without Frank, I probably would've ended up in the NSL (the forerunner to the A-League).[97]"

Bernie Mandic, one of the most significant Australian agents in history, introduced Trimboli to Base Soccer in 2001 and after spending a year bashing down the door of chairman and founder Leon Angel for an interview, he finally landed a gig. Within a year, Trimboli not only survived the cull after Base Soccer went through a management buyout but was named Chief Executive. "My lucky break was in 2005 when I moved Patrick Vieira from Arsenal to Juventus (20 million euro transfer).

That deal takes you to another level in terms of name and reputation."[98]

Approach to the agency business

Trimboli tries to keep low key and away from newspapers; focusing on his work and not looking for headlines or media attention. "For me it's not about being the biggest, it's about being the best for the people you work for. Reputation is important. Trimboli's bulls--t detection radar" has been fine-tuned after 20 years in the cut-throat industry."[99] When it comes to business, he's economical with his time. Meetings are short and sharp; hotel lobbies and his Soho, London office are preferred destinations. Trimboli knows how to swivel to new markets like China (and more recently, Saudi Arabia) when necessary. Trimboli remit is all about "establishing and maintaining strong links with the biggest football clubs"[100]. Further, Trimboli will always be above the hype of the agent industry and he is quoted in saying that "it's nice to be recognised in the upper echelon of a fiercely competitive industry. We're confident (as Base Soccer) that the people who need to know about us do know about us"[101].

Vince (Vincenzo) Grella

Vince Grella, a key member of the Golden Generation, pivoted to the player agent profession. Grella established himself as top NSL talent with Carlton Soccer Club before progressing through the ranks with initially smaller Italian clubs in an excellent career as a player. Now residing near Florence, Italy, Vince would gravitate to agency under the guidance of Frank Trimboli and become part of the Base Soccer agency, with a remit to scout and recruit talented Australian players. Initially, Trimboli tried to convince Grella not to work with Base to avoid being tarnished by the agent's industry. Grella responded by stating, "Look as long as I stick to what and who I am, I want to give it a shot."[102] Grella hired a tutor in England to assist his FIFA agents' exam preparation and he also applied to the Italian FA to get accredited based on his former licence in Australia. He is an Italian citizen but had an Australian player agents' licence (pre-2015).

Background

As a player, Grella knew football dressing rooms well, therefore the agency transition was easier than most in looking for talent. He is motivated by assisting young players and passing on his playing experiences. He managed one of the most exciting tyros in Australian football, Daniel Arzani. At 19, Arzani was rated as a player who may have a career path likely to result in an eventual EPL move. Grella convinced Arzani, whose dancing feet had left a trail of bewildered defenders, to seek an opportunity in Scotland with Celtic. However, an injury cruelly hurt Arzani's momentum at that time. Grella also managed Danny De Silva, who went to Italian club AS Roma.

Vince Grella's agent philosophy

In an interview with me on 20 March 2020 where the main topic was the Australian scouting ecosystem, we both agreed that in Australia there was very limited player scouting being undertaken. Advisors like Grella must consider Australian conditions where clubs rarely give three-year deals to talented players and are forced to make the most of the young talent that they have due to salary caps and squad sizes.

As a European-based Australian agent, Grella also wanted to give Australian clubs a feel of the worldwide transfer market to make better recruiting decisions. He is of the view that most times, you need to convince a European club to take a punt on Australian players, as they have so many other similar players in Europe to choose from.

Furthermore, in a captivating interview on the *Football Nation Radio* show, *The Football Bosses* with Tony Pignata and Michael Zappone, Grella set out his approach to the agent's game by saying he was always there to help players go in the right direction and give them a good pathway. As a realistic agent who knows the difficulty of the player market, Grella was clear that as opportunities are limited for Australian players in Europe, we now see many players coming back to Australia as an easier option.[103] In terms of Australian player development, Grella was circumspect around the reported lack of young players coming through, suggesting that the issue is not the young players coming through, but the opportunities that they have. He is also big on player resilience and temperament, and he prefers to give full and frank feedback in order to let young players work through difficulties. For Grella, the question young players should be asking is, "Do I deserve more game time?" He encourages them to stick it out. "In today's 'want it now environment', a lot of people don't want to hear the answer."[104] Grella was involved in getting James Troisi on loan to Melbourne Victory from Juventus. Additionally, he not only helped convince Matt Derbyshire to make the move to Macarthur FC, but actually facilitated the 34-year-old's transfer. Grella used to play with Derbyshire at Blackburn Rovers. Knowing players in the game creates a small circle. In fact, agency is a 'who-you-know' business in many ways.

Grella understands the demand for Australian players and even with his access to CAA Base Soccer's networks and resources, he knows how hard it is to promote the Australian market. He has travelled to Belgium regularly since retiring and focused on agency. Grella observed that "The (Australian) players who went there, the vast majority went on to bigger and better things. The quality of the players was high. It's not an easy league, (it's) a tough league to play in. It's a strong league. Arguably now it is better than the Dutch Eredivisie. Physically more demanding, a bit more tactically rigid. In the past, with their freedom of registering non-EU players, it was a good country to get into the market. Why don't we send more players there? They're signing better players than we can propose (for) them."[105]

Grella has now pivoted to football club administration after being appointed as the new CEO of Italian club Calcio Catania. The move by Grella from the top end of player management (CAA Base) to hand back his agent's licence is a "big call." However, it also signifies and acknowledges that influential Australian agents like Grella can smoothly transition to clubs as football directors or even CEOs.

Chapter 12:
Project Asia – Nathan Hall,
Scott Ollerenshaw and Tony Grdic

Asia is such a vibrant continent. With its interesting cultural dynamics and complicated layers of doing business, it can be a challenge for football agents.

However, Asia is positioning itself as a significant stakeholder in the football ecosystem with strong leagues in Japan, South Korea, Saudi Arabia, the 2022 World Cup in Qatar, and until recently, the player wages in China. In fact, the value of the English Premier League's overseas TV rights were greater than the domestic England broadcast contract for the first time in the 2022/2023 season, mainly due to new deals with India, China and other parts of Asia.

In footballing terms, Asia may not be yet the powerhouse of player development like Europe, however the rise of Japanese and Korean players, as well as Australian players, is changing this narrative. For Australian players and agents, Asian leagues are a natural destination, as specific league criteria such as the Asian visa spot provides an opportunity for experienced Australian players to be counted outside the club's allowable foreign player quota.

There has been a demand for Australian players over many years in Asia, especially a strong centre-back, a natural striker or sometimes a big midfielder or winger, due to their athletically strong attributes, diverse sides to their game, technical foundations and work rate. At one stage, there were six Australian defenders in the South Korean K-League including Matt Jurman (Suwon Bluewings), Dylan McGowan (Gangwon), Aleksander Jovanovic (Jeju United), Tomislav Mrcela (Jeonnam Dragons) and Adrian Leijer at Suwon FC. Previously, Alex Wilkinson, Sasha Ognenovski and Robbie Cornthwaite had very good careers there.

In China, at the peak of wages in the Chinese Super League from 2015 to 2017, we had many Australians showcasing their talent, including Tim Cahill (Shanghai Greenland Shenhua and Hangzhou Greentown), Michael Thwaite (Liaoning Whowin), Trent Sainsbury (Jiangsu Suning), Apostolos Giannou (Guangzhou R&F), James Troisi, Dario Vidošić, James Holland and Robbie Kruse (all Liaoning Whowin).

Recently, many Australian players have been tempted by the Gulf leagues like the UAE Pro League and Saudi Arabia Pro League or the leagues of Malaysia where many former NSL players gravitated towards the end of their long footballing careers.

To work as an Australian agent in the Asian market, you must have connections, cultural insights, patience and the ability to ensure your players deliver on the field. Asian football is always changing. Big-value player contracts were previously offered in China while enticing wages were previously offered in Thailand and Malaysia. However, the pendulum has swung and now Saudi Arabia is now the big market with rewarding player contracts also available in Japan and South Korea.

I interviewed three different Australians with varied backgrounds on their journey working as agents in the Asian football landscape.

Nathan Hall

Just off the plane in Dubai, United Arab Emirates (UAE) and into a cab to head straight to the club's offices, Nathan Hall is on his way to negotiate a deal for a player with an Emirati club, with just a few hours left in the transfer window to come to a deal. In Nathan's mindset, he must have the player's instructions down pat, understand the negotiation strategy of the club and their expectations, and work to get a deal over the line. At the back of his mind, the key question circulates. What would your ask be? As in many negotiations, the visible (face-to-face meetings and providing in-depth information) is important. But in the UAE and Asia, what may be invisible (understanding the hierarchy, reciprocity, building trust, hospitality customs, and player characteristics) can be the key to success.

From dealing with players and clubs in Thailand, India, the Philippines, Cambodia or the United Arab Emirates, Hall is one of the Australians at the forefront of Asian football. With his easy-going nature, ability to listen and read the cultural nuance, Hall has developed a thorough understanding of the Asian football mosaic. To deal with Asian football stakeholders, you must think and act differently depending on the location; having patience, respect and being able to manage expectations are at the forefront of any negotiating strategy. Agency in Asia can be a toil in virtual anonymity. And unlike Europe, not hugely glamourous.

Background

Nathan Hall was initially a coach in the Thailand professional leagues. He held the assistant coach roles at Thai Premier League clubs Thai Port FC and TTM Chiangmai at just 27 years of age.[106] This was an achievement, as Hall never held a position of note back in Australia but he does have an Asian Football Confederation (AFC) 'A' coaching licence and coached at more exotic clubs including Indian I-League club United Sikkim and Amicale FC from Vanuatu.

His Asian coaching experience and his dealings with club management and owners resulted in him exploring player agency as part of the Australia-based entity Asian Sports Promotions. In 2017, with his array of connections in Thailand, Hall represented famous Brazilian player and coach Carlos Dunga. With his leveraged approach, Hall met the Football Association of Thailand president and submitted the Brazilian's resume for consideration for the Thailand national team position. He advised the Thai FA that they were Dunga's second choice, using a key negotiation strategy of informing them that his client had interest from more than one party. Hall told them that Dunga wanted to start negotiations with a Chinese club that had tabled an offer first. He had an offer of 3.5 million euros a year from them, which was far more than the Thai FA's offer. He advised them that if the Chinese deal didn't happen, he would be ready to talk with the Thai FA.[107] This managed the Thai FA expectations while ensuring that Hall was following Dunga's preference.

Asia is very much about relationships and trust. Hall always emphasises that if a player leaves on bad terms, it affects the agent as he or she still needs to deal with the same clubs in the future. Further, how you set up a deal is different to Australia where gross salaries, relocation fees, flights, accommodation and car expenses leave the agent with little in fees. In Asia, you may sometimes have to pay (from your agent fee) a coach, the local agent and football director to get a player in. You need a thick skin too, and an understanding of family, as you always get around to talking about your family during negotiations. Many agents' wine, dine or lunch with coaches and football directors, and you must obtain information about the workings of the clubs. For example, is the manager subject to the president's control or is there a pecking order at the club? As a now FIFA-licensed agent, Hall maps out all the parties involved in the negotiation and recognises saving face or giving face will be even more important if a negotiator must take an offer back to certain constituents. Hall's track record in Asia is impressive, having completed over 40 player transfers into Thailand alone. Recently, he also placed Australian players Harry Hore and Ryan Williams into Asia.

In his own words

On Hall's background and how he moved into the football agent industry

I'm a former professional coach that worked in Thailand, Indonesia, India, Bangladesh and Vanuatu from 2009-2014. After taking Amicale F.C. of Vanuatu to the 2014 Oceania Football Confederation Champions Final, I decided to take a hiatus away from the coaching/technical side and fell into the agency work by chance. A very good friend of mine, and still my business partner to this day, was putting 15–20 foreign players into Vietnam each year, until the Vietnamese Football Federation decided to reduce the foreign quota from five visa players to only two. This drastically impacted his business and forced him to look into other markets, namely Thailand.

Initially, I organised some meetings for him with coaches and directors of clubs in and around Bangkok and helped broker three or four deals in that initial window. Like any business, if the client does well, you keep the door open for repeat business and things just grew from there. It was probably after 12 months that it turned from a side-hobby to a real business that was making money. From 2016–2018, I spent a good four or five months each year traveling and investing significant amounts of money to build my network in South, East and West Asia, and as a result, have been directly involved with around 70 deals in 15 different markets, and indirectly probably close to 100.

Nowadays, because of the plus one quota in most Asian leagues, I focus a lot of my efforts in brokering Australian/Asian players throughout the region, and I also organise winter and summer training camps (as a boutique business offering) throughout South-East Asia for professional teams, which is something I really enjoy.

On his role as an agent

In a nutshell, it's managing every aspect of your client's career to allow them to concentrate on what they do best, playing or coaching football. Primarily, our role is to negotiate the best possible employment contract for the client and depending on the level of person you are managing, potential commercial and endorsement deals.

On his day to day as an Australian player agent working in Asia

In normal times, there is significant travel. Probably a standard weekday would be getting up early, having a coffee, checking WhatsApp/Viber/email etc., trying to get some exercise in and then knuckling down in front of the laptop for most of the day/night liaising with players, clubs and my partners.

On the weekends, I try to watch as many games as possible. In Thailand, that could sometimes be watching the first 60 minutes of a 5 p.m. match, and then racing to another game on the outskirts of Bangkok to catch the 8 p.m. match.

My partner and I are both avid travellers. So, in the "non-busy" periods, we like to travel somewhere near to relax, see the local sights and indulge in plenty of good food.

On the most rewarding aspect of the agent business

I've been fortunate enough to have brokered deals for many Brazilian and South American players that have come from extremely humble backgrounds, many can't even afford a flight ticket from Sao Paulo to Bangkok. Through my connections, plus of course their qualities, we have seen their life and finances change significantly to the point where they can pay off their debts, buy land and build homes for their families, and invest the rest of their money in other areas.

I have also been involved in looking after numerous Australian (NPL) State league players who were one week playing in front of a few hundred people and a few months later lining up in the AFC Cup in front of tens of thousands. These are unforgettable moments that fill both the player's family and me with immense joy and happiness.

On key agent learnings

A lot of things keep me up at night as a person with bad OCD (obsessive compulsive disorder). I used to have a tendency to try and make every deal in Asian Football, and at times work on far too many things at once, which as you get older isn't great for your blood pressure and general health.

During the last 12–18 months, I have made efforts to slow myself down, seek more of a work/life balance and focus my energy on working solely with hungry, motivated, diligent players that are determined to open new doors and are willing to listen. That is a very important trait.

On how player contract deals are structured in the Asian markets

The paramount difference would be the single ownership model of most South-East Asian clubs in comparison to the European model comprising of multiple departments and often a president who is often more honorary than hands-on. In South-East Asia, the president will often be heavily involved in player signings and general day-to-day decisions. Of course, being directly responsible to key stakeholders who are spending their money, instead of an organisation's money, helps to cut through some of the red tape that agents face.

Take Thailand for example. Most foreign players signing with T1 Clubs will receive housing, transport, medical insurance, multiple flight tickets and often very generous incentive schemes that are separate from their remuneration package.

If we compare this to the salary-capped A-League, all of the above would need to be covered by the player in an obviously expensive country.

On the future of Australian agents in Asia

I can't speak for other agents, but the players and coaches I work with are treated like family. I haven't changed my mobile number for 15 years and they know they can call me at 7 a.m. on Monday morning or 9 p.m. on Sunday night to talk about whatever they want. I look at myself more as a football mentor, instead of just an agent. I have had players, families and friends in their homes not just to speak about contracts and business, but to have a nice meal as friends and a chat about life.

I can't see real estate agents going anywhere and with football being one of, if not THE biggest product in the world, its agents aren't going anywhere either.

What are the challenges in promoting young Australian footballers to clubs

It really depends. If a young player has all the ingredients to become a top-level professional in the future, plus some European heritage/passport, then like most, I would be encouraging him to pursue tangible opportunities outside Australian shores. For players with different circumstances, the advice would probably be to stay here, listen to their coaches, keep working hard, get as many games as possible in the A-League (or whatever league they are playing in) and build up their experience and statistics before looking at the next steps. Let's be honest, if our players aren't able to produce in our domestic competition, then what chance do they have of doing it week-in and week-out in Europe or any top Asian league.

On the wisdom he learnt about the football agent business that still applies today

Work diligently, stay positive, enjoy what you can and manage your expectations so you aren't left disappointed.

Scott Ollerenshaw

How does a former National Soccer League (NSL) player who ventured to play in the Asian leagues become a football personality and TV pundit in football-crazy Malaysia, a country which was a leading Asian football power in the late 1970s and 1980s?

Answer — the ability to speak sincerely and give a refreshing and informed view of clubs, players and the leagues. I am referring to Scott Ollerenshaw, who is well-known in Malaysia and parts of South-East Asia as a football commentator, TV analyst on *Astro SuperSport* and football tournament operator (Borneo Cup International Youth Tournament). Scott was also involved in the agent game. He obtained a remit from the Football Association of Malaysia to recruit and identify players with Malaysian roots and to promote Australian players with an eye to opportunities in Malaysia. An ambassador-type agent or intermediary, Scott is passionate about Australian football and the success of its players within the South-East Asian market.

Ollerenshaw played for Malaysian Super League club Sabah FC from 1994 until 1997. He scored 110 goals and won the Golden Boot award twice, becoming a club legend. Recently, Ollerenshaw has been appointed as Sabah FC's technical director, head of the youth development program to unearth new talents and he also acts as an intermediary for the imported players. For him, Malaysia remains a more attractive destination for many foreign players because the English language is widespread and western comforts are closer at hand.

Background

Ollerenshaw tapped into the booming Asian market by setting up a player agent business, Australasian Sporting Enterprises, with its own intermediary registration. His agency operation also brokered deals into China for A-League players like Daniel McBreen and Bernie Ibini

However, it was in the Malaysian mixed-heritage player market and Malaysian club scene that Ollerenshaw was able to excel and provide opportunities to Australian players like Brendan Gan and Matthew Davies. He was appointed as a consultant by the Football Association Malaysia (FAM) to locate foreign players with a Malaysian connection or heritage. Ollerenshaw played an influential role in bringing Brendan Gan from Australia and Junior Eldstal from England to Malaysia to represent the country. Australian-born Matthew Davies, a former Perth Glory defender, followed after getting his Malaysian passport. Ollerenshaw described the process as complex and multi-faceted, yet very rewarding. "It's a long-drawn process to get a player to apply for a Malaysian passport. A lot of paperwork is needed, and several government agencies are involved and this is why we need the support of the FAM and the Sports Ministry. This is a legal process and is in accordance with FIFA rules. The main football criterion is that these foreigners must be better than the locals and they should be able to contribute to Malaysian football."[108] In essence, Ollerenshaw and the FAM engaged in something similar to what I call the Morocco model, where about 12 players in the Moroccan national team who competed in the 2022 World Cup were born in the diaspora: Spain, France, Belgium, the Netherlands. etc. The Moroccan FA made it official policy to recruit them into the national teams.

In another unique agent operation in the Malaysian league, Ollerenshaw assisted Second Division Malaysian club Negeri Sembilan in revamping its foreign player signings with an all- Australian cast, while also assisting in relaunching the careers of the Australian players. Former Melbourne Victory, now Melbourne City winger Andrew Nabbout, ex-Sydney FC striker Joel Chianese, one-time Newcastle Jets defender Taylor Regan and English-born ex-Wellington Phoenix midfielder Alex Smith all joined the club for the 2016 season to work under Australian coach Gary Phillips. Phillips' objective was to rebuild, remodel and restore the glory of Negri's proud history and stated that "while I can't yet officially announce our new signings, the fighting qualities typically associated with the Australian psyche was something we felt was missing in previous campaigns. I know the new players will come out swinging, desperate to reinvigorate their own careers and future ambitions."[109]

For Ollerenshaw, the Malaysian league option was an alternative for many uncontracted but talented A-League players who did not want to always fall back into the Australian National Premier Leagues.

In his own words

*On his background and moving to the Malaysian League
as a player and then into agency*

I was obviously a football player in 1994. There were a lot of Australians who were going over to Malaysia because they could make more money there. I was no different to Alan Davidson, Mehmet Durakovic, Alistair Edwards and Abbas Saad. I came over here and ended up at Sabah. I started playing, (and) did okay. Earned three times the money that I could back in Australia. Stayed here for four or five years playing, met my wife here, she is Malaysian and ended up staying here.

Once you retire, you have to work out what you're going to do to earn a living, because it's not like you're playing in the top level in Europe where you can make enough and you don't have to work anymore. Suddenly, you get a phone call, and somebody wants a player, you just do it, it just grows into that. But for me, I never saw it as a full-time gig, just because I found I struggled with some of the integrity of the industry.

On the agent business in South-East Asia

It's just a ruthless industry. When people are trying to earn a dollar and survive, yeah, I struggled with that at times. When I say 'integrity', I mean other agents, players, clubs, the whole thing. It's just part of the business; a hard-nosed industry. If you've been involved for a long time, you know where I'm coming from. At this stage of my life, I'm 55 now, I've become sporting director at Sabah FC, I'm enjoying not being involved in that part of the industry.

On the day to day of being an agent in Malaysia

You're just on the phone all the time. A text will come through that Perak FA (club in Malaysia) are after a foreign centre-back, must be under the age of 30, must be six-feet tall. The budget is around USD12,000 a month. As that text is going out, the same text is sent to about 1,000 people. And then you can imagine it's like the cavalry. Everyone's on the phone. It's just mayhem, it's just crazy. But that's what happens. In Asia, whenever a club puts out that they want a type of player, in that half an hour, I reckon one million texts go out between a thousand different people trying to get in on the deal.

People don't realise that for any deal to go through, there's about ten boxes that need to be ticked. People don't realise that talking about salary, agreeing on the salary, agreeing on the bonus, agreeing on a transfer fee, agreeing on the length of the contract, which are all complicated topics, takes time. I've seen deals fall through because the club is only prepared to offer economy tickets for the family, but the player demands business-class tickets. The club says no, and the player says, "Alright, I'm not going." I've seen nine boxes ticked and then the wife finds out that they didn't have her favourite perfume in that town, or her favourite shampoo. She's not prepared to consent to the deal because she can't wash her hair properly.

It can take a long time in negotiations, and that's why the average Joe Blow thinks, "Oh, he's only an agent, anyone can be an agent." You have to be skilled at negotiation. You've got to be patient, you've got to understand.

In Asia, you have to understand the mentality of the people there. And the culture is a lot different. For example, losing face in Asia is the end of the world. You can't do certain things in Asia that you would do in Australia.

On dealing with clubs in Asia

In Asia, if you fight too much for the players' rights at a club, that club will just sometimes blacklist you. People have to understand that agents are caught in the middle, they're representing a player, but at the same time, they have to develop relationships with the club. If they push too much on the side of the player, the club may just blacklist you as an agent.

On the player-signing decisions made by clubs in Asia

Sometimes the coach is not even involved at all. It's about the secretary general, or the CEO, or the actual president, and those people will just say, "We like the player," and they'll do all the negotiation. The coach's job is just to coach the team, aside from a few clubs where the coach will have the power. But at most of the clubs, it's decided by the president or the CEO or the secretary general. That's just how it is. And it's not just in South-East Asia, that also happens in China and other Asian markets.

There's a lot of people along the line that have their influence. Many agents will work for one particular club because they have a procedure that is in place. They don't even have to talk about it, everyone knows what percentage they get and how the gravy train works. People can say it's not fair, but that's just how it is.

On his involvement in the mixed-heritage players project being pursued by the Malaysian FA

It was more luck than good management to be honest with you. I was running a sports tourism business at the same time as doing the agency stuff on the side, and I was running a yearly lawn bowls tournament, as well as my Borneo Cup tournament. Junior Eldstal's mum emailed me and said her son had both a UK and Malaysian passport. He was doing a sports tourism business course and needed first-hand work experience. She asked if he could fly to Malaysia with his friend and do some work. I had the bowls tournament coming up and had them doing some basic stuff — lifting orders, running errands, etc. Halfway through the tournament, I said to them both, "I'm playing indoor soccer tonight, do you boys play?"

We played futsal that night and Junior was impressive. Robert Alberts was (the) coach at Sarawak, and I told him about Junior. He said, "Fly him down." After a week he called me and wanted to sign him.

That's how I started and then suddenly we got Brendan Gan (who was with Sydney FC in 2008) who's played in the Malaysian national team, Junior of course has played in the national team, (and) Matthew Davies (ex-Perth Glory player) as well. About seven or eight went on to play for the Malaysian national team. Then you've got your other players like Curran Ferns (ex-Melbourne Victory Youth player) and ones that didn't quite make it that far but are still very good players at Malaysian club level. In the end, it became like a just explosion, they came looking for me. I became known as the mixed-heritage player agent.

We had support from the Federation, which was fine, but you have to prove that they have Malaysian heritage. You need certification and proof like the parent's passport and the parent's birth certificate. It's just a challenging process that you have to go through.

On the reputation of Australian players in Malaysia and Asia

Australians are known. Whenever they look for an Asian player, they want an Australian centre-back if they can get one. Our centre-backs are respected, they know Taylor Regan for example. Our centre-backs are known as very hard-working, disciplined and they know they're going to get a certain level from them. I would say we're not as respected as we used to be in the NSL days. But Taylor Regan's done really, really well over here. Brendan Gan, he's done well, Matthew Davies as well.

On dealing with other Asian-based agents

In this industry, you have to be prepared to work with other agents. Apart from the mixed- heritage players, I don't think I've ever done a deal without being involved with another agent. If you can do a deal and it's only you and them, that's a good result. It's not unusual to do a deal with three or four agents involved. And you have to be prepared to work with other agents. Otherwise, it's very, very difficult. It was challenging at times. The combination of clubs, players and other agents is sometimes very hard.

On player talent identification

Players came to me and then I researched them and worked out if they were going to make it or not. I'd call Tony Rallis (leading Australian agent[110]) or Zeljko Susa and say, "Have you got this player?" If they don't want an Aussie, then you've got to go to other agents. Then they'll send you something and you do that research and you might ring up a coach who's worked with the player. It's good to have the network of coaches to talk to.

I wasn't in love with the business enough to actually go through a process beforehand to find a player before there was a request from a club. I wouldn't go and do all this research on a player, hoping that a team might want that sort of a player. I wasn't in love with the agency business enough to do that.

On reigniting the careers of Australian players
Andrew Nabbout and Joel Chianese

Andrew Nabbout was at the crossroads of his career. Negeri Sembilan wanted to get four Aussies in. Tony Rallis and I got Taylor Regan, Alex Smith, Joel Chianese and Andrew Nabbout. All four at that stage were struggling to get a gig in Australia.

At the halfway mark of the season, Negeri Sembilan were in second spot. They're one point from being top, and the top two teams go up. The team manager calls me up and says they are slightly worried about Nabbout and Chianese. Both were scoring and creating chances. (But) They felt the boys were missing a few chances to score. I told them it doesn't matter (that) they were missing a few chances. In football, if you're creating plenty, then you're going to miss chances. We were not going to terminate them and bring in other players.

I told them that if they did, "It'll be the biggest mistake you've ever made. You will not be promoted, and you will lose two fantastic players. If you keep them, I guarantee you'll be in the top two and you'll go up next year."

Within twelve months, Andrew Nabbout was representing Australia, starting in the first 11 at the World Cup. And Joel Chianese's career has gone from strength to strength in the A-League. He got a big move to India, made some money and did really well in the A-League. Andrew Nabbout continues to do well. All four of them did really well. Taylor Regan's gone from Negeri, he went to Adelaide United, came back to Malaysia at Selangor FA and spent two years there. It's (Selangor) one of the biggest clubs in the country and now he's at Sarawak United. They may be promoted from Second Division into the First Division. So, he's done really well.

Alex Smith went to Johor Darul Ta'zim F.C. (JDT), played there for a couple of years and did well. JDT are becoming a powerhouse club in Asia. Those four boys mean a lot to me because they've become friends of mine as well. I have a lot of respect for all of them.

On Australian youth player development

The best thing that happened to Australian football was when they were forced to bring in younger Australian players because of the pandemic. It forced a lot of clubs to start using some of their youth talent. Before coronavirus, not many of the coaches would take a risk on any of these kids. The coronavirus inadvertently helped bring in some players. In terms of Australian youth development, we need a new structure. For me, it's fairly simple, if it isn't broken, don't try and fix it. So why did we get rid of Ron Smith's AIS program? The way they ran things and the system they had in place was effective. It's now up to clubs to have their own programs. I just think we've lost our way.

Then it was the Dutch coaches, we had to follow the Dutch. We stopped doing what was working for us. It's as simple as that. The problem now is that it's not going to be easy to go back to what we did in the '80s with the AIS. I think they should do a case study on what worked and what didn't work. And start from scratch or a blank page.

Tony Grdic

Arriving in Zagreb, Croatia, in the chilly month of November, it was straight down to business. I was there to meet Tony Grdic, an Australian and former Sydney United player who forged a career in Australia, Croatia and China, and the father of Australian youth international player Donci Grdic. Tony has been living on Croatia's beautiful Dalmatian coast for over 20 years running his tourist resort away from the Australian agent scene. Yet with a stable and seasonal life on the Adriatic, Grdic has much time to work in the agent field. Tony played an important catalyst role in opening the lucrative China market to Australian players and agents. Further, by being based in Croatia during their golden period of talent, he has also developed an understanding of how smaller footballing countries develop and promote their talent to bigger European markets and clubs.

Background

Grdic was recently selected in the greatest 11 players of Chinese Super League side Hangzhou Greentown for their 20th anniversary. He travelled to China to receive his award and was one of the earliest Australians to have an impact before Chinese football exploded in monetary terms. As former player and now agent, Grdic observed that Australians have been popular in China ever since Joel Griffiths won the title with his impressive performances in 2009 with Beijing Guon. The high point came in 2016–17 when the Chinese Super League was the biggest spender in the transfer market. Carlos Tevez, Oscar and Hulk were on over 20 million euros each.[111] However, football in China is now facing severe financial issues and Grdic recognises that at this juncture the good days may be over.

With Asian clubs wanting to spend less and get more performance out of foreign players, Grdic appreciates that foreign players can often be scapegoats if they do not perform at all times.

In his own words

On his unique playing career

I was at Hajduk Split at the time and not many players were going into China from Europe. I got a call from my friend here in Croatia asking if I might like to go. Ante Milicic and I were supposed to go together. We travelled together but I stayed, and Ante didn't.

At the time, my agent was just starting, and I was one of his first players. He grew very much in China and afterwards was one of the biggest Chinese agents. I stayed there for three years and wanted to stay longer. I would have stayed there for the rest of my career. The problem was that at the time, China didn't make the World Cup. The Federation changed the rules all the time and they cut down from four foreigners to two and I was a defender. Nobody kept on defenders and that's how I left China.

After, they had the Asian rule where Australian, Japanese players and Korean players could come. I had an Australian passport. But I was pretty much finished. I would have made a lot more money if that rule was (made) earlier. The Australian passport allowed Aussie players to make money they couldn't have dreamed of in Europe.

I was there from 2001–2003. I was named in the best 11 in the history of the club, the best defender. I've got all those awards from the club.

On moving into the agency and intermediary business
and not coaching

I never wanted to be a coach, maybe that was my big mistake, but I always wanted to be involved in football. That's why I started doing intermediary and agency, because I don't have the nerve to be a coach. When I look here in Croatia at coaches, you have to be the director, you have to be the psychologist, you have to be everything for the players. When the players say, "I don't have boots, we don't have equipment to train with, we didn't get paid," the coach has to deal with all that stuff. I'd only fight with the president and the directors of clubs (from an agent's angle) because I wouldn't let them manipulate the players.

I'd rather stay in tourism, there's less headaches. But I've got a lot of friends, they're all coaches and under stress. To be a coach, you have to be ambitious for that, and I take my hat off to my friends who are coaches now.

On Chinese football

The atmosphere at the stadiums was fantastic. They'll cheer you on if you just do a header. In Europe, no one would even look at you. It's just a different style. I remember whenever I had a good game, I couldn't get out of the stadium. Crowds would want to touch you or get autographs. Sometimes, I had police escorts to get out of the stadium. It was great. It's a different culture, it's very hard at the beginning. I did get sick of it in terms of living, it's always crowded, everything's crowded. And then when I went back for a holiday in Croatia, I couldn't wait to get back. China's very special. It was so funny, the people would just crowd around you, and just touch you and touch their hair. That type of stuff, it gives you a good feeling. They treat you very well. The clubs treat you very well, so you should play well.

On why Australian and South Korean player traits were popular in China

I think it's the physicality. Their main players were Koreans, with plenty of Korean coaches. The Chinese Football Association wants their players to play like Koreans because they're very strong. The problem with some Chinese players is that they're the best players in the world when you have training sessions with them, but when it comes to the game, they have a blackout, they're much different. When they see a full crowd, they don't perform as well, because of the nervousness. It may be a little bit of stage fright which they have not ironed out. That's the difference between Chinese, Japanese and Korean players.

They have a different mentality and that's what the Chinese Federation wants. They want them to be like Koreans or even Japanese. But I don't see that happening. The Chinese players there, the national players, are paid very well. They get paid millions, but some of them may not even be able to play in a decent European Second Division side.

They don't have players outside China because why would you leave China to play in the Bundesliga Second Division for less money? You would in the past make triple the money in China and you're treated like a star. They play at home because they get paid very well. (The) Japanese are different. Japanese and Koreans, they can play in Europe and that's why they're strong national teams.

Australians are popular because Australia won the Asian Cup. They're very strong boys, and very fit, and they like those players, they like players with character.

Australian agent Ante Alilovic and big Chinese agent Fan Shide brought a lot of the Australian players in. Obviously, they wanted Tommy Juric and it was a disappointing decision of Tommy's not to take the deal. I told his father that many times. He was only 21 or 22 at that stage and I know what it's like in China, if they don't like you (due to performance-driven expectations), they may get rid of you after one year of a four-year deal but they have to give you all the money as FIFA regulations apply to all club contracts worldwide.

On Fan Shide —
the biggest mega-agent in China

Fan Shide's advantage was that he lived in France for ten years and he knows the French language very well. He has French connections and he brought Nicolas Anelka through them. And of course, France has connections in all of Europe. And that's how he started doing it. Look at all the French coaches or players previously at Shanghai Shenhua, he brought them all.

On player deals that fell through

I've done a few deals that didn't go through. I had one coach as well. The coach was supposed to get on the plane, they were waiting, and the TV people were waiting at the Shenyang, China Airport. The deal was done, and he didn't even arrive, I thought he was on the plane. He told me, "I didn't want to go."

I had one boy calling me for a month wanting to go to China. So, I made a deal for him, he was supposed to be on a flight at 10 in the morning. He calls me and says he can't go because his wife's going crazy about not wanting to go. After six months, he gets divorced and he has missed his opportunity.

On the difficulties younger Australian players face when
coming to Croatia for trials

In Croatia, they train at least five times a week. In Australia, they'll train two to three times a week (generally). I think the younger Australian players who come to Croatia may sometimes think it's easy, but it is very, very difficult for them and a different style of playing as well. Australians are mostly physical players, not always used to the Croatian-style tempo and technique.

I came here to Croatia when I was 17-and-a-half, I'd just finished school in December 1992. I was one of the first players to come and I was still a youth player. It was an exceedingly difficult time for me in the first year.

On how tough it is to be an agent in Europe

It's competitive, however it's a lot easier than in China. For example, in China it's connections, connections and connections. You've got 100 things to worry about as an agent in China. Here in Europe, it's more straightforward. But in Europe, it's very important to scout young players and get them in your agency's portfolio. There's a lot of talent. All you need is to have one or two or three very top players as an agent and you can make a sustainable business.

On Croatia's player development
(a small nation with a formidable track record)

Dinamo Zagreb do it well. They sell their players for ten or 20 million euros. And then those players get sold on again for another 50 or so million euros. Dinamo Zagreb always make a fortune selling players and they have a very good youth system. They bring all the best talents from the whole region. It doesn't matter if you're from Serbia and Bosnia. Doesn't matter if you're worth anything, if you're a prodigious youth talent, Dinamo will be interested.

But the problem for Dinamo Zagreb is they have so many talented youth players and only a couple will have exceptionally good careers. They'll make a lot of money from them, but the others may fail or not be selected, and it's very hard for them to go to another smaller club. It's a shock for them, that's the big problem. This process sometimes chews up a lot of great talent.

It's not just Dinamo, it's Hajduk Split as well, they can chew up a lot of great talent. Hajduk take all the talent from Sibenik, (it's) an hour away and in my area in Croatia. If I have the chance to speak with the parents, I sometimes say, "Don't always go to Hajduk Split, you may curtail the momentum of your son's career."

Hajduk have money, and they find a job for the parents as a relocation sweetener, but they have another 20 excellent players in the team, and don't sometimes care who will succeed as long as one or two or three make it.

Some players that go from my hometown here in Sibenik sometimes fail or don't get selected, and then they sometimes lose themselves, it's happened many times. It's still happening and that's why I didn't want to give my son Donci (an Australian youth international) to them. I didn't want to give him to any big club.

I had offers to take him to some clubs, but I said no. He is better to stay here and fight his way to the first team. And that's what he's done now. Sibenik rate him as a club project and he's now playing in the first team. Generally, in Croatia, if they want to make money from transfers, they have to force young players to play. Every club has at least one or two very special players, and they can sell these players and have their yearly budget paid off. Croatian players succeed because they improvise. They don't have everything like in parts of Australia where they have the playing fields and the better stadiums. They (Australia) have some of the best training facilities in the world (good sports conditioning and recovery services). Croatia doesn't have much. We don't have a proper national stadium. It's got to be shut down. We've got a national team of all these big players, but they have to overcome adversity and that's why they succeed in Europe.

When Croatian players go to Real Madrid or a top 40 team in Europe, it is a dream. They look at the fields, (and) they perform because they're hungry for it. They have to be hungry. All the kids play on the street here, like many in Brazil and Argentina, in the barrios. You get all the special talent out of there. They want to succeed. That's the main reason why Croatian players prosper. They know where they're going, they appreciate it and they give 100%. They don't whine about anything because they're used to it.

On the playing talent Australia is now producing

The problem in Australia is that they don't force the young players to play, they're not giving them as much chance. (The) Example is my son's generation; I only see a handful of them playing at senior level. In Australia, there's no relegation, what have you got to lose? There's nothing to lose. You should develop your players and try to sell them in Europe. But the problem with the Australian national team now is that there's not as many players playing in Europe. Before, they were all playing in Europe, and that's why Australia was so strong in 2006 (albeit Australia is slowly again getting stronger now in international tournaments).

On where Australian players sit now in the European league pecking order

I don't think it's the quality that is the problem. Since the A-League started, the rating of Australian players has dropped a bit because many players are not leaving Australia. Some players are getting very good money and they're happy with it and they say, "Why would I go to Europe now? If I can have the same money here in Australia, I don't have any ambitions to go to Europe."

They were semi-pro and now they're professional, they're living like professionals in Australia. I don't know what the money's like over there, but I'm sure they're earning much more than the players were in the NSL 20 years ago. Maybe triple or quadruple the money or even way more. For Australia to succeed, they need to send a lot more players to Europe.

On what makes a good agent

The most important thing for an agent is to try and transfer the player. If the player and agent are fighting after the deal or fighting after they finish football, then something's wrong. In Europe, it's all about contacts as well. The clubs open the doors for you, but you have to start from scratch and build your way up. If you have a talented player, you sell him or her to one club and then the doors open for other players. Tomorrow you'll have that contact. If you have a contact and they have to decide between your player and another player and they're the same quality, they'll take your player. That's the main difference.

Chapter 13:
Where Samba Meets La Celeste
– Steve Panopoulos and
Jose Martinez

Steve Panopoulos

Sometimes we Australians underestimate ourselves on the world football stage. Yet Australians have been doing great things in world football all the way from Eddie Krncevic being top scorer in Belgium in 1989 to Ange Postecoglou coaching at the Scottish powerhouse Glasgow Celtic and now Tottenham Hotspur.

The journey of a player from the famous South Melbourne FC team which played at the World Club Championship (in Brazil) to becoming a successful agent in one of the leading football countries is an intriguing and compelling story that I had to explore. He is Steve Panopoulos, the agent working in one of the most exciting, talent-laden, rich and sassy football markets in the world. An Australian in among the colourful Brazilian cities, carnivals, beaches, the Amazon and the passion of football.

Remarkably, in an article by Ange Postecoglou in *The Sydney Morning Herald* in 2013, he revealed that one of the highlights of South Melbourne FC's participation in the World Club Championship was that "during the World Club Championship, Panopoulos was able to convince David Beckham to swap shirts — not an easy task given the competition for this honour — but later he also came away with a more prized possession when he met his future wife in the lobby of South Melbourne's Rio De Janeiro hotel and (he) is now a successful player agent."[112]

Background

The Brazilian football agency market is affected by two significant factors. Firstly, the demand by worldwide clubs to recruit talented Brazilian players to improve their winning percentage and game style. Secondly, the objective for Brazilian clubs to transfer their talent to Europe for huge transfer fees. For an Australian agent to make a career in agency in Brazil is no easy feat. The Brazilian player market does not know you and networks which tend to mainly speak Portuguese look at a person's playing, coaching or administrative credentials.

Yet with all these challenges, Panopoulos has made a successful and long-term career in player agency as owner and director of management agency SP7 Sports based in Rio De Janeiro. SP7 Sports even has its own VIP corporate box at Flamengo home games to entertain clients and international visitors. Panopoulos has loaded up the A-League on occasion with Brazilian talent that supporters want to see live, such as Alex Terra who played with Melbourne Heart and Fred who played at Melbourne Victory and then Wellington Phoenix. Panopoulos convinced Terra by selling the joint attractions of football, money, the lifestyle and the coach. Panopoulos mused that, "What really did it for him was the lifestyle in Australia, after speaking to friends that had been to Australia, they spoke really well of the country, the city of Melbourne was a huge factor, and the clincher was John van't Schip."[113] When Fred signed a six-game guest stint deal with Wellington Phoenix, it was Panopoulos who set up one of the first loans into the A-League. Panopoulos said, "It has been a long process with a lot of discussions between myself and Wellington, and with DC United (of the MLS)."[114]

In his own words

On his football playing background

I grew up in a Greek/Australian family in Melbourne's eastern suburbs; Mount Waverley and Oakleigh area. My dad took me down to Oakleigh Soccer Club to play as a junior when I was about 10 or 11-years-old, which was actually late, I should have started earlier. When I was about 14 or so I was picked for the first time to play for the regional squad. All the dads got together at the time because the vast majority of the players were Greek background, the coach was also Greek, and we decided to all leave our current teams and form an under-15's team at South Melbourne. About a year later, I left South Melbourne because the inaugural VIS squad was selected and was picked by Ernie Merrick (VIS coach). He had seen me and thought that I should be part of it. I left for the two-year scholarship. A year after being there, Jimmy Pyrgolios, the South Melbourne coach, had seen me in some sort of game and asked me to come back to South Melbourne.

I went back and in my first year made my debut. I had a great career in South Melbourne and I only left before that last terrible year of the NSL where everything was a mess. I had the chance to play in the World Cup Championship in Brazil and that was where my life changed. I met a girl and then sometime later she came out to Australia. She stayed and we got married and had a family. Our first son was born in Australia when I was sort of winding down my career. Missing the family was part of my decision to retire. I retired early. I was thirty. We came back to Brazil with the idea of spending a year with the family.

I was sitting on the beach one day, doing nothing, and when I arrived home my wife passed me a number. She said some guy called and wanted to speak to me.

It was Ernie Merrick. He had just gone to coach Melbourne Victory in the new A-League. He had asked about me and my dad told him that I was in Brazil. I called him back and he said Melbourne Victory were not doing too well and was there anything I could do to help out? Do you know any agents? I told him I would see what I could do.

Rewinding two years before that, my wife and I went to Brazil every time the NSL season would finish so she could be close to her family. And during one of those trips, my wife's new single had been recorded and I went with her to sign a contract with the record label. They wanted to release it to Europe. During the conversation, the guys started speaking English, and asked what I did.

One of the guys introduced me to his brother, who was an agent. I had a little highlight tape and I gave it to him. About two weeks later, after I had gone back to Australia, he called me with an offer to go play for Maccabi Haifa in Israel. I didn't accept it. but I kept in contact with him.

On becoming a player agent

Two years passed and I made contact again. I told him about Ernie Merrick. It was around December and we tried to put a few players forward to Ernie, but it didn't happen. A few months later, he came to Brazil. It was the first A-League season and Melbourne Victory were second last. We spent 10 days together, flew to a few clubs, saw a few games, and that's basically when we found Fred, Alessandro and Claudinho. We came to agreements, the contracts were put forward, and soon after, we flew out to Australia.

And that's when it all started happening. It was actually during the time that Australia had qualified for the 2006 World Cup and Australia were doing their last camp before leaving; playing against Greece at the MCG. Melbourne Victory were training, and Australia trained straight after at the same ground. I was sitting there and Mark Viduka came up and said, "Ah Greco." I used to play against Mark, we were both born in the same year, and came up together when Melbourne Knights versus South Melbourne was the biggest derby in the NSL league. I spent time with him at the AIS, so we knew each other and respected each other.

We went to the game (with this Brazilian guy) where Australia played against Greece with 100,000 at the MCG, and I had to translate for the Brazilian players. We talked a lot about getting together as partners and the stars aligned. It was just perfect timing.

We started putting together ideas to start up a company. Six months earlier, he had done a deal in Belgium, and met an agent named Steve Davis, who was a representative with mega- agency Stellar Group in London. In Belgium, he was their representative. While he was doing this deal, there was a guy from Stellar Group, one of the chief consultants called John Lewis, and he'd met my Brazilian colleague. The stars aligned again, because I'm Aussie and Stellar is English. So, they came out to Brazil, we talked and we came to the agreement to become an affiliate of Stellar. We opened a company called Stellar Brazil as part of the Stellar Group.

And we grew really quickly. Stellar Group put a considerable amount of money into us to get started and set up an office in Rio De Janeiro. In Brazil, you've got to have a lot of money to get started because to get young players, which is Stellar's philosophy, you've got to pay to assist them with expenses. You've got to give money to the family. Almost a monthly salary. So, we needed Stellar's investment. We started with three or four players in 2006.

By 2012, we had about 130 players. By creating a critical mass, you build credibility and respect. I did the Rafael and Fabio deals with Manchester United. The two twins. Rafael the right-back, Fabio the left-back. Fabio played a few games. Rafael did really well. Rafael was a starting player for a long time and they made a lot of use out of us. We sold him straight out of (the) Fluminense Academy where they hadn't even got close to becoming senior players. That made a lot of waves, it really projected our name.

It was always a lot of stress. Money creates a lot of stress because in our business, it's sometimes all about the money. There's always moving parts. There're always people involved. There're always people that put their hand up and say, "Look, I introduced you to this guy or that guy," looking for a favour.

Basically, I came here with an Australian mentality. You know, what you say is what you believe and what you do. We were partners on paper, partners in theory, but I started gravitating to the business of international transfers. Obviously, I speak English and a lot of players I was talking to in Australia were going off to South Korea, Saudi Arabia and the USA. Dealing with the younger players, the local (Brazilian) players, wasn't really giving us a lot of profit. What was really sustaining the business was international deals.

In 2012, I made the decision to split away from my Brazilian agency partner. I started my own company, which was SP7 Sports. In a nutshell, I took all the learnings from my experience as a newer agent, like having too many players, overpromising, spreading yourself too thin, (and) spending your time on poor players, and tried not to repeat them.

Instead of spending 80 per cent of my time putting out fires and maintaining the business, I inverted it. Now I spend 20 per cent of my time putting out fires and 80 per cent of the time producing deals.

I have a maximum of 25 players. If I'm going to bring a player in, someone goes out. It's like a boutique agency, no more partners. I have a network of contacts and people that work with me, (but) not on a permanent basis. I only have one person on a permanent basis, which is basically my guy that does everything that I shouldn't be wasting my time on (like administration). I work with people I trust and each player has to have value. And that doesn't mean that after I'm going to make 100 grand ($100,000) off every deal, it just means there's value in some way — future value, real value. I'm not going to have players just to have them, otherwise I could have 300 and be wasting my time.

On dealing with mainly Brazilian players

I would say 50% of my business is looking after everything for my players — their contracts and their financial status in Brazil, and we've also got lawyers and accountants that look after that. I've created such a massive network and 50% of my business is as a broker and an intermediary. My best education as an agent was with super-agent Jonathan Barnett. He's the owner of Stellar Group and an unbelievable man. He's an amazing agent.

When I broke away in 2012, that was around the time when FIFA was trying to back away from having the responsibility of the licence fee for agents. It was up in the air. I wasn't going to spend a fortune getting a licence from FIFA when it could maybe change in a year's time. When it was finally sorted out, I became a CBF-accredited agent (Brazilian Football Confederation). So, there was a little period there where I had nothing, no accreditation, but it was because I just waited for the mess to be sorted. And to be honest, it didn't change my business in any way.

On focusing on the big Asian markets

I really do very little business in Brazil. I've probably got two or three players here and usually it is from one Brazilian club to another.

Brazil has thousands of players with a big export market. What's changed more than anything has been just the evolution of the internet. Before I'd get on a plane and fly to South Korea, to China, and to Japan where I do most of my deals. I'd take a suitcase full of DVDs for agents that I've made contact with over the years through phone, email and had face-to-face conversations; basically, building relationships.

Now, the internet, Facebook, Instagram and WhatsApp have created a new generation of viable agents who sit in front of their computer. They've got no business operation, they've got no office, they've got no company, and they've got absolutely nothing. All they do is send people messages, saying, "Hi, you know I've got this player." It's created a new breed of Facebook agents LOL!

On the day to day in the life of an Australian player agent based in Brazil

Obviously, the day to day changes based on what time of the year it is.

Coming up to a free transfer window period, it's a lot of preparation. I try not to get my phone into my hand straight away because the moment I get online, then it doesn't stop for the rest of the day. Basically, I'll get up, have some breakfast, answer a few messages from the Middle East Gulf Region and Asia, then I get into my emails. I spend most of my day in contact with the people that I have partnerships with. When I started, I wanted to expand my network of contacts as much as possible, so I'd go to South Korea, (and) have 20 meetings with 20 different agents.

In South Korea, I've got one main company that I work with that I have a 10- year relationship with, a good friendship. I usually have one or maybe two in each country and it's just constant contact either through WhatsApp, (or) through emails, always talking about transferring players. I speak to nearly all of them every day when preparing for the next transfer, and then I'll head off to the office. I've always got people coming to see me, there's a handful of trusted agents and scouts that I work with here in Rio De Janeiro that see me as their doorway to Asia. There are good agents here in Rio De Janeiro that I trust and (who) look after good players, but they don't have that connection to Asia like I do. Instead of them forging their own contacts and creating a pathway, they ask me to take the players. There's a big company here in Brazil called OTB, they're well respected. They've got a player in the national team and around 120 players. In the past, they've actually invited me to be part of the company.

I did a deal with them about a year ago and formed a really good relationship with one of the partners. He started calling me and asking about players. "What do you think?"

This began happening on a regular basis and at one point he said, "Steve, can I just tell everybody to speak to you about our players?"

We formed an official partnership in which I'm the representative for their whole company into the Qatar, Saudi Arabia, UAE, China, South Korea, Thailand, Japan, Australia, Greece and Malaysia markets.

If I do a deal, it's a normal 50/50 split of the commission. But if somebody calls them and they ask for my advice, I become basically a glorified secretary, just giving information, and then I have a smaller percentage of the deal.

On what is the most rewarding aspect of the agent business
and any sliding-door moments

There're probably two or three things that I look back on as pivotal changes in my career. Obviously, the Manchester United deals, which is something that everybody wants to do — to go to Old Trafford and meet and have lunch with Alex Ferguson. It was a huge team at the time, Cristiano Ronaldo was there and Ole Solskjær. That was an experience.

I'd also say one of the defining moments that really started to push things up for me in the early days was my main market, South Korea. The first player I took to South Korea went to Suwon and for some reason he didn't do that well there. But he had one good game against Jeonbuk and when Suwon released him, Jeonbuk contacted the player. He went there in 2008 and helped the club get to the finals and they kept him to the next year. In 2009, he just killed it, he was the Most Valuable Player (MVP) of the league and Jeonbuk were champions for the first time in history. That was massive. It was Luis Henrique and there was a huge bidding war between Jeonbuk and FC Seoul, who were much richer. We kept him at Jeonbuk for way less money and the president said, "You're not going to regret it." He would bring me back every year as a present, he'd pay for my flights and I became the official representative of Jeonbuk Hyundai at that moment in South America.

All the Brazilian players that went to Jeonbuk from 2009 to 2013, were through me. Jeonbuk just kept investing and growing and it became the unbelievably massive club that it still is today. I started bringing Jeonbuk back to Brazil. I'd bring them all the way to Brazil to do their pre-season training. They came here three years in a row and in 2011, they were champions again. They then made the AFC Champions League Final.

Then I sold players out of Jeonbuk, to UAE and brought in Leonardo. I brought him to Jeonbuk in 2012 and he's probably the best player in the history of the club. He stayed there for five years and then I sold him to Al Jazira in 2016. But then the relationship got a little tougher in 2013, especially when I sold Eninho to Changchun Yatai in China. Taking Leonardo to Korea changed everything for me because when I would go there and set up a meeting with any president and say that I was the agent of Leonardo and Eninho, they would say, "Bring me a player like them."

Probably the most satisfying deal, nothing to do with financials, was one of the first deals I ever did. I met an agent who was actually a Greek guy, and he had a good relationship with a guy that was an owner of a Third Division team. They needed a young guy and a scout there gave me a player. A year later, he's scored nearly 50 goals. He was then sold to a First Division club for nothing and he remained with that club for about five or six years. In his final year he was the top scorer in the league, and I sold him at that time to Shandong Lueng in China for a huge amount.

Chinese football was exploding, and he went to Shandong, did really well for a couple of years, and then forged his career through Asia and Saudi Arabia. It was one of the most satisfying things because I took him out of nowhere to the top of Asia where he became a millionaire.

On what keeps Steve up at night

When a player of mine, any player, as their contract end nears, it keeps me up at night. It kills me. I had a case recently where I had a player in the UAE, at Al-Fujairah and the club decided to terminate his contract in his last year. He had been there for two years, and they wanted to terminate his last year. We were pretty confident he'd go back into Saudi Arabia because he had played really well there. I terminated his contract, well, we agreed to terminate, and another Saudi club was keen. (but) Because of COVID, the season finished late. Then at the end of the season, the club had a really bad run and was relegated, so the deal fell apart.

It's October, and I've got nothing for the player. The markets dried up, the UAE is closed, all the markets are closing. I'm not getting anything done and the player is messaging me saying he is worried. That keeps me up at night, even though I've done so much for this kid. He started off in Malta, making nothing and now he's making a lot of money. The responsibility I feel to every player is massive.

Dealing with the cultural characteristics of Asian clubs, whether it's Thailand, the UAE or South Korea

South Korea is a market where you've got to be firm, but with the respect that you have to show culturally to everybody in the club. To the president, the coach, (and) the manager, (respect) is so important there. To break that ice and have a relationship is the hardest thing. The moment you have the relationship, things just flow. I built a lot of personal relationships in South Korea with a lot of clubs.

In China, you don't really develop a relationship with any club. There's always going to be a Chinese agent who's got some influence or connection with the club. It's totally different.

In the UAE, it's similar to South Korea, with the need for respect to be shown to the people higher up in the club.

On identifying talented players

I don't sign young players. I don't get the junior players. I don't have any at the moment. Some agents have young players, (aged) 16 or 17. I don't ever pretend to be a scout or to be a talent identifier. I'm a salesman, I know how to identify products, and I know exactly what my buyer wants. That's what I do best. I know exactly what my guys in South Korea and all of Asia are looking for. I can identify the product that they're looking for, but I don't identify talent. Even though I played the game, it doesn't mean that I can spot young talent.

I identify the characteristics, the mentality, the physical attributes first and then, based on that, identify their background, their CV, their history and what they've done, how many games they've played, etc. Then I'll take it to my guy in South Korea.

On the most difficult part of the
player agent business

The most difficult part for me is when you're dealing with unreasonable agents. I hate that. I hate dealing with an agent where after I look at his player, he or she demands astronomical figures which have nothing to do with reality.

I hate agents that are trying to bluff me. I like agents that are in the same boat and we're going in the same direction. I prefer an honest and upfront agent.

I prefer honest agents and the contacts that I've built, and the trust when a guy comes to me and says, "Steve, he's making 300. Right? That's what he's making. He'd be happy to go, make it 400, 450? But how much can the club pay you?

On dealing with the Australian football market

I'm always in contact with Australian clubs because I know so many people there. But I've stopped doing business in Australia because I don't want to, it's just not viable. When the A-League was new, Brazilian players weren't making much money (in Brazil). So financially, it was a great market to go to.

That's changed and the Brazilian market and league has exploded. We've now got Brazilian clubs buying players like Gabriel Barbosa from Italy, buying players from Europe to come back and they are making astronomical amounts. Brazilian Serie A and Serie B league players are making good money. At the same time, some European markets have gone down in salaries.

Brazilian players heading to Australia is financially very difficult, and at the same time, you've seen the increase financially of the second-tier Asian markets. They are one of my main markets at the moment. I've got six players, and if I offered any one of them to an A-League club, none would take them. The six players are making between USD300,000 to USD850,000 per year.

There was a player that I showed to Kevin Muscat when he was at Melbourne Victory as coach. He offered around AUD300,000 (as was the Melbourne Victory budget at the time) and I signed him into Thailand for USD750,000 plus all the perks, business-class tickets, huge commissions, etc. Financially, for the player and me, it's just not attractive anymore (the A-League), and they're not taking chances on younger players that are fairly unknown like they did in the past, like with Fred (or Carlos Hernandez). It's just become a difficult market to deal in at the moment for me.

On the wisdom Steve has written in his notebook about the football agent business

Look, to be honest, when I first started, there wasn't a certain philosophy that I would go by. I developed it based on my experiences. I learned 100 per cent of my football business through my ex-partner, 20 per cent of what to do and 80 per cent of what not to do.

For me, it's simple. Tell it as it is, you're always going to come out better at the end. It might not be what a player wants to hear, or a club wants to hear, but just tell it as it is. Otherwise, it's worse.

On the challenging and demanding football agent lifestyle

I'm a grafter and I work hard with my players and with my contacts. I'm very particular about the way I work. Even with highlight videos. There's a lot of companies in Brazil where you call them and ask for a highlight video made for a player and you pay them the set amount.

But I edit the videos, and I make my own DVDs. For me, that's my success because I know the player I see every single moment. I'm not some young scout apprentice getting ten bucks (dollars) a day to watch videos and having to deal with deadlines to put a video together. I take my time. I put in a lot of effort, a lot of care. That's my product.

I've never lost a player. I think my biggest attribute is the relationships I build. That is why I choose players very carefully. My relationships are my base. I just watched 24 games of a player in the last three days. They are the things that I pride myself on, relationships with players and clubs.

In 2016, I went to watch the last match of the season between Jeonbuk Hyundai and FC Seoul. Jeonbuk had to win to be champions. They won and a few days later, I had two players in a Second Division club called Gangwon. They had a playoff game that they needed to win. They couldn't draw. They won in the last minute and I was at the game.

Back at Jeonbuk, they were playing the first leg of the AFC Final against Al-Ain. And I remember staying with the family of my player Leonardo. He scored two crackers that night and we won 2–1, it was unbelievable.

I flew to watch the second leg against Al-Ain. And after scoring two goals in the 2-1 win, he was the hottest player in Asia. I spent five days there before the game and I sat in the lobby having meetings every hour. Dubai was full of agents from UAE, Saudi Arabia, Japan, South Korea, China, everywhere, and everybody wanted Leonardo.

I would have had 20–30 meetings, and that was such a great moment because I had everything in my hands. I went to the final and Leonardo was fantastic again. Jeonbuk were crowned AFC champions, which was unbelievable. It was a huge moment and I had the biggest player in Asia on my hands.

I flew back to Brazil and Al-Ahli of UAE were after him. They sent me an offer and it looked good. We basically were progressing to an agreement that I would sign just after New Year's Day (if everything was met) to finalise the deal. I was actually sitting at the Rio beach at 5 p.m. in the afternoon and my phone rings and this guy from the Royal Group, owned by Sheikh Mansour's family that runs Manchester City, asks if I was taking Leonardo to Al-Ahli. He said, "I want him," and (that) there was no deal unless I flew to Dubai.

I literally left the beach, walked straight into a travel agency to buy my ticket and flew that night. I arrived at my hotel in Abu Dhabi, slept, and at 11 a.m. in the morning, went to Al Jazira's office.

I had an offer for ballpark $3.25 million a year for the player from Al-Ahli and we signed with Al Jazira for $4 million a year. A two-and-a-half-year contract, $10 million. The deal was done in ten minutes. The best deal of my career by far.

It was the icing on the cake of an unbelievable six months.

On his observations on the way younger players should develop themselves now

Things have changed, PlayStation et cetera and all these kids are wearing their brand new Adidas boots before they can even kick a ball. They go to some academies but they're not all able to develop players effectively. If you really want to develop as a player, and the parents are serious about it, create a culture of development.

Australia doesn't have anyone to take the players. The clubs don't always have the structure. People are going to those academies so they can take a picture and are then promised a trip to Barcelona. The parents pay for it, as if they've actually got someone in Barcelona to look at them. People are wasting their time, that's not development.

On being part of the Stellar Group with super-agent Jonathan Barnett

My relationship with Jonathan Barnett became strong because when we started out, he already knew that he wanted his son (Joshua Barnett) in the business. I basically put him under my wing and was with him every day. I'd take him out, we'd go to the beach in Rio, I'd teach him a bit of Portuguese. Jonathan was grateful because of that. He recently sold his company for two-and-a-half billion pounds (I think) to Creative Artists Agency, I believe. There's no one like him, he's the best and biggest agent ever.

Jose Martinez

In terms of the agent landscape, Uruguayan Jose Martinez has had as much influence as anyone. The tenaciousness and spirit of Uruguayan football is reflected in Jose's approach to the agent business, and his values and philosophy on the world game.

Background

Martinez brought former Adelaide United and Melbourne Victory player Marco

Flores to the A-League. To complete this deal, he had to get A-League decision-makers to South America to watch the player live. Martinez described the groundwork for the Flores deal. "Marcos was impressive and I showed (Adelaide United football director) Michael Petrillo the DVD of him playing in Chile in December 2008. When Adelaide wanted to see him, the FFA was running Adelaide at the time, so Carl Veart came with me to Chile. It took me a while to convince them about Marcos, but in November 2009 they signed the paperwork in La Plata, Argentina before he arrived in 41-degree heat in Adelaide in January, 2010."[115] This was an exceptional occurrence in the A-League at the time, as rarely did A-League club staff go and scout players internationally.

Subsequently, Martinez promoted Uruguayan stars Cristian Rodriguez and Diego Lugano to the A-League. Both were "two of the finest players Uruguay has produced," according to Martinez. He offered them to clubs that had been targeted.[116] Unfortunately, the players never received a final A-League contract offer.

In his own words

On Jose's background and how he became an agent

I am a newspaper publisher and editor. I haven't been around as long as the other agents, I started in 2005 when the A-League started. I was doing my coaching badges before that, coaching youth. I wondered about being an agent and rang the NSL, they said, "We're going to create an A-League for everyone." That's when I did the test in 2005.

I passed the test and then brought one of my first players from South America, he was with Queensland Roar at the time. That was Osvaldo Carro.

On initially paying for a player's trials

I brought Carro for a trial (I paid the expenses). He was playing for Plaza Colonia, Uruguay, where he now coaches. He was my first one but the one that gave me the best satisfaction was Marcos Flores. I went to South America in 2009 with Carl Veart from Adelaide. We went over and saw him, (and) Michael Petrillo was the football manager at the time. We went back again the same year with Michael and signed a contract over there. Another player I brought from Panama was Yau to Sydney FC. He didn't play much, just a few games. And then he came back for a second stint.

On why the South American players pipeline has been more
a trickle than a stream into the A-League

The main reason is money. A good South American player, no offence, is not going to come to Australia. That's a fact. The money is not so good.

That's the problem. When we first started, we had a meeting in Melbourne with a few agents, (in) 2006, just after the A-League started and I mentioned Gabriel's Batistuta salary in relation to the cap. They laughed when I said that. No one is going to come for peanuts and the talented players, they're not going to come here to Australia for average money. Yes, I acknowledge that we did recently see some South American players who fulfilled the A-League club squad requirements at the time like Adrian Luna, Marcelo Carrusca and Bruno Fornaroli.

Bruno is now a superstar here. He's now, I am guessing, getting marquee money, but the first time I talked to him, when he first came, he was only getting the standard wages for foreigners. Australia can be a good launching pad for South American players. Carrusca has started a fantastic youth academy in Adelaide, which I think blends the Argentinian coaching style and philosophy with the local style. Luna got a good opportunity to go to another Asian league (the Indian Super League) to play. The A-League can provide a window for South American players to new experiences.

On his observation of how coaches here see
many South American players

It took me a long time to get into clubs and a lot of the coaches don't want South American players unless they go through Europe first. That's a big problem, because if they go to Europe, that means they're a very good player. If they come to Australia after Europe, they are usually past 30 years of age. The language is another problem, if they don't speak or understand English, they don't want the player.

On what has happened to Australian player development

No players should be paying money to play at any level. Simple as that. In Uruguay and Argentina (young players), they don't pay a cent. If you're stopping players from going to the top because they don't want to pay to play, I don't agree with that. They shouldn't be paying to play football. But that's how the system works here, plus you've got more competition in sports. Australia is a sports-loving country.

On developing coaches in Australia

I think everyone should invest very good money in coaches, not just for a week or two, but for a long period of time. Like Oscar Tabarez, who brought on a revolution in Uruguay after they lost to Australia in 2005.

He took over in 2006 and helped create players like Edinson Cavani and Luis Suarez. The Australian coaches are very good. Ange Postecoglou who was in Scotland (Japan then England). There's a lot of potential here but they have to be taught different ways. Not only the Dutch way (which we took on in the recent past) but maybe also some elements of the South American way.

On sending Australian talent to South American academies and clubs

It's very hard for Australian youth. There's a lot of very good talent here and they can do well in South America, but it's a very hard life in South America. It's not easy there. Here, the kids have it somewhat easier. Very good facilities. But in South America, it's not like that. You have to go by bus, (and) the food is not the same. It's a different style. So, you have to be very, very strong to go to South America as an Australian player.

On the A-League playing style

It's a better level than when I started. I think it's a higher level. They've bought some good players now. The style is maybe similar to Europe or English football, but now they're trying to play from the back like the South Americans do. Australia's got its own style, a little bit towards English football, but not as much as when they first started. I don't know if that's because of the players that come here, but all I can say is that it's a higher level now.

Physically, the fitness level is very high here, which is good. It's very good. Many South American players find that that level of fitness is too high, even Flores initially found that a problem and had to adapt.

On the difficult parts of the player agent business

The difficult part for me is dealing with people who want me to bring somebody like a Ferrari at the price of a Fiat. That's the main thing, money talks. If it's a very good South American player, no offence, but he's not going to come to Australia. He's going to go to Europe or Mexico first, or more often the MLS. Mexico is a step before Europe. Sometimes they go straight from Uruguay to Europe.

There are a lot of very good agents in Uruguay, very good agents; former players that can take players from the little club in Uruguay to Italy or Spain. They've got connections because they're former players (like Paulo Montero, ex-Uruguayan international and Juventus player, and now an agent). Many of these former players are agents now. Everything in South America is all about football. It's all about football, on the streets, on the beach, everywhere. And that's the difference here. That's why maybe the talent is not there yet.

On the reaction of Uruguayan and Argentinian agents to Jose being an Australian agent

They saw me as another window, opening another door (to) another market. They only deal with top players. They don't deal with average players that won't make it to Europe. They saw me as a good step to get into another market. But when they find out about the money, that is a problem.

They couldn't understand the tax rates. They couldn't understand how high they were and the superannuation rules as well. Until Australia wakes up and says that no kid is going to pay money to play football, the football will continue to suffer. A salary cap? What's that? When you explain to them that it's a budget limit, they understand, but they can't believe it.

On changes to the agent business over time

It's very hard to live on just this agent business. That's why I had my newspaper at the time (Noticias y Deportes in Sydney, Australia). My market is very, very narrow, it's just South American players.

When they (Football Federation Australia) introduced part of the agent's fees into the salary cap, that hurt us agents again. There's no way out.

On his proudest achievement as an agent

Marco Flores was the best player in the A-League at one time. He got the Johnny Warren Medal that year, that's the proudest thing. I had a very good reception after that, but going back to the money thing, no skilful top South American player is going to come to Australia for peanuts!

Chapter 14:
Changing the Agent Benchmark
– Buddy Farah

Australian agent Badui (Buddy) Farah operates Benchmark Management and is now synonymous with the Denmark market. The Denmark leagues are seen in agent circles as an informative indicator as to whether a player can launch a good career in Europe. Buddy has used them as a model for several Australian players to launch their European professional careers. Denmark football respects rising young players, buys at a low price, sells high and has a more favourable system for football work permits.

Buddy is a candid and fascinating agent. He conducts most of his football business overseas and understands what European clubs require. He has tasted the shift in the benchmark of which Australian players will be considered by European clubs.

Background

In October 2020, Buddy appeared on *The World Game SBS* podcast with Lucy Zelic. He provided an all-encompassing analysis and observation of the A-League, agent industry and Australian player development and pathways.[117] His commentary on the industry highlighted, among other things, that not all A-League clubs can find an unknown gem. It is the agent who compiles the scouting and gets the player in front of the decision-makers. Buddy has also said recently that many Australian kids "have been given quite a lot too early, which makes a more complacent nation."[118] Culturally, Buddy also laments that Australia is only slowly adapting to the transfer market and is restricted by the salary cap.

"Our roles are far greater than 10–20 years ago. We're more life coaches, psychologists … psychiatrists! I'm pretty hands-on with my players, it is a pretty much (an) around the clock job. You have to become a friend, not just an agent, you have to see the other side of the fence. What might he or she be going through?

Pressures at home? Married with kids? There are different levels of pressure. Wives and children might want to know where their dad's and their future might lie. Are their children already in education?"[119]

He laments the decline in younger Australian players coming through. "We are just not producing the talent and it is an alarming situation. Being an agent and dealing with these European clubs on a daily basis takes a lot of hard work to try and convince them about the Aussie boys. They know of the reputation of the Australian kids as sports people, that they can play multiple sports, have great hand-eye co-ordination and have strength, but they wonder why they can't compete on the world stage."[120]

Buddy is also another agent concerned that the recent Dutch influence in national youth player development has done nothing for the Australian game in the short term, stating that "the Dutch have done us no justice. They have been getting hefty pay packets and the results have not been coming and this has also carried over into our coaching."[121]

He sees a potential solution. "Overseas clubs are now looking for ready-made players and not many players can walk into a team in Europe straight out of the A-League. The solution may be Denmark for some of our young players. There is keen interest from a number of clubs over there looking at Australian kids. It is a place where young Australians can adapt easily to the football and the lifestyle. It is not too dissimilar to here. There are no issues with the lifestyle, the food, or communicating."[122]

Buddy has also started to represent elite Australian women players with the A-League Women's competition under pressure as overseas leagues gain budgetary momentum. He was involved with the move of Ellie Carpenter to Olympique Lyonnais, the powerhouse of women's football. His late-night phone calls and Zoom meetings got Carpenter's deal over the line. Carpenter stated that she "can't thank Buddy enough for all his work in getting it done. When the opportunity arose, I told him that's where I want to be, and he made it happen, which is quite amazing."[123]

In his own words

On his background and how he ended up being a player agent

I transitioned from my secondary education to a full-time professional contract at Marconi in the old NSL and then went on to represent Australia at the Sydney Olympic Games in 2000 as a squad player. I played for Lebanon at international level before they changed the rule around only being able to play for one nation. At

28 years of age, I was unlawfully terminated by an Icelandic club that I was contracted to and the agent at the time, who was a lawyer based out of England, was meant to be representing my affairs. Little did I know that he wasn't. He was representing the club's affairs and took me to an independent tribunal regarding my breach of contract.

The tribunal ruled correctly on me being unlawfully terminated but wouldn't rule on the money I was owed in compensation. When I then took it on to the players' union, they told me that the agent had taken me up the garden path.

He knew that an arbitrator wasn't going to rule on the compensation, and I had no other choice but to take my case to the Court of Arbitration of Sport (CAS). I didn't have the money to pursue it. That was the end of my playing career. I decided to return home and I had six weeks of soul-searching. I decided to take a different path and retired from the game.

Within twelve months, I brought Gianfranco Zola to Australia as the promoter of his charity match, and that sort of opened up the floodgates for me to get involved in the management of professional footballers. I went on to represent Archie Thompson in the latter part of his career. Archie is one of my best mates. I represented Jade North throughout his professional career and Mark Milligan.

And then one thing led to another. I was one of the first agents conducting transfers in China with European players. I was bringing players from around Europe to the Chinese market as well and was quite successful. We sent Mark Milligan to Shanghai Shenhua at the time and our name started to get out there. I started receiving calls from more and more players. In my 18 years as an agent, I have now represented close to 15 Australian internationals and that gives you a fair bit of insight.

This game is reliant on agents making an impact for our players and being able to be somewhat bullies (in a good way) on the world stage. I know from my time floating around the world that there is respect for agents that actually want to get out there and work. But there's a lot that sit behind computer screens and there's certainly ones that shouldn't be part of this game. They create a bad name for the rest of us.

On dealing with the East-Asian football market

When I started doing business in China, it was at the infancy of Australia being part of the Asian Confederation. I was in Germany at the time doing some business and my German partner was doing a lot of work in China. He was bringing in a lot of former German players like Karsten Janker and George Alberts. Through him, I was introduced to a doctor who was pretty big in athletics in China.

Dr Sofia Lu her name was, and then she made a connection for me with a Chinese agent that was based on the border of Russia. He opened the floodgates for me in the Chinese market and I had success bringing in Mark Milligan to play for Shanghai Shenhua, before Joel Griffiths was fortunate enough to be contracted to that club as well.

I was doing all the business dealings for Shandong Luneng in their transfer market acquisitions of players out of the Italian Serie A, the German Bundesliga and the Brazilian top-flight.

I was doing the job that they required of me and the players were also doing the job that was required of them on the pitch. It allowed me to do some really good business in China.

It also opened different markets in Asia and at the back of my time playing for the Lebanese national team, I was able to learn Arabic. That also opened opportunities for me in the Middle East and I started doing a lot of business there as well.

I think it was certainly on the back of Mark Milligan and Joe Griffiths' successes in the early days at their Chinese clubs that allowed other Australians to join the ranks.

I actually brought in their first Asian player, and he was a former teammate of mine for the Lebanese national team. He had a 10-year playing career in the German Bundesliga with Bayern Munich, Hamburg, Freiburg and Cologne. I started to bring in Brazilians and different foreign players to their club soon after.

On the Middle Eastern football market

They can be a little more rogue in the Middle East. Do they have a clear understanding of the game? Well, they are definitely starting to develop and adapt, because they're putting their resources in the right places and they're changing a lot of their recruitment approaches inside football departments.

That allows them to bring in seasoned professionals from strong footballing environments. But I wouldn't say that they are too far away from the mindset of the Chinese. I think they're quite similar. Different cultures, but quite similar in the way that they think around having immediate success.

On his day-to-day activities as an Australian agent

I wake up in the morning and I deal with a lot of stuff coming from different time zones.

I'm also engaged by different clubs around the world. I'm on a retainer with an

MLS club, a German club, a South Korean club and a Scandinavian club, so I work on behalf of them, as well as on behalf of my own clients.

Currently I've got 14 Australian players playing in different countries. I deal with any enquiries that might come from the player overnight. Then I'll have certain messages and emails from agents and clubs that I also deal with.

The middle of my day would be more dealing with my locally based players, their enquiries and that would consist of watching a lot of games that I would have missed over the weekend.

The back end of the day is preparing for what lies ahead in the evening with the different time zones. I have business in North America, South America, Asia and Europe. The days are consistent with football business but I am a full-time agent. I'm not a guy that runs another business and does this on the side.

On spending huge blocks of time overseas as an Australian agent

I spend seven months overseas a year. I have a home in Germany. The two years of the pandemic were quite challenging because it was the longest (time) I've probably spent in Australia in my 47 years. It's allowed us to reset with our children, which is fantastic. But it was different because we didn't have too much football going on in Australia.

On the most rewarding aspects of the agent business

We provide a holistic approach. We're not just there doing their contracts. I've helped players get through divorce cases. I've helped players that have gone through depression and mental health challenges. My biggest satisfaction and this is why I entered into this world, is not the monetary side of things. I lost close (if you count it all up) to nearly two-and-a-half million dollars as a player at the end of my career to dodgy agents. For me, it was more being able to provide opportunity and I'm of the mindset that if you do good things by people, good things come back to you.

The most satisfactory aspect is taking a kid from Australia, which is a really small football market, to the jungle on the other side of the world and helping (them) build a career and making it a successful one. Jade North for instance, and Mark Milligan both came out of it with big profiles and they've been able to stabilise themselves financially.

When I look back and I think that I'm a big part of that, that's the biggest satisfaction. It's certainly not the monetary benefits but seeing and being part of an individual's growth.

On players that were underestimated initially by some Australian clubs

I've got a couple at the moment. Zach Duncan was a boy that was practically let go by Brisbane Roar, only for them to come back and ask him to trial when they found out that he was in Europe.

He's at the beginning of his European career, but his trajectory at the moment is looking quite good. I've taken another kid from Adelaide to Midtjylland in Denmark, where he's now starting to hit the scene with their senior team. There will be quite a number of players who get lost in the system that will kick on. I was the first Australian agent to have an Australian player contracted to Bayern Munich, and this kid was a highly talented one that they had massive plans for. Two years into his four-year contract with Munich, he was practically shown the door (released) at 24 years of age. He is now back in Australia.

His name is Julius Davies. He played at Melbourne Victory as well. That boy doesn't play soccer anymore. After Bayern, he spent two years at Hoffenheim. He was moved out of there as well, ended up back in an A-League environment and I took him from Victory to Brisbane, where he won a title.

On recruiting players for his agency's portfolio

Character is massive because character and desire sometimes outweigh the technical ability of a player. It is the first thing that I look at and secondly, the upbringing of that particular player. Where has he come from? Who are his parents? How have they raised the kid? The biggest challenge we're finding as agents is that you're no longer dealing with just the player. You're now dealing with the brother, the sister, the mother, the father, the grandfather. Everyone wants a piece of the pie these days, they see it happens overseas. Neymar gets looked after by his dad. Messi gets looked after by his dad (at the top level it can work as you have advisers as well). You know, some think my son, or my brother is an aspiring young player, maybe I can make some money out of looking after him. That's happening quite a lot these days (at the lower levels) and people aren't realising that you're better off just being the parent or the sibling and letting the real people (the good agents) do the business.

I was Awer Mabil's first agent. I managed Awer for six years. I took him to Midtjylland and I did all this business and I've seen it from his perspective. I was one of the first Australian agents to work with African-Australian kids. Awer was the first African-Australian to be transferred out of the A-League into Europe, before Thomas Deng, before Bruce Kamau. I've had quite a lot of success with the African-Australian players and many are very well-educated. Yet many players from all heritages, have families that may have no intellect of the agent's unique role and maybe say "We can do this ourselves."

If players want me to be their agent in Australia and just Australia, well, I'm not the person for them. I have an ambition to take my players outside this country. Whilst the domestic game is not where it should be, players will never make a living or enough of a living to sustain not having to work post-football.

I use Archie Thompson as a perfect example. Archie spent seven years of his playing career in the A-League as a marquee and still has to go out and work. From my perspective, if I have a mother or father bringing a kid to my table and they only have an ambition to play in Australia, well, I'll tell them to sign with another agent. What becomes challenging for the parent is getting that kid to the next level abroad because that's when you really need the network. That's where you need the right agents in your corner. Because ultimately, if I'm a parent, I don't want my son or daughter to play football in Australia for the rest of his or her life. I want my son or daughter to go and experience real football. And most of the real top football is abroad, it's not always here.

As the game grows and as the money increases, more parents and siblings will think they're going to be able to do the job of agents. I've seen it a lot, but when they give it a go, they find out that it's too hard. Well, guess what? They're running back pretty quickly.

On having a strategy in place on how to deal with assertive or unrealistic player agents, in particular from Europe

I think an agent by being assertive, rude and disrespectful is only narrowing the opportunity that he's going to create for his player. What's going to happen is that you're going to get 10 phone calls and you're going to be the same person on every single one of them. You reckon the world is small, the world of football is even smaller. So, word will get around very quickly that that's not the guy you want to be dealing with. And there's quite a number of those people. It is very easy to reach out and ask about certain people. I tend to make my enquiries (as a club agent) before I make that first call to that particular agent in regard to that particular player. I need to understand firstly who I'm dealing with. That way, when I do deal with the person, I know how to attack it.

On club and player research

The internet allows you to do that as well. Over 18 years, I have built a decent network around the world that in most countries where they've got a football presence, I have a presence. In those countries, the top agents or the ones that are quite active will know most of the people involved in the game.

On structuring deals and his negotiation strategy

I try to get to the point pretty quickly. I think it's important to try to cut out all the bullshit in the process and see who you are really dealing with on the other end. My experience is that if they really want the player, they will come as close as they possibly can to your demands. What are the positives that could come out of the player actually signing with this football club? Do the positives outweigh the negatives? Is it a situation where you might have to take less than what you could potentially get if you really want the deal done? Every opportunity is looked upon differently. I like to be straight up and transparent from the outset. I don't necessarily want to have to go back and forth 10 times before I reach a deal. In some cases, you understand that that will happen.

But in most of my cases, I've just gone in from the outset and just said, "Look, this is the target we're trying to achieve and this is the reason we're trying to achieve it." I give them a case breakdown on why I'm asking for that particular deal and that particular structure. Usually, they'll be transparent with me and say, "Yes, we can do it," or no, "We can't do it." We find the medium in between and then all parties are happy. I find that's how you keep relationships.

On the niche Denmark market

When I was 19, FC Copenhagen offered me a four-year contract when I was playing in the NSL at Marconi. The three weeks that I spent in Denmark are still vivid to this day. The level of training at the time was unbelievable, I'd never seen anything like the level or quality. It was a really good era for a lot of those Danish players. But I went away from that experience understanding that it would be a perfect place for Australian players to kick off their careers. One, the country is very similar. They share a very similar culture to us. An English-speaking country, five million people, one of the best leagues in Northern Europe, some of the best talent coming out of Northern Europe, a physical league, which was also very similar to our league. That all allows Australians to adapt very quickly and (Denmark) sat well with me because of my own experiences.

A majority of those FC Copenhagen players ended up as either sports directors, head coaches, player agents or chief scouts. I had strong relationships from my time

THE STORIES OF AUSTRALIAN FOOTBALL AGENTS

there, and when I retired, one of the guys that had become a club scout really liked the mentality of Australian players. He came to Australia. It was during my first few years as an agent. His name was Peter Christiansen, sports director of FC Copenhagen, and he's one of my best mates. He watched a young Mariners team that had Mustafa Amini, Matt Ryan, Trent Sainsbury, Bernie Ibini, and Graeme Arnold as coach.

They were training out at a little backfield with goats on the pitch. He just liked the fact that these Aussie boys went about their business without any complaints. On the back of that, he identified Amini and Ryan. And as a matter of fact, he was the first person to table an offer to the Mariners for Mat Ryan to sign for a Danish club.

Mat (I believe) agreed to the deal. He was meant to be flying to Miami for pre-season with the team, however that deal did not go ahead as someone else took him to Club Brugge. The rest is history.

Amini signed at Dortmund and this chief scout at the time was monitoring him and said to me, "When his time's up in Germany, I want him here in the Danish Superliga. I think he will have an enormous career here and could potentially open the floodgates to the Aussies." And that's exactly what happened. Amini and Mabil were the first two players from an Australian background to move to strong clubs in Denmark.

I was their agent and they did a fantastic job. They both made a very strong name for themselves and then I started filtering more players in. AGF Aarhus have had four Aussies in their history. I've brought all four of them in. Amini, Zach Duncan, Alex Gersbach and now young Jim Reece. Midtjylland have had three Australians in their history. Mabil, Husein Balic, and Antonis Martis is contracted to them, but then went on loan at Macarthur Bulls.

FC Copenhagen have recently brought in one of my young boys from the Western Sydney Wanderers. I feel like it is the perfect launch pad for Australians, and that has shown with the success they've had and the level of game time they get. I had a young kid make his debut for AGF only a few weeks ago in the Danish Cup. He was playing NPL football here and offered a trial because of my relationship with a number of people there.

He went there, and first and foremost, it was the character that they liked. I come back to how I dissect players. Character is the most important thing because in some cases, the character will get the boy over the line, rather than just his football prowess.

It's worked very well, and there will be more and more going over. There's another Australian boy going over to a Danish club at the end of November, and there will be a few more between now and the next European summer.

On supporting other players by providing
a reference

I get calls from all the Danish clubs because they know who Buddy Farah is. I've almost become the person that they call in regard to any Australians that get presented to them. Even if I'm not their agent, they'll always give me a call and ask, "What can you tell us about this particular player?"

Nathaniel Atkinson from Melbourne City was proposed to them prior to the Olympics. And they were keen on acquiring him. They said, "Buddy, what can you tell us about this kid? We'd really like to have a go at him. What do you believe his value is?" I gave them his value and also (vouched for) his character and (provided) some insight on him. They tried to have a go at him but maybe Melbourne City outpriced them.

It was the same thing with Lawrence Thomas. When Thomas signed in Denmark, Sonderjyske called me up, the head coach was close to me.

On working effectively with a club on a deal

I'll give you a perfect example. Adam Taggart. Taggart was Golden Boot in the K-League. I work for Suwon, that's a club I'm retained by. I'm over there because I've brought in Terry Antonis and Doneil Henry to them. The sports director turns to me and says, "We've the K-League Golden Boot at our club, what's going to happen regarding a new deal." So, what do I do? I pounced. He was off-contract in February. So, guess what? I sold Adam Taggart to Cerezo Osaka.

On marquee players in the A-League

I brought William Gallas to the A-League, to Perth Glory. I was watching France vs Australia in the international match where Australia got whacked 5-nil and I had a call from Gary 'Bongo' Williams (another Australian agent). Gary knew I was in France, and he told me he was sitting with Didier Drogba's agent who looks after Gallas and a number of the boys playing for the French national team.

I told him to ask if he had any players. Gallas had just retired from playing in the Premier League with Tottenham. I was sitting in a café in Paris and I said to him, "Well, there's a club in the A-League that's keen on a marquee, can I propose William to them?"

We got on the phone to William Gallas and he met me in Paris. We share the same birthday and I told him that anyone born on the 18th of August is an automatic mate of mine. That was how I broke the ice. I told him that I could make something happen. The rest is history. I ended up doing the deal for William Gallas, became a friend of William, and continued doing business with his agents.

On Australian player development

I'm always looking for good players within the A-League landscape and trying to get them to the next level. The biggest satisfaction is taking a player from Australia to Europe. That's really where agents have to do their work. I do use the A-League as a launching pad for us to be able to scout vigorously on the best talent and then get them abroad. I still believe that A-League clubs need to do things better internally in regard to their football departments and who they employ and how they go about their business.

I still feel that there's not enough of a scouting department within most A-League clubs. Single-handedly, I believe I have brought in 12-and-a-half million dollars in transfer fees to the A-League. The Melbourne Victory have been massive recipients, obviously with Mark Milligan's transfers, they've picked up quite a lot of money out of that. I believe I have had a lot to do with the progress of the A-League.

On how Australian clubs value players

John Constantine loved doing business with me back in the days when he was the owner of Newcastle Jets. I also worked on a plethora of transfers with Western Sydney Wanderers — some worked, some didn't.

What I find from experience is that sometimes A-League clubs are lacking information as to the value of the players. Secondly, I don't see why A-League clubs should be stopping international transfers for our young Australians. You know, for me this is a development league.

This is a league that is there for our kids to get that opportunity and move on to the next level. This is not a league that a CEO should be knocking back Buddy Farah when he comes with an offer for the transfer of a young talent. (But) They often want more transfer fees (it's business).

We're seeing that in South Korea and in Japan, but they're able to produce better talent than us on an international level. They are now far superior to us. They are doing well in the top leagues in Europe. You look at the Premier League, Serie A, Bundesliga — the Japanese and the South Koreans have done well. I sold two Japanese players to the Bundesliga. I sold Hiroki Sakai from Kashiwa Reysol to Hannover and then from Hannover to Marseilles. I sold another from Kawasaki

Frontale to Bochum and these transfers were USD1,000,000 plus.

I sold Amini to Dortmund for AUD$350,000. The value of Australian players sometimes does not always stand up to what these A-League clubs think they're actually worth.

On what challenges exist in promoting Australian youth talent to European clubs

Training compensation. One of my players at the Western Sydney Wanderers, a highly talented player already given a scholarship, was scouted by FC Copenhagen. He was flown over with his father. He spent two weeks there. He's one of our best talents. They threw him in the under-19s at Copenhagen. He was probably the second-worst player on the pitch. Then they threw him into the 17s at FC Copenhagen. He was probably in the top three. Copenhagen turned around and said the €150,000 training compensation doesn't justify what we're seeing in this kid, yet we would love to keep him here.

They were happy to do a loan deal with the Wanderers where if he makes it to the senior team, they pay the Wanderers ballpark AUD230,000/240,000. How can a 16-year-old kid be worth AUD250,000 when he's never played one minute of first team football (it's not Wanderers fault they have to look after their interest – it is the training compensation system)? Many agents ask this question. He didn't sign at FC Copenhagen. Was he better staying at FC Copenhagen and being in the 17s and 19s and working every day like a pro, giving himself every chance to play first team football at Copenhagen?

I ring Borussia Dortmund, Bayern Munich, Midtjylland, FC Copenhagen, Ajax Amsterdam, FC Groningen, (and) Twente Enschede, and the first question they ask me is, "Buddy, what's the training compensation?"

A kid who has spent three years at A-League academy will want me to take them to Italy to a Serie A club. Well, guess what mate? You're going to have to be exceptional because if that Serie A club wants to sign you, they know there's three years' worth of training compensation. They can get an Italian kid on their doorstep for nothing. That's restricting our development. I took Zach Duncan overseas and the Danish club wants to sign him. Brisbane Roar don't want to sign him, but when I take him overseas, Brisbane get wind of it. When he signed at the Danish club, Brisbane Roar were the first ones to ark up and demand compensation. They took the Danish club to FIFA and won.[124]

On the Matildas and Ellie Carpenter

I've played a part in the Matildas' development, look at Ellie Carpenter. When I first managed Ellie, she was a girl from Cowra earning half-a-million a year (since banking an estimated AUD1.2 million in 2022 to play for France's Olympique Lyonnais).[125] We've got quite a number of them now playing in England, and they're a global brand. I look after Kyah Simon as well. The game for women is certainly expanding.

My concern is what's coming through after this batch of girls is gone. We're relying on our youth to come through on the international scene and start putting our country on the map, but the problem is the lack of camps that are happening and lack of resources and funding that they're putting towards it (the hope is that the legacy impacts of the FIFA Women's World Cup in Australia and New Zealand in 2023 will bring new funding). How are we going to compete with South Korea and Japan? Even the smaller nations are now pumping more money into women's football.

Chapter 15:
Port Wine, Pasteis and Ronaldo
– Vlado Bozinovski

Vlado Bozinovski has been an agent for over a decade and is based in Porto, Portugal — the home country of Jorge Mendes (super-agent), Jose Mourinho and Ronaldo. Bozinovski's superlative technical abilities as a midfielder player have translated to his agency business. He can intrinsically pick the right players. This is a rare quality as an agent. He researches potential players in a holistic manner and has developed his own blueprint of the types of players he seeks to represent. He will not divert from this blueprint that has served him well. He is right at the heart of the biggest export markets. Porto, Benfica and Sporting Lisbon cumulatively have transferred over 1 billion euros' worth of talent to other European clubs in the past 6 years.[126]

Background

A former Socceroo midfielder, Bozinovski played at many clubs including Club Brugge in Belgium and four clubs in Portugal. He became a football agent after retiring at the end of the 2001 season.

Portugal as a player market is always buzzing with talent identification activity due to its brilliantly run youth systems. It is common knowledge that football in the land of port wine sometimes feels like it has more scouts than players.

Bozinovski's presence in Portugal allows him to view the football development richness and ingrain himself with the Portuguese football mindset that has a lot of circular reasoning. Talented players in Portugal are seen as complex projects by agents and scouts. All possibilities are considered.

In 2017, Bozinovski was instrumental in bringing Nick Ansell from Melbourne Victory to Portuguese Primeira Liga outfit Tondela. Bozinovski can assist players like Ansell to transition effectively into Europe because he is based there. Ansell was grateful for the connections that Bozinovski had in Portugal, stating that "I haven't really been brought out here and left alone, Vlado's been with me every day at the moment which makes it a lot easier. It hasn't been a hard transition. Vlado and I thought this was the best time to give it a shot and you never know how things are going to go."[127]

The understanding of talent held by Bozinovski is also exemplified in the move of Ivory Coast- born Adama Traore to the A-League. Bozinovski alerted coach Miron Bleiberg to the possibility of Traore being available for Gold Coast United (then part of the A-League). "Vlado had been to watch the under-20 team in a tournament in Toulouse against France," Bleiberg said. "He said there was a striker and midfielder worth looking at. I watched the DVD but the player I liked most was the left full-back, Adama, and we got him to come here to start the club."[128] Traore ended up having a great career at Melbourne Victory with his signature runs down the flanks, his speedy recoveries and the ability to effect tackles.

In his own words

On becoming a player agent

I was always conscious that I was going to continue in football after playing and it was either going to be as a coach or an agent. I stuck to the agency because I was very tired of traveling. I played in many countries, with lots of traveling time away, and I was quite tired.

Agency would give me flexibility both personally and professionally, which is really why I chose that path.

I did do some coaching courses. I believe in my ability and my experience that I could pass that on to other players, but thought that through the agency, I had more control of how I work and who I work with. You don't get many choices.

I didn't want to deal with other people's issues, I wanted to do it my way, and that's why I stuck to agency.

I gained my FIFA agent's licence in Portugal during my last year as a player when I finished up in Singapore. When I finished playing, I stepped into agency and thought I'd settle back in Melbourne with the family. I actually built a nice home in bayside Williamstown in Melbourne, but I needed to work. I needed to stay busy. Europe was calling.

I live near Porto, in a beachside area. I have good access to both Porto and Lisbon. Quiet, quite pretty, good food, good climate, everything can be done from there and it is pleasant.

On the type of players he manages from his Portugal base

I've managed players from many countries; Japan, Paraguay and Brazil. I've done the rounds, gained my experience. I speak a few languages and that's helped me along. I went to South America; Paraguay and Uruguay. Those sorts of countries are about trying to discover talent early, talent that the bigger agents are not looking for.

When you start, you can't be going for the biggest and best because the biggest agents have (already) got them. You've got to start from scratch like any other business.

We realised early on that players are quite difficult. Privileged, a good life and all the rest of it. But if you want to be a professional football player and travel and play in different countries, you have to sacrifice. I didn't feel that the Australian players always have those qualities and some players simply go abroad because they are programmed that way. Then after six months, they're back in Australia. I didn't want to deal with that bullshit, to be honest. I didn't want to deal with any bullshit, (pushy) parent bullshit, so I went and did it my way.

On talent identification and taking on new clients

I can generally tell what sort of a character the player is. I see certain things that he says, not to the opposition, sometimes to his own teammates and how they deal with situations. I look for grounded, humble and disciplined athletes.

That's number one. He doesn't have to be the best player for me to approach him. Sometimes the player is one that nobody else has even looked at and I see something that I'm looking for. Number one is the personality and the character of the player.

Talent for me is not enough.

On Jorge Mendes, the Portuguese super-agent

Jorge Mendes and some of the other bigger agents haven't actually had a top football playing career. What they do have is a powerful business sense. Mendes is a brilliant mind, a brilliant businessman and very creative.

On using his Australian-based brother as a scout and partner agent

I run my business from A to Z. I scout them, prepare them, teach them, coach them on and off the field, and then I'll transfer them to the league, to the club, depending on the conditions and the characteristics needed. I do it a little bit differently. I don't have a lot of players and I've never wanted to because I'm doing this in Europe on my own.

I have my brother, John Bozinovski, who lives in Melbourne (who represented players like ex- Brisbane Roar player Devante Clut). And although we work together, I'm doing all the European agent work. Sometimes we travel together, South America and Africa, and it's hands-on. I guess it's a little bit of a mix, agency and managing. John works mainly on the Australian market and Arabian Gulf/Asian markets.

On being a mentor-type agent

I'm not money-driven. I have a passion. I played for passion and I'm in football for a passion. Of course, I get rewarded handsomely for my hard work. But it's through the passion that I enjoy taking a player that nobody even cared about, preparing (him) and then seeing him having success. It's more than the money that I'm earning from commissions, and that's the enjoyable part.

On facilitating international deals for players he has directly scouted

It's always a process, and I manage a number of players from different countries. A lot of players have their own agents. I took one Paraguayan player, a 20-year-old, to Turkey after scouting the boy. I met his family and spoke to him.

While I'm planning his trip to Turkey, he had an agent which he didn't disclose. This came as a surprise. One day, I called his home and his mother answered and she said, "Oh, he's travelled. He's gone to Turkey." They'd organised everything with the club president.

I got myself on the very next flight to Turkey. I actually found him in the Frankfurt Airport, he was catching the same flight from Frankfurt to Istanbul. He said that the agent had told him I knew about it. In the end, I worked out that there was a sneaky South American agent involved.

I started some of my early agent work in Africa. It was very difficult, the safety and conditions and all that to spend two or three weeks in Africa. I had a meeting there regarding a boy who was almost 20. He was football-educated at one of the biggest names in Ivory Coast, ASEC Mimosas.

At 18, he was ranked the fourth or fifth left-back for the club. He was always loaned out. When I arrived there with my Ivory Coast agent partner to have the meeting, I simply said, "I want this player, I want to take him to Portugal." The chairman and the coach looked at each other and sort of smirked. They didn't know me, it was the first time they had met me. They thought, "This guy's a banana.

He's taking the problem off our hands. Let's just give it to him." When we spoke about figures, whatever numbers I threw, they said, "Yeah, no problem, take him." Today he plays League One in France and has played for the Portugal national team.

He was a national under-18's starter playing First Division in Portugal. And to this day, that chairman is a good friend of mine and he always tells this story to others. He respects me because of my vision and what I saw, what I picked up that nobody else could.

This one boy now supports a family of 20 or 30 back home. That's where the real pleasure comes from. Okay, I've made a lot of money with the boy and so has he. But what it's done back home to that family speaks volumes.

On networking as an agent, and his agent style

I played for many years in many countries, and there's a number of players that are now agents. One in particular with whom I work in Mexico and South America was a teammate in Portugal and Turkey. That was almost 30 years ago, and we've continued to be good friends. Most of the agents that I deal with closely I've known previously, that's the way I operate. I'm very selective.

I do it my way with my particular group of people. And I don't go around showcasing. That's not my style. I keep it simple, honest and the people I work with, I have trust in them. That's the most important thing.

On player preparation

I prepare the player to be as attractive as possible, and in most cases, they come to me. They see my player, they like him. The clubs that I'm looking to place them at usually come directly to me.

The best strategy is to have the player as well prepared as you can, which can then give you more than one option. When you have that, it's obvious that you're going to get the best deal possible.

On dealing with different international markets

I've placed a number of players in Turkey and I've played there. I know their culture very well. It's a very difficult country to deal with football-wise, and (there are) some very difficult people to deal with in the football business (like everywhere). They like bargaining, they like negotiating. They're like playing strategic negotiation tricks sometimes and are looking for something spectacular.

But the people that I deal with generally, they know me, they know my style and generally they respect that. They understand that I won't be sitting there taking bullshit. We either do it the proper way or we go elsewhere.

The way I manage myself has given me that edge. When people talk to me, they know who they're talking to. I guess it's a balancing act, but that helps me. I don't take nonsense.

In Portugal (like everywhere in the world), they're also football stakeholders who can be sneaky. They may say one thing and then change it next week and next month. That's difficult. But again, I don't work with a lot of agents or a lot of clubs. I want to work with people that if I say or they say yes, it's a yes.

I don't want to be dealing with people that aren't honest. They'll probably turn around and just waste your time. So, I stay away from that. I filter it and I'd rather not do a deal than do a bullshit deal. I'm not 20 you know, I've got grey hairs. I'm 58. I haven't got the time to waste.

You need to know the cultures, you need to be able to manoeuvre and work through things. Different cultures equal different ways.

On seeing a change in the players in the last 10 years in terms of their expectations

I believe there have been changes, particularly to the player's general outlook. I think they're sometimes quite spoiled and sometimes have a weaker mindset. I guess when you have so many agents, so many options, you start to be a little complacent and probably believe too much bullshit, because everybody's telling you what you want to hear. I've seen that even in Portugal. Dealing with parental expectations is impossible.

When I work with a player, I speak to them. I try to meet the family to understand what's in the background. More times than not, if I'm not happy with what I'm seeing as a person, I'll move on because I know I'll be disappointed.

There was an Australian player who had A-League experience with several clubs. I took him to a big club in the United Kingdom when I was in Europe. He was in Australia during the off- season and I said, "Listen, you have to make sure you work at a certain level, because when you get to England, they'll be already moving, they're a different level fitness-wise. Make sure you're doing this." He arrived to play a practice game in the reserve team and he couldn't last 30 minutes. He was unfit.

It's that professionalism, it's that seriousness that is missing. Some Australians are good at blaming others. And they're always looking for excuses. It might seem like I'm anti-Australian but I'm not. I've tried with many. Some have let me down.

On Australian players coming through

The talent I believe is less than what it was. To be honest, I found some Australian players and their parents are very amateurish. They don't know what it's really about. Someone like my brother and me, when we talk to you, we will tell you what we want to tell you, not what you want to hear. They don't like that. They get offended. Some of them have no problem with telling you the way it is. At the end of the day, you'll be as good as the decision you make, and you'll be as successful as the decision you make.

I say this often to Australian parents. "Listen, if I have a toothache, I'll go and see a dentist. I'm not going to go to a carpenter." Don't come and tell me how to do my job. If you want to tell me how to do my job, you don't need me. You need someone else. Or perhaps you don't even need an agent. Maybe you should be the agent. Parents have tried, and they nearly always fail miserably.

On how he deals with a difficult situations as an agent

I'll give you an example — one of my players in Portugal. He started off in the under-23 B team, and he was ready to step up to the first team.

He was more than ready, but the coach and directors had brought in another player in his position at the start of the season who was very popular. I knew that when he did get his chance, he had to be prepared. That's my job, to make sure that he's prepared.

Don't worry about what anybody else is saying. Just focus on yourself and do your job. The player playing his position was sent off, remarkably in the last minute of a game, he was sent off.

The coach looked at four or five different options, determined not to put my player in there. In the end, he decided to play him. The president called me and said, "Vlado, your boy will be playing tomorrow. Just talk to him, psych him up and make sure he's ready." I said, "With all due respect, he's been ready for a long time. The boy is ready. You don't have to worry." He played the next day, they won their game and he became a starter.

At the end of the season, he was transferred out.

On Adama Traore

I guess the best story in Australia is Adama Traore. He was picked up when he was 19 in the Ivory Coast and wasn't ready for Europe. He's a left-back. Very good offensively, but defensively, (he) needed work. John and I thought maybe the Australian market was the first step for him.

We offered him to a few clubs and the only club and only coach that listened to us was Miron Bleiberg. Bleiberg saw our vision, believed in us and believed in the player. He gave him a chance. After only a few games, everybody was raving about him, at 19. That's probably a good story to show the Australian mentality. It's very, very narrow. When we think about how many Africans are playing in Europe's top clubs, and there's so much talent, we desperately need to implement something in Australia where we actually bring more quality young African players in. They will be one-fifth of the price paid for any other foreigner.

That was our pitch, but they didn't believe us. Nobody wanted a bar of it because they were too young. They didn't have a CV. They couldn't see and didn't want to see that vision.

The difficulty of being an agent in Australia

Sometimes Agents are not always understood and respected in Australia (it's getting better). Like they almost they don't need agents. That's how they see it. Agents are a pain in the bum to them for whatever reason. It seems to work in the rest of the world, but it is what it is.

In Europe, if you've got a good player, they'll listen to you. They know they need agents. They have to cooperate and work with agents. That's how they see it. Unfortunately, in Australia we are still behind with that.

On the agent business currently

One thing that annoys me is that all agents are painted with the same brush. It's alleged that they're all dirty and they cheat and they lie. Some of them do. Some of them are real bastards, and they'll cheat you for a dollar and promise you the world.

It's not easy for a father, a parent or a player to make the decision because they don't have the experience. They don't really know what the football world is all about. I guess the best advice is to do as much homework as you can on the person that you want to trust with your son or daughter's career.

Talk to some players managed by that agent. The player might say, "He's fantastic. He does everything for me." I think that's a simple way to help parents to select.

Number two, when you've selected, let them do the job. Don't get involved. We know every father thinks their son is the best player in the world, but then they want to comment on football, and they want to get involved in the decision-making.

Let the professional do his job. That's my advice to parents in Australia, in particular.

On whether Australian players should go earlier to Europe or try to make it in the A-League

Some players are ready, some players are not. And it's not easy. If it was easy, everyone would be picking Messis. Some players have the talent but they don't have the other characteristics needed to be a professional footballer and succeed for 10–15 years.

On the Latin style of football and its impact on Australian players

Australian players have a difficult time with Latin-style football. There's been a couple of Australians in Portugal and they haven't succeeded. Mexican football is interesting, not too many people know about. It's a very, very competitive league. There's a lot of quality and they pay very well. I would say the most talented and creative Australian players would have a chance there. Generally, I think some Australian, Canadian, American and New Zealand players are still a little bit too robotic. Not enough creativity, not enough awareness.

It comes from culture as well. African and South American players spent hours on the streets and that just naturally brings you that awareness and understanding of certain things, the readiness that you need.

On Australian youth players trialling at some private academies or lower league clubs or talent camps in Europe

It is a business. They'll promise you something but you have no chance of making it. It's a big business for them, so they'll tell you what you want to hear.

Parents get sucked in and nothing will happen from it. The reason, and I'm generalising, is that those players were never going to make it. They didn't have what it takes. They went because the parents paid. And of course, the businessmen took them because the parents paid. It's not an honest business when you're promising someone a career.

My brother's son started football late. He was previously in athletics and tennis. In his 12th year of high school, he was dreaming of being a Beckham, playing overseas, being a star, and his grades started going down. It was always school first with him and I happened to be in Australia and went to see a couple of his games. I actually took him out to train, just to test him. Both John and I saw that he didn't have what it takes and we had to sit him down one day and tell him. It was cruel, really cruel.

When he was playing under-18s at South Melbourne, he had terrible reactions to certain decisions and was so far out of reality. He's thinking Beckham's level when he shouldn't even be kicking the ball.

When I know you won't be a great player, you're wasting your time. You won't be a footballer. I'm not going to lie to you. It destroyed the kid, but today he's a very successful surgeon.

You have to be honest. We can't play jokes with young people's lives and futures.

On Tyler Boyd

When I talk about discipline, dedication, sacrifice and professionalism, I think about Tyler Boyd, the ex-Wellington Phoenix player. He was a New Zealand international at 18.

I offered him to a few clubs because I did want to take him out of there sooner rather than later, and nobody was interested.

I decided to take him to Portugal. He is an absolute professional. The hardest working person, he listens. He's a New Zealander with an American mother and New Zealand father. He had speed but not much of an understanding of the game at all when it comes to the European level.

I took him to Turkey on a loan for six months, (and) he absolutely killed it when I transferred him into Besiktas. He got his American player approval from FIFA and was called up into the US national team. It's just mind-boggling.

I made all the decisions. The father supported everything, even when I had to get stuck into Tyler. Whatever I said, the father would back up. We were a team. We weren't one against the other, this was a team effort. The father, myself and the boy.

On how he analyses every game of his players

It's important to know that I analyse every game of all my players. I actually make short videos to explain to them what was good, (and) what was wrong.

I understand their structure. I understand how they play. I understand what the coach wants from my player, which is why I can make certain players get to places quicker. I'm an extra coach and a support for both the club and the coaching staff

It's not just about cutting a deal and then dropping the player off.

Chapter 16:
Unique Approaches –
Brad Maloney, Boris Ivanov,
David Mitchell and Eddie Krncevic

Brad Maloney

There was always speculation within Australian agent circles that someday the Australian Players Union (now known as Professional Footballers Australia) would set up a player management arm. Finally, in 2010, it was time. The Professional Footballers Australia (PFA) Player Agency arrived under Brad Maloney, a former player and Johnny Warren Medallist, and head coach of the under-17 Australian national team. But what role was the PFA agency going to play? It is a difficult and sensitive scenario to develop a player management agency arm and then simultaneously represent players against agents and clubs in any disputes.

Background

The PFA launched its Player Management Agency in response to an overwhelming demand by Australia's elite professional footballers. It has had a far-reaching impact on the Australian football agency scene. A key example of where its agency framework came into focus was when young players from Australia's academy system, including the Australian Institute of Sport, turned to the PFA to negotiate and receive advice about playing contracts with Australian clubs. The PFA's inaugural chief executive Brendan Schwab stated that "we are worried about young players signing deals with agents that see them charged excessively for negotiating A-League playing contracts at close to the minimum wage. Some agents will charge 10 per cent of gross income for such an agreement, which sees a young player charged $3,000 or more for a deal the PFA can do for nothing. The better agents will not charge young players much, if anything, but invest in them over a 3 to 5-year period and reap the rewards down the track."[129]

Initially, the PFA agency created opportunities for the players that were unrepresented. It was more of an advisory service for players and was not profit-driven, nor did it intend to provide competitive tension in the player agent marketplace. However, the PFA subsequently moved fairly quickly away from agency and into providing a more advisory and interventionist role as a union, where players knew that if they were having difficulty with their agent or club, they were in no way compromised.

As Schwab said to me in an interview, "The PFA was always down the line with the agents, whether assisting them with their player moves or assisting the player to resolve a dispute with their agent."

To understand the motivation behind the PFA setting up a short-lived player management arm, I interviewed Brad Maloney (now Australian national under 17 coach - the Joeys) on 6 July 2021.

In his own words

On why the PFA set up a player management arm

Among the PFA group, we saw the need for a player management arm. We already had the legal team in place at the PFA. The PFA had, since its inception, advised players in their career path and was engaging in contract negotiations with clubs already, so it was a natural progression. I went through the exam process with FIFA and gained a FIFA agent's licence.

On becoming an agent

I managed the project and set up the agency at PFA. It was always about helping players and as the PFA had a good network through its affiliation to FIFPRO (the world footballers' union), we thought we could help. Through the PFA, we had experience of contractual disputes and cases, and were directly aware of the concerns of Australian players' trials abroad not going well, and therefore wanted to help the younger players. In particular, those players whose parents did not have the expertise and knowledge to avoid players going on club trial junkets abroad without any outcome.

On the Australian Institute of Sport's football program and player development

With the AIS closing down and National Youth League competition on pause, there was a consequential decline of Australia's player development model. Clubs had to absorb the talent and also work on development. The AIS polished many players to be ready for the club pathway and it gave players exposure to the media, sport science and the development of a professional mindset. In the AIS program, the environment assisted Australia's respective national teams, as did the players' attitudes, which were built on persistence and an Australian fighting spirit.

On the PFA remit in providing player agent services

Younger players needed professional opportunities. Therefore, as the PFA's agent we would advise the player on opportunities and aim to get them regular employment. The PFA agent model was providing service to off-contract players who needed somewhere to turn. My aim was to get on the phone, using our network, to open opportunities through our contacts in Australia and abroad.

On international opportunities for Australian players

As part of developing opportunities for players, and the PFA's objective to open doors, I travelled as the PFA's representative to Europe a number of times; to London, Sweden, Paris and Denmark to speak to football managers and clubs. I provided advice to Jarred Lum formerly of Sydney FC. Jarred was a brave player, so I opened the door for him to Hong Kong and Asia. He had a 10-year career and I continued to help him on the periphery. Further, the PFA management arm, with its legal department, could help with final contract terms, especially as many Asian football clubs back then had weird clauses in contracts which were more difficult to negotiate than A-League contracts. Australian club contracts were smoother and more amicable to easier negotiation.

On his approach and philosophy as an agent

For players who approached the PFA for assistance, my philosophy was to advise them on their football options and also ensure they received support for their own state of mind and wellbeing. Before a player signed a contract or received an offer from a club, I went through the options; both the pros and cons. My style of player management was to look at the stability and financials of the club and to advise the younger players that they had to play every week; it was less about a huge salary and more about performance. I would also do my research on the club, as it was key for players to establish themselves by being in the match-day team. My player-agent approach was to always be honest about my assessment of the club and ensure the player understood the reasons behind any move. For me, agents have to be honest, knowledgeable, have expertise, the right contacts, go into bat for the player, have near 24/7 availability, understand talent identification, and have the ability to weigh up offers.

On how long the PFA agency operated

The PFA player management arm started in 2010 and went for a couple of years. In 2012, I wanted to get back into coaching so the PFA agency ceased. Finally, I have to say the agents' business environment, both here and overseas, is ruthless and a very competitive and hard-hitting industry. It is very hard to place players who have been let go from their clubs as there are just not enough club employment opportunities.

Boris Ivanov

Stamford Bridge, November 2016, home of Chelsea Football Club. It's the Wyscout Forum where football clubs and agents meet in a speed-dating format to discuss recruitment and player deals. I am there with another Australian agent, Boris Ivanov. It's a long way from home but if you're Australian and want to do international agency business, then the Wyscout Forum is one of the best places to network and make connections with decision-makers. I notice Boris gravitating towards Belgium and Dutch clubs. It makes sense, as both have been admirers of Australian players for many years and are markets we must pursue. Ivanov is about presenting and consolidating these opportunities for Australian players. However, as he has said to me in the past, many do not want to take these opportunities, especially at some lower league European clubs. As Boris says, "comfort equals mediocrity."[130]

Background

Boris is the principal of TF14, a Melbourne-based player agency and one of the few agents (along with me) who contributed to the seminal Crawford Report in 2003, which aimed to reset and restructure Australian football. Having invested a lot of time into meeting clubs and club directors in Europe, Boris has developed his own unique approach to agency. Firstly, he focuses on markets like Scandinavia and the Benelux region where Australians have had a good track record.

Secondly, Boris brought international youth football directors, coaches and scouts to Australia to identify lesser-known Australian players looking for pathways into Europe. He focused on clubs that would provide pathways and suited the Australian playing style. Boris believes that Australian male footballers (if they do not hold a UK passport) will find it harder to transfer into English teams due to Brexit compared to Australian female footballers. This is due to the relative strengths and rankings of the A-Leagues — Men and Women — and the Australian national teams. He is of the view that, "effectively, for non-national team male players, England will no longer be an option — it wasn't for many previously either, only those with EU passports had access — unless they hold a British passport or can access a heritage visa. For non-national team women, it will be harder but still possible due to the strength of the W-League (and the Matildas) and the points you attract in playing in that competition."[131]

Boris developed TF14's talent identification program. In 2017, coaches and scouts from 10 different clubs flew to Melbourne and conducted five days of training sessions in the hopes of scouting prospective younger Australian talent. "Representatives from Croatian powerhouse Dinamo Zagreb, Dutch sides Heerenveen and Twente Enschede, Serie A side Atalanta, MLS franchise Chicago Fire and Danish second-tier side Esbjerg"[132] were among the clubs represented by coaches and scouts to select potential trialists and signings.

In his own words

On his background in football

I got into football a little late, maybe when I was about 10 or 11, playing out in the southeast of Melbourne for a club called Vermont. When I was doing my postgraduate degree at Melbourne University, I decided to join Melbourne University Soccer Club and that was really where the love affair for football began again and where I became passionate about the game. I played at Melbourne University for a long time. I ended up being on the committee there and then was president for six years. I think there are something like 14 men's teams and six women's teams. Running that was a big part of my life, I really loved running the club and managing it. I felt I was giving something back.

I also completed a Bachelor of Business at Deakin University and ended up working predominantly with Australia Post in marketing, strategic planning and international business and development. I travelled the world and that gave me opportunities to explore other fields. I followed the Socceroos everywhere, to the qualifiers in Japan, to the World Cup in Germany, and these things just made me want to get into football more and more.

After 17 years at Australia Post, I thought it was a good time to make a change in life. At that point, a family friend of ours' godson was playing for the AIS and he asked me to go and have a look at him to give him my thoughts on what sort of player he was. I went and had a look and I thought, "Yeah, this kid can play football." That was Matthew Theodore.

Matt ended up signing up for Melbourne Victory. Things didn't work out for him there and I spoke to Matt and asked, "Do you want to work together?" He wasn't happy with the representation he was getting. Once I got my Australian Post redundancy, we jumped on a plane and went to Sweden. We had organised trials and I had some good contacts there. Matt had a good CV, he'd been in the AIS, he'd played Australia under-20s. He trialled there at Trelleborgs for a couple of weeks. They liked him but didn't feel he was suited for the game in Sweden.

Matty was a small player, short in stature, not physically dominant. Then we jumped on a plane to Holland. I'd always been an advocate of Dutch football, followed it closely and I basically went sales 101 and cold-called every Second Division club in the Netherlands. I got two trials for him. They both liked him, but one of the clubs had already put an offer out for their last position on the squad, so they couldn't take him.

He went to Telstar and did extremely well. Straight after the trial game. I knew they'd want to sign him, which they did. The technical director spoke with me, and he wanted to know if Matt was a free player.

At the time, I didn't know there were licences, or what it took to be a proper agent. I was just using my networks and my commercial and professional skills.

The director wanted him, but what about training compensation? I'd never heard of training compensation in my life. I went back to the hotel and Googled "training compensation." I contacted Melbourne Victory to try and get the training compensation waived because he'd had a professional contract there. It just shows you the level of knowledge in the game back then and maybe still now to an extent. They advised him that, yes, this training competition thing exists, and that they're entitled to money. The process took two weeks to resolve. Telstar signed two other players and there were no spots (left) for Matty.

We then went to Greece, sorted out his EU passport there in a village up north, and then to Bulgaria. We waited to see what other opportunities came up because it's a cheap country and I was working on various things. I got him a trial with PAOK Salonika through a friend of mine. We organised a trial for him in Bulgaria with a club in the First Division. He did really well, they wanted to sign him, but didn't have money. They had a big derby coming up with one of the other Sofia, Bulgaria teams.

The TV cameras were there and some of the players put on their tracksuit tops with the pockets back to front to show that they weren't getting paid. It was quite amusing. We came back to Australia after that, and it was at that point that I realised I really enjoy the agency work but needed to learn more about it.

On becoming an agent

That's when I applied to do the FIFA exam and went through the process. I was probably a little too overconfident to start with. I thought, "How hard can this be? You know, I've got postgraduate tertiary qualifications in finance!"

You pay your $200 or whatever it was back then. There's a lot of paperwork, all the regulations of FIFA basically, and you realise it is a law exam and tough. I studied really hard to make sure I was across everything. I went to the exam in Sydney and felt pretty confident going in. There were probably about 20–25 people there.

I think only two of us passed that day. I obtained my professional indemnity insurance, then I needed to learn more about the game. I joined the Australian Football Agents Association which included Ritchie Hinton, John Grimaud and Lou Sticca.

Then it was about building a profile. How do I build my player base? Obviously as a new agent, that's not easy. It took time, but I did it through my contacts, my networks. It has been a rollercoaster ever since, some good successes early and then losing players. I had an impression that if you do things the right way, players will stick with you. I believed that if you have a good plan in place, if you're delivering results for the customers, customers very rarely leave you. They understand the strategic vision. I had to learn the hard way that 22-year-old boys don't think like that. Well, very few of them do. They don't see the big picture. I started off a few players, one now that's made his debut for the Socceroos recently, Kenny Dougall. I got Dougall and Alistair Quinn to Telstar in the Dutch Second Division and everything was going well. At the time I was very focused on one-year agreements, with the intention that if things are going well, we would work together for the long term.

I quickly found out that players don't always think that way and they can quickly jump ship when some powerful (in this case) Dutch agents are circulating. Losing Dougall to other agents was pretty heartbreaking because you invest so much. You believe you're doing the right things with the right intentions, and you feel a little bit hurt by that. But you learn your lessons and that people think differently. I still have a decent relationship with Kenny, so that's good.

But it was definitely tough at the time. Now I make sure that I protect myself more. You realise that you can have the best of intentions, the best strategies, but unless you've got contracts in place and longer-term contracts, you know you're really setting yourself up to lose players. Even when you have a two-year contract. Working with younger players, you work hard and that's the hardest step — getting their foot in the door, but you don't make much money at that point.

You make money down the track. And if they leave you after one year, it costs you in the long term.

On Boris' day to day as an agent

For a long time, I was a full-time agent. For the first seven-and-a-half years, I just focused on agency. That enabled me to develop networks around the world and domestically, and (I) put the effort in. That's the start of your preparation for a window. Two or three months before the end of a season, I reach out to my contacts and start communicating about what they are looking for. I don't want to throw names at clubs for the sake of throwing names. What I like to do is sit down, either in person or via the phone, depending on travel, and find out exactly what are the requirements of the club. What positions are they looking for? What age profiles, what budget profiles?

I get as much information as possible so that I'm not wasting their time with the players that I'm offering them. I try to work in the most professional manner that I can, rather than saying, "Here's 50 players that I can offer you," and you may not need any of them and they may not be at the level or of the age profile or the positions that you're looking for. Then I reach out to my network of partners and agents and say, "Hey, do you have this player, this is the requirement from Club Brugge or this is what Heerenveen need. Do you have something?" Obviously, for the Australian clubs, you're going to reach out to your international network more, for international clubs you reach out to both your international network and your domestic network because everyone has different players, needs and different contacts. It's also very important to have relationships and contacts with other agents.

On some lessons learned and taking on new clients

Character is such an important element. I've also learned that talent in itself is not enough. I don't think in Australia we have any truly exceptional talents from a global perspective.

There's a wide variety of people that, if given the opportunity, could easily play professional football, not at the very top level, but easily in the A-League. They could play in a secondary European league or a Second Division, something like that. But they need the opportunity. I started to walk away from looking at just what appeared to be the most talented players if their character was questionable. You'd sit down and talk to them and you just didn't gel. There wasn't that relationship, trust, faith. You'd see how the parents behave. There's a lot of crazy parents out there and to be quite frank, I don't need them. I don't need to deal with a crazy parent who thinks their son or daughter is Messi or Sam Kerr. I've dealt with enough craziness, parents asking, "Where do you have contacts?" I say, "Germany or Holland." Then they turn around and say, "Fantastic, Germany would be great. We've got family around Munich. So yeah, maybe a trial at Bayern, that would be fantastic." That's not a joke, that is how some of them think.

That's the deluded level we sometimes have here, and I don't bother with those sorts of people anymore. I want to get to know their character. Make sure we get along, because even if that other player is a little more talented than this one, (it) doesn't mean they're going to make it. I think character is the key to determining whether you make it. Yes, you need a base level of ability, but you need to show resilience and a never-say-die attitude more than anything else. Lots of talented players don't make it because they can't deal with homesickness, they can't deal with a change of culture, they can't deal with any of it. I'd much prefer to get the person that's mentally ready, maybe a little less technically or tactically ready.

Every country plays and sees the game differently. Just because you're deemed not good enough for Holland doesn't mean you're not good enough to play in Sweden. Just because you're not good enough to play in the A-League doesn't mean you're not good enough to play in Belgium.

On his talent identification process

The way we view talent here is very different to the way talent is viewed in Europe. Very different. Australian clubs look at players in a similar way. In Europe, that's not the way. A Spanish club looks at a player from one perspective, very differently to a Norwegian club, very different to a Bulgarian club or a Greek club or a Hungarian club.

The trick is, when I look at a player, I wonder where I can place them. They may not be the best player, but they've got potential to play in a certain country. A physically dominant player who I may not think is technically great, I'm not going to take to Holland, but I'll take them to Sweden where being physically dominant is important.

It's very important that you understand the strengths of the players, the leagues that they will suit in terms of the way they're played, but also understand what the coach's requirements are. Sometimes, they do want something a little bit different.

You've got to look at each player and see what the strengths are, factor in their passport situation and understand the regulations and restrictions around different parts of the world.

It's important to be an accredited agent, to understand all the FIFA restrictions on movement and each country's separate restrictions, and who can play there. There's been so many examples of players that haven't made it in Australia that have gone on to play overseas. I use Kenny Dougall as an example. He wasn't deemed good enough for the Brisbane NPL competition but ended up playing for the Socceroos and then a Dutch club wanted to sign him on a professional contract. Christian Volpato was cut by two A-League clubs and he's now playing for Roma.

These are common occurrences. It's because we have, at the moment, twelve clubs in the A-League and twelve people that are making the decisions. They sometimes all see the game very similarly because they've been brought up in Australia. In the old NSL, you had so much more variety of play because you had a variety of coaches from different parts of the world, and more clubs giving more players opportunities. There are hundreds of players that could easily play in the A-League, but they're not given the opportunity that other players are. Some people say, "If you can't make it in Australia, what's the point of going overseas?" I totally disagree with that. Yes, the competition may not be as great, but they all view the game in one way.

You go to the Netherlands or go to Germany. Let's take Germany, they've got close to 60 professional clubs, so it takes one in 60 to like you and see something. There's more competition, but the game is subjective. It just needs someone to see something in you to give you a chance. I think you're better off going somewhere where there are more eyes on you; constantly looking, constantly scouting. There's not much scouting here. If you're playing in Belgium, you're surrounded by Holland and France, scouts and clubs will all be watching. They'll see you. All it takes is for one person to think you've got something. If a coach likes you, they can give you opportunities. I always wonder, "How is Denis Genreau capable of playing at PEC Zwolle, yet not capable of playing every week at Melbourne City?" (maybe he was in a big squad with similar players).

The difference is that John van't Schip believed in him at City and took him to Zwolle. The coach trusted him, believed in him and gave him the opportunities.

On the most rewarding aspects he found in the agent business

It's very rewarding helping players achieve their dreams. If I can help a player achieve that, I'm chuffed. I'm absolutely over the Moon.

It's not about the money, it's about helping players achieve something. That gives me great satisfaction. When I see a player like Beattie Goad making it to the Matildas, it gives me a great sensation. She went to Stanford University in California. I'm not sure what she wants to do long term, come back to Australia for a medical degree, I think. We got her a club in Germany and playing in the Bundesliga every game provides an opportunity to be part of the Matildas and play for the national team.

On negotiating a deal for a player

You always want, where possible, everyone to leave the table quite happy with the deal. I think you need to understand the value of your player quite clearly. How good are they? How needed are they in that team? Understand the other options that club has because that affects your negotiating power. You need to understand the market completely. Negotiating in Australia is completely different to negotiating in England or mainland Europe. The negotiations in Australia are far simpler and less complex. You don't have various bonuses that you're throwing in because of a salary cap.

It's much more complicated negotiating in Europe. Negotiating in England is probably one of the most complex things. I did a negotiation for Kevin Bru, Jonathan Bru's brother at Ipswich, and that was a really thorough negotiation, requiring an understanding of the level of salaries in the UK. I pulled Ipswich's annual report for the last few years to see what they were doing in terms of their wage spending. What was their profit situation? They were telling me they were in a bit of a difficult financial situation. I needed to confirm that. The level of negotiation is all about me being prepared and thoroughly understanding the market conditions, as well as the club.

I don't believe that the player always has to get the most amount. I think they have to get a fair amount. You have to explain to the player what their market position is and get them to be realistic. I aim to get them the best outcome without damaging the relationship with their employer as well. The three things for me are market conditions, club conditions and value.

On how to deal with difficult players, parents, other agents and clubs

With difficult parents and players, I push back and say, "Look, this is the reality."

I used to be probably a lot more amenable and agree with things. Whereas now, I just tell them like it is. "Your son or your daughter is not that good, that is the reality." If they're not happy with that, that's fine. They can walk away. I'm confident enough to know now that I really don't need the player as much as they need what I know I can do for them. It's cutthroat in that sense. If they don't like it, no problem. Go to someone who tells you what you want to hear.

In terms of difficult agents, it's pretty clear early on who a good agent is. If an agent's been difficult, if all they're talking about is how much money they want to make and let's get a deal done quickly, they're usually not looking after the client's best interests or building a long-term relationship. That's not the sort of agent I want to work with.

I just don't respond to them after a while or just say, "Thank you very much, I think we don't work that well together."

Difficult clubs are a tough one because at the end of the day, we need them. We need to have a relationship with them. I try to be as diplomatic as possible. I continue to maintain a diplomatic relationship with them. I wouldn't turn around and argue with a club or be aggressive in the sense of being unprofessional.

Whilst they may be difficult to deal with, you have to keep pushing in a nice way to remain in communication. That's fine. If they don't call back, you message them again, not straight away. You just stay on top of it, but always in a very professional manner.

At the end of the day, if they don't want to deal with you in the right way or they refuse to do it, that's their problem, not mine. (At) Least I can hold my head high, saying (that) I've dealt with them in the best way possible. There are plenty of other clubs in the world.

On Boris' Australian talent and trial showcases held in Melbourne

The showcase idea came to me because I'd developed good relationships in Europe and, through flying over there, door-knocking, cold-calling and using all my networks, I was able to get players' trials overseas.

However, it wasn't easy. The first barrier is just the mental one. Europeans think Australia is 100 years away.

They don't want to drag a player over to Europe for a trial. They say, "There's other players here." They don't understand that Australian players have limited opportunities and will do whatever it takes. The clubs have a negative impression, so it's always very difficult getting them to overcome that.

The clubs aren't keen to pay for Aussies to fly over. They've got players of equal quality, so the players here would have to pay their airfares and accommodation and be there for that opportunity. You might only get one or two trials locked in, so players would be paying a lot of money to be seen by one or two clubs.

My thought was to turn it on its head. I'd been working with a lot of very talented players at Richmond Soccer Club in Melbourne at the time. They had a great program in the youth area previously, and I really wanted those kids to have an opportunity. I spoke to their parents and the players. I said, "What about if rather than costing you guys $5,000 each to go overseas, we bring some professional clubs here; the head coach, the sporting director, the head scout, people that make the decisions? You pay $500 and between 30 of you that will pay for the airfares and accommodation. That was the thinking behind the talent ID program, to get players seen.

I tried to bring different clubs from different countries to give players the best opportunity to be seen. I've done about six or seven of them now. The common themes are that our players physically are very good and technically, they're fine. Tactically, they have not progressed enough. What they do on and off the ball, where they are positioned, how they react, how they change position has been, without a doubt, the main negative feedback. The other key element that's been noticed is that the talented 12 to 14-year-olds in Melbourne have been viewed as highly as the youngsters in Europe.

The problem appears to be as they get older. The level drops, and I think that's the big challenge for Australian football, to understand why that is happening. At 12 to 14, our top players are good enough to play in Europe. Then, as they get to 15, 16, 17, they're okay, but dropping, and then at 18 and over, it gets really tough.

I think it is due to the number of hours of training. If you compare the amount of training they're getting overseas to here, it is no wonder our development is suffering. There are some good coaches, but overall, the quality of coaching is not the same. The quality of players, the depth of players is not that strong. Get more games, the best playing against the best. If you're training with guys that are well below you, how are you going to ever be pushed to that next level?

It's definitely opened the eyes of parents, because they get to talk to the sporting director of Mechelen or the head scout of Heerenveen, (or) to top development clubs like Dinamo Zagreb and Atalanta. They learn about the expectations there, (and) how things are done there.

A number of players have got deals overseas from the program. But it's always going to be the minority because they're only going to take the best of the best, but it opens opportunities. One boy got picked up by Mechelen to trial, and he was very unlucky not to sign a contract. He was doing the program for the fourth time, and that was the first time that a top club had seen him. You may not be ready at a certain age. But you might be ready later on, that's resilience and character, you've got to have that, you've got to keep working, got to keep getting better.

No club in the A-League had looked at him, the sporting director of Mechelen said, "He's got something," and flew him over. He trained with their under-23s at the time. He lifted to their level. Sadly, the Belgian Federation had just made a rule that they were going to under-21s and he was turning 21 soon after. He was too old, and they were not going to use an over-age position for a guy coming from the other side of the world.

So Mechelen think he's good enough. But an NPL club, let alone an A-League club, doesn't think he's good enough. That shows me sometimes there is something fundamentally wrong with our understanding of what a player's level is and where sometimes football is in this country (of course it is a game of opinion).

David Mitchell

The agent business has become more diverse, with many agents or intermediaries becoming scouts, club advisers, introducers or club referrers. David Mitchell will not ever describe himself as an agent, however his introductory intermediary role in referring some of the best Australian talent to clubs in the Netherlands cannot be overlooked. David brings a rounded perspective to the representation business; a top ex-player and coach, he was appointed as an exclusive scout for Dutch powerhouse Feyenoord. That's a rare position for an Australian to hold.

Background

For a decade-and-a-half, David Mitchell was a professional footballer who carved a successful career in Europe, the United Kingdom and Asia. He played 44 times for Australia, scored 13 goals and appeared in three Socceroo World Cup qualifying campaigns. His playing clubs included Rangers (Scotland), Chelsea, Millwall, Swindon Town and Newcastle United (England), Eintracht Frankfurt (Germany), Feyenoord (Netherlands) and Selangor (Malaysia). Further, Mitchell coached Kedah FA, was the head coach and director of football at Perth Glory Football Club and is a Football Australia Hall of Fame recipient. He set up an intermediary services company named COACHUB Talent Identification and Management Services. It focuses on the football talent ID process that creates pathways for elite-level young footballers and also provides professional club advisory scouting, player testing, contract negotiation and intermediary services. Mitchell's appointment at Feyenoord involved representing their interests in South-East Asia and working as a scout for the club in the Asia- Pacific region. He was behind Brett Emerton's move to Feyenoord from Sydney Olympic in 2000.[133] His intermediary endeavors also included being Feyenoord ambassador for their brand in Asia.

In his own words

On David's background and his move into scouting

I was coaching at Sydney United and playing when I first came back from overseas. At Sydney Olympic there was a young 17-year-old Brett Emerton, a fantastic young player who had been taught how to play from an AIS point of view and had been through there with Ron Smith and Steve O'Connor as mentors. He was a great lad from a good family. He had the potential to go overseas. I went to Sydney United to play and coach and that's where I picked up Mile Sterjovski and a couple of players there that were coming out of the AIS that I liked. When I went to Parramatta Power, the opportunity to sign these players was there and I tried to sign Brett Emerton. I suggested Parramatta were to sign him for one million dollars off Sydney Olympic, which I knew would be splashed all over the place. Also, because I knew that there was real interest from Feyenoord, and they would probably have paid one-and-a-half million dollars for him. I could see he was a talented player. I told Rob Baan, who was the Feyenoord technical director, and he took a real interest in what I had to say. Then I parted ways with Parramatta Power, where I had signed Brett Holman also as a young player. I scouted the best young players because I wanted them to come in and play in our youth team and hopefully, give them a pathway into the first team, or overseas if they were good enough.

Holman was offered $50,000 at Sydney Olympic, Marconi offered him $55,000. I think Feyenoord offered him $60,000 and then I think Olympic came back with $50,000 plus Thai Airways business-class tickets around the world. There were a lot of clubs chasing him and we at Parramatta Power only offered him a $15,000 scholarship.

He came in and trained with us, with the idea being that once he developed, we would put him in the first team and then give him a proper contract. If he was good enough, he would go overseas. He took our offer over all the other clubs and his agent was Alan McGrouther at the time.

On being appointed as the Feyenoord scout

When I left Parramatta Power, the opportunity came about to sign with Feyenoord

Rotterdam as the Asian/Australia scout. They pay you per month and you scout players and inform them who is good and who isn't. They had a certain system of how to look at players. The Dutch are well-known for how they scout players, and I think the Dutch league is a great league for Australian players to go and play because it's a league where your technical ability can come out and also your physicality is valued. They always appreciated that Australian players were quite physical and very fit. The Dutch are very thorough in what they do, and they're very good with their own youth and development.

On elite players he has helped through
his intermediary role

Holman was very quick and he was a great young player. He could actually put players under pressure upfront and was dynamic, he could read the game well and put other people into play and could score goals himself. But he struggled when he came to Parramatta Power.

He was training every day, sometimes twice a day, and then we realised that he needed vitamin pills and potassium and iron. His blood tests showed that he needed to eat properly to enhance his training. We monitored him, and then he became really professional and a fantastic player.

It was Rob Baan who initially did the deal with Brett Emerton. He flew over here, had a look at him, (and) did the deal with him at the club. The next one was Brett Holman, and there were a couple of other players that I sent over there. There was also Michael Brown. Brown and Brett Holman signed together. Feyenoord has a sister club, Excelsior. They would come and sign up for them and play there at Excelsior and develop before signing with Feyenoord.

Brett Holman had a five-year contract and Michael Brown had a two-year contract. They were really keen on Brett Emerton, but saw potential in Michael, and he had a British passport. It made it easier for them to acquire Michael with his British passport than it was with Brett.

Michael was a talented player, and he could see things and make passes, (but) unfortunately, Feyenoord had really good midfielders in his position and he couldn't break through. He left after two years, but Holman stayed and then Feyenoord was struggling a bit financially. They sold Brett Holman to another club, from Excelsior to a club called NAC Breda, which a guy called Mario Been was coaching at the time. I had played with Mario, he was a Feyenoord player and a coach, and he knew about Holman. Brett did fantastic under him, and then went to AZ Alkmaar where they won a Championship.

On why the demand for Australian players by
overseas teams has somewhat declined

You've got the rise of Japanese players and the rise of the South Korean players in our region. Everyone's caught up. It's about winning. With the under-16, 17, 18 teams, it's about getting to the next stage (professionalism), and before that, obviously from twelve onwards about developing players, let them learn by teaching them the game.

In Europe, many different players have got an avenue through Belgium football. They've got agents that work there, they get them in there then they play in Belgium, (for) two or three years, and then they can go anywhere, so there's a bit of a pathway (Australians don't always have that).

For Australian young players, they also need to understand that an A-League head coach doesn't always have the time to actually work on someone's ability, they've got to be ready to play immediately. There might be a young player given chances that plays five good games and five bad games. Well, those five bad ones might cost the coach his job (this mindset impacts the pathway and playing opportunities).

On mentoring players

You try to guide them. You tell them that they are going to be lonely sometimes. When an Australian player goes overseas to a club trial, (other players at the club) they're like, "Who's this guy, he's taking my spot," so they're not really friendly to you. It's not a friendly environment until you actually prove yourself as a player and teammate, (then) they go, "This guy's all right, he gets stuck in." You need to highlight to your players (that) this type of treatment does happen.

With Brett Holman, the good thing about Feyenoord was that they had a family that looked after you (foreign players) in an apartment. They set the rules and you've got to stick by them, and if you don't, they tell your boss at the club. Brett Holman still has friends there today. He calls them his second mum and dad in Holland, he's still got close relationships with them.

I also try to give advice to players to link up with good coaches. Good coaching is not about going through your hard drive and thinking, "Right, okay, where did we go wrong?" It's there and then and that's the flamboyancy we miss. Some coaches might not be able to do a spreadsheet, but they know the game and they can actually articulate what they want the players to do.

On why players should always be upfront and transparent

I told players not to misrepresent. Don't say you've done this and done that, because if you haven't, they'll pick it up on Wyscout or other platforms. These guys (clubs and agents) are professionals and that's their job. They don't want to lose their job or business. They love working in sport. They love working at that elite level. They don't want to be embarrassed by sending a dodgy player and not being given all the details which means they have been misled. They (Agents) have to be 100 per cent sure before they send you as a player to a club that everything is correct and it is what it is.

On the need to have an Australian football
home base or central hub

The A-League started a whole new ball game. Frank Lowy came along and made changes, and that was great. But the biggest problem in our game is that we haven't got a place called home in Australia, we haven't got a patch of land. Football Australia needs a home. You've got Football New South Wales who have a home at Valentine Park that was donated to them years ago. But I think we should look up somewhere like the Central Coast or maybe down in Geelong for Football Australia's home. A training camp where teams come to play, train and prepare. We haven't had the money to do that.

Eddie Krncevic

Eddie Krncevic, former professional player and Australian Soccer Hall of Fame inductee in 2001, represented Australia on 35 occasions and played in Europe for 14 years. He was undoubtedly the first player from Australia to make it big there and he was the top goal scorer in Belgium at Anderlecht in the 1988/89 season. During his professional career, he scored over 250 goals and also played at Duisburg (Germany), Cercle Brugge (Belgium), Mulhouse (France) and Dinamo Zagreb (Croatia). Krncevic's foray into agency was through Eurogoal Management Group Pty Ltd, based in Melbourne, and he once travelled with Edgley International's (an artist management company) chief scout, Angelo Vendetti, to Europe to scout players.

Eddie's background in the world game as a player at a first-class, elite level would have allowed him to forge considerable contacts throughout Europe. He can speak five languages (English, French, Dutch, Croatian and Italian), which is a huge advantage in the agent industry.

Background

Krncevic was one of the first agents to be mandated by an A-League club to put together a playing squad. He also engaged in recruiting players for well-regarded clubs in the Belgium leagues and brought a coach's perspective to the agent industry.

In the early days of the A-League, the New Zealand Knights appointed Krncevic as their international player agent. This was a rare occurrence in both New Zealand and Australian football. He assisted the NZ Knights in signing Victorian NPL players like Jonas Salley (South Melbourne FC) and Simon Kovacevic (Sunshine George Cross).

In relation to his Belgium connections, Krncevic wanted to "help Belgian clubs reveal great talents." He provided an opportunity in Belgium for players like Andy Vlahos and journeyman goalkeeper Caleb Patterson-Sewell, who ended up playing in six different countries and for at least 14 different clubs in Belgium, England, the United States and Portugal.

At 17, Patterson-Sewell headed to Europe for a trial with Belgian giants Anderlecht. He would later go on to play academy football for English sides Sheffield Wednesday and Liverpool. He would say later, "I had an agent from Australia, Eddie Krncevic. He played for them, and he took me across there. It wasn't a very long time there, but then I went to England. I didn't have a European passport. But we found a loophole, where if your parents are working in the country, they can't stop you playing, you just can't play in any games where they're taking gate receipts. So, I could play all the junior football, including reserve team football, as long as they weren't charging."[134] Sometimes agents need to be inventive, and Krncevic set up the pathway for Patterson-Sewell.

Krncevic was adamant that A-League teams give young players opportunities. He was advising Croatian clubs on Australian talent like Mate Dugandzic, Steven Lustica and Daniel Visevic and stated, "It's development and the politics of not giving these boys a go. If we're going to recruit foreigners, they've got to be better than our boys. There are many that are not up to scratch and they're taking our kids' places. Give our kids a go and let them develop: they might not set the world on fire straight away, but they might in one or two years."[135]

Krncevic's agent philosophy was also about giving players the stage to perform and develop careers, as long as they remained focused and disciplined to grow as players. In his column, 'Krncevic's Krunchlines,' which appeared in Australian soccer newspaper *Goal Weekly!* in 2006, he wrote, "I recently returned home from spending the past five weeks in Europe on a footballing visit to Germany, Belgium and the United Kingdom. There appears to be quite a few young players and interesting players coming through the ranks who seem to have a good future in the game. Believe it or not, the success of Australia's World Cup qualification and the A-League is causing quite a few people in Europe to really take note of where are up to Down Under."[136]

Krncevic is a "great believer in giving young talent a go at the top level. Vince Grella, Mark Bresciano, and Simon Colosimo were 18-years-olds when they were given a first crack at top-flight football when he was coach at Carlton SC."[137] In 2006, Australian football was recognised as a world leader in sports science, yet according to Krncevic, many in Europe were not convinced at the time about the beep test that was being used in Australia. He said, "From my experience, hardly anyone in Europe bothers with the beep test. You're either quick or you're not quick. I had lengthy discussions about some of the fitness methods used in Australia with Bayern Munich chief Otto Hitzfeld." Otto chuckled to Krncevic about the reliability and validity of both the beep test and the Cooper test (running around in circles in 12 minutes).[138] These tests are now standard around the world.

In his own words

On slowly transitioning into agency

I sort of dabbled in it a little bit when I was coaching with Marconi. I had a friend of mine, Mike Eisenhoff, who wanted to start an agency business, and he was good friends with the Mark Edgley Group. He was talent scouting and I was guiding them. One of the first players we signed was Danny Invincible who went to Kilmarnock in Scotland.

I remember speaking to Tony Popovic and Hayden Fox and them saying, "If you're involved, we'll sign it." That's how it started. I had had enough of the politics by the time I finished coaching and decided to get into player management. I actually got my licence in Sydney. I sat the exam. A lot of people failed.

On his first deals in the agent business

Andy Vlahos was one of my first ones. I moved him to Cercle Brugge, a club I played for, Danny Invincible was in Scotland and Steve Laybutt (RIP) in Belgium, it just started with those (players). The players back in Australia were quality players and Belgium was a good country for them because it's got the right mentality. They like Australians. But it's too hard working from Australia. You've actually got to live in Europe if you want to be successful.

On providing agent-consulting services to the New Zealand Knights

It was actually Lou Sticca who guided me through it because he did the same at Sydney FC. I went to the United Kingdom, watched some players and brought Michael Turnbull over. There were a few players that I recommended that came. I can't remember all of them now. They did alright but the squad wasn't totally strong.

On building club squads as a consulting agent based
on player types and characteristics

It's obviously based on the positions they need. I'd consult with the coach.

I think you need to know their characters outside of football. I think if they're a shitty character, don't do it. When I signed the pre-contract with Pisa in Italy while I was at Zagreb, the president wanted to meet me. I spent about a month with them. He said the reason why we do this with all our players before we sign them is to find out what sort of person they are. I don't care how good you are. I've spoken to so many agents who have asked me, "How can I deal with this player?" His mentor or father's involved, his wife is involved or the dog is barking the wrong way. Character is so important. You need to be a sports psychologist when you speak to someone to find out.

"What are your goals?" is what I ask the players straight away. "What are your ambitions?" If they say, "money," I don't want anything to do with it. I'll use Marco Bresciano as a reference. When Marco was at Carlton Soccer Club. I went and watched him play and brought him in. "What are your ambitions, Marco?" "I want to play for Juventus one day," (he replied). He went to Empoli, came back after a year and he brought a bottle of whiskey back for me. He was earning AUD40,000. I said, "That's not bad per month." He said, "No, no, that's a week, but I don't care about the money. I just want to make it." That's what you want to hear as an agent or as a coach.

On the AIS and youth player development

One of the biggest mistakes Australian football made is not having the AIS there. I took all my players from there. They had a program there which made it easy for a coach. Right now, you've got different programs and different clubs.

I haven't seen anything exciting come out in the last 10 years. Correct me if I'm wrong, but I haven't. They had it down-pat. The program was excellent. Why isn't the A-League youth system successful?

There's not that much here. Competition-wise. If you want to succeed, you go to Europe like so many Australians have.

On his agent trips to Europe

To stay in contact with the clubs, I met up with people, (and) connected with different agents as well. There were some good English agents. They were probably more correct, but it was difficult dealing with the Italians and the Germans. The French were okay too.

On whether being an ex-player
at the elite level helped him with agency and scouting

I think so. Without being conceited, I can tell you within five or ten minutes what level a player will be playing at. There's no doubt I do have that ability. You either have it or you don't have it.

Zach Lisolajski (invited to the Young Socceroos squad) of Western United and now Perth Glory is a prime example. I think other clubs were watching him, but no one made a move. Then as soon as they heard he was going to Newcastle Jets, his father got a call from other A-League clubs. That's not necessarily doing your scouting job properly. You would think A-League (that) clubs would be. They've got to get out to the smaller clubs. It's not just NPL. You've got to have a look. I saw Chris Taylor, Oakleigh, Victoria NPL coach at a game in Sydenham, Melbourne. He said, "Who's that kid (Zach), I want to sign him straight away."

He said he was one of the best talents he had seen since striker John Markovski. A big statement. But you've got to get out and see those lower-level clubs. There's always someone that stands out physically, technically and that reads the game well. That's how you do it. But it isn't very uncommon here unfortunately.

On playing younger players at senior level

If you remember the old NSL days, you had to play three players under the age of 21. Rudi Gutendorf (ex-Socceroos coach) brought that in. All the younger players got the experience. Maybe that is an option? We need a Second Division, definitely. I think that will focus more on player development.

We could do an under-23 Second Division. You can have five senior players, three on the team sheet, but the rest have to be under 23. Then you'll see development. They do it in Indonesia in both Second and Third Division. That's their rule. They've got some good footballers there.

On coaching compared to agency

The problem is politics. It's dealing with committees who think they know everything. It was horrendous. Johnny Warren said to me after I told him I wanted to get into coaching, "You better be strong, they don't want to let you in."

I'd come from Europe but they made it hard in everything I tried to do. At Carlton, I was the first person to go full-time, and we had a good football team. We played good football, ahead of our time in my view, yet we ran second.

Then the following year a lot of players were sold, like Bresciano. I was playing kids the second year, we were playing well, but had no experience. My contract ran out and I went to Marconi for two years, then South Melbourne. At Marconi, I knew I was going to possibly be terminated. I had a three-year contract and after two years, made the playoffs.

At South Melbourne later, I had a young team, they sold everyone and George Vasilopoulos was president at the time, he was great. He said, "I want you to go to the press and tell them we are building a new team." We got into the playoffs, the only player I signed was Con Boutsianis. We won 12 games straight and then I had a meeting with a few board members. I said, "Look, you want to build; you build from here."

On players who make a difference

I did follow one player a few years ago, Daniel Arzani. I followed him because he made the difference. I look for individuals, great players that can pop, dribble past others, players that are going to go places. And obviously it's difficult. But I used to go and watch Arzani and just keep my eyes and ears wide open.

He was unlucky he hurt his knee. If you're out for a year, it takes two to come back. If you're out for three months, it takes you six months. I thought he was good. Archie Thompson was another one too. I coached him, I played with him. You love players like that.

On the salary cap

I think it is clear where Australian football is at when you watch the Asian Champions League. The Japanese are 10 years ahead, 56 professional teams, their programs are solid. Obviously, they've had the right financial backing. I understand that. But there's still a salary cap in the A-League? It has to go.

Chapter 17:
Legacy Agent – Dragan Jevtic

The name Dragan Jevtic was an important one in the agent stratosphere. He successfully completed player contract deals in the A-League and Asia and had developed a track record of bringing good foreigners into Australia. I met Dragan at a football networking function and noticed he had a European agent outlook and demeanour. Tall, self-assured and coolly dressed in his turtleneck sweater and sometimes a lounge suit, he seemed to speak with authority on football markets. He was similar to some suave European agents I had met on my agent travels. He had a natural feel for the football industry, the agency game and the player market.

It was sheer synchronicity that I met with Jevtic for a coffee and subsequently started to provide regulatory advice services for his player portfolio. This included advising on matters concerning Andrija Kaluderovic and designing best-practice transfer release clauses to incorporate into his players' A-League or Asian contracts in case they received a major club offer from Asia.

Sadly, in March 2016, the 37-year-old Jevtic passed away suddenly. His death left his players reeling, his Australian agent peers stunned and football club directors in limbo due to the proliferation of his player representation activities.

Background

Jevtic's influence in the Australian football market was immense. He was a powerhouse agent who specialised in recruiting players who were looking for fresh challenges, while also facilitating the move of creative foreign players into the A-League.

At his A-League agency peak and as a sign of his influence in the market, "According to Football Australia's own reports on intermediaries, in 2015-16 Dragan Jevtic acted for six players from Sydney FC."[139] Those players included Filip Holosko,

Miloš Ninković, Mickael Tavares, Jacques Faty, Shane Smeltz and Miloš Dimitrijević. Jevtic brought Diego Castro to the A-League, and at one time all Perth Glory foreigners were either managed by Jevtic or managed under a joint venture agreement with other agents.

Jevtic used his "strong ties with European football (and his Serbian heritage) to help Australian clubs sign visa-players from top tier leagues while still in their prime and was widely regarded as one of the best agents in the A-League due to his record of bringing quality foreign players to the competition."[140] Indeed, he was somewhat plugged into the worldwide Serbian professional football diaspora (agent-coach-player network) where they all try to help each other.

It was not just at Sydney FC and Perth Glory where Jevtic did his best representation work. He also brought in other players like Youssouf Hersi and striker Stein Huysegems, as well as managing Australian players like Bruce Djite, Danny Vukovic and Mile Jedinak.

Jevtic is credited with reinventing Hersi's career, who stated that, "He was so genuine and positive that it really convinced me to give Australia a go, and I'm so glad I did. Dragan was far more than agent; he was a friend to his players and a totally honourable man who always made sure his players was looked after."[141]

Hersi, who is now an agent himself, observed that Jevtic "had a great eye for talent and he wasn't just liked by the players. The clubs he dealt with respected and trusted him."[142]

In essence, Jevtic was an agent who played a big part in developing, diversifying and strengthening the A-League.

From an informed perspective

I interviewed Terry McFlynn, former football operations manager and general football manager at Sydney FC (and now the new Auckland A-League franchise football director) who dealt with Jevtic during the peak of his agent activities in 2016. McFlynn was also a football intermediary and FIFA football agent with Mercer Consulting and understands the agent perspective.

On how A-League clubs assess foreign players put forward by the well-networked agents like Jevtic

We run the recruitment database. It's mainly for visa and foreign players. On every foreign player that comes in, we'll do a competency report on the player. That would be presented to the coaching staff and coaching team along with video footage. We probably look at 150 players before making any decision. Because the investment is at a marquee level, you need to be homing in on the one that you want. Then you have a backup and a second backup if the deal hits a snag or anything untoward happens.

On how Sydney FC began dealing with Jevtic

I think my first interaction with Dragan was actually while I was still playing, and Dragan had brought in a player named Nikola Petkovic. Nikola came to Sydney and he struggled a little bit settling into Australia and a different style of football to what he was used to. He played in Turkey and Serbia as well. Dragan actually spent quite a bit of time in Sydney helping Nikola settle into Australian life, (and) into the football club. Dragan then brought Miloš Dimitrijević, another Serbian player, into the football club. He was a fantastic footballer, and his father was a wonderful footballer as well, playing for Red Star Belgrade.

At the end of that season, I retired, moved into the backroom staff and was working with Graham Arnold, Rado Vidošić, Tony Pignata and Steve Corica on the recruitment side of things. We had quite a few of Dragan's players in the team, but it wasn't really until the start of the next season when I got more involved dealing with him. I was actually back in the UK doing my coaching badges. The CEO, Tony Pignata, called me and we did a lot of competency reports and a lot of footage on the type of players we were looking for. Dragan had presented two players. One was Miloš Ninković and the other one was Filip Holosko. Both fantastic footballers and they were exactly what we were looking for at the time; a number 10 who could play in between the lines, face forward and make things happen, and a winger who was quick, direct to get to the by-line, able to play crosses into the box and play in the final third. Dragan presented both players through the recruitment committee at that time, which was Tony Pignata, myself, Graham Arnold and Han Berger. We put the budget together to sign both players and they were fantastically well-received by all the rest of the players. The quality of training went up tenfold and we went on and won the 2016/17 Grand Final, won the Premiers Plate and the Cup Final. Dragan was very easy to deal with. Very relaxed, very laid back. He had a lot of confidence in the players that he presented and they were fantastic footballers.

On how Jevtic understood the A-League foreign player placement market

Dragan's player stable had good quality foreigners that were a better level than most of the local Australian players. He was basically bringing in good quality foreign players that would definitely make a difference, have an impact and raise the standard of the A-League.

He also brought in a guy called Ranko Despotović. That was in the January transfer window when we were struggling a little bit for firepower upfront. Ranko was playing in the Second Division in Spain, doing very well, and Dragan was able to bring him to Sydney FC and he did extremely well for us in the back half of the season. His goals got us into the finals that year. I think he really knew the landscape and the standard of the league. He knew the players that he could get his hands on were better than what we had here, even though they probably weren't all top-level European players at that time.

*On how Jevtic understood the budgets of Australian clubs,
including what possible marquee money was available*

I think he really understood the salary cap. He understood the landscape and he knew the politics of the clubs he was working with. I'm sure he had many players that he could have presented that were out of our budget, that would have blown the salary cap, but he didn't do that because he was realistic and realised it had to work for everyone. When he was dealing with both Holosko and Ninković, I actually thought it was a question of which one we wanted. Ninković is possibly the best player ever to play in the competition. But he actually joined Sydney FC in year one as a salary-cap player.

I think Dragan's ability to sell it to Miloš, (and) get Filip Holosko into the team as a marquee and Miloš inside the salary cap was amazing. Dimitrijević was still inside the salary cap, (and) Petkovic was as well.

We signed Mark Janko as the other marquee. We were actually building a team to be successful. I think Dragan had a longer-term plan that Filip would move on and Miloš could then become the marquee. He understood the club's plan. He understood his role in that plan in terms of managing his players and the expectations from the financial side.

On Jevtic spending time around an A-League football club

He spent a lot of time at the football club. Obviously, when we went to Melbourne, he was at all the games. He was allowed in the hotel, meeting up with the boys. About once a month he'd be in Sydney just to catch up with the boys, have dinner or coffee and just make sure everything was okay with them and their families. He really did look after the players, not just before finding them a club. There was an all-round thing with Dragan where he looked after the boys when they were in Sydney and their families.

On Jevtic being a day-to-day agent manager and a problem-solver

I remember part of my role as a general manager of player welfare was integrating the new players into the club during an induction period, and part of that was finding them accommodation. Apartments, houses, schools for the kids, whatever. And a lot of my dealings with Miloš Ninković and Filip Holosko's families was done through Dragan. Dragan was present for all those conversations and all the decisions that were made as a family.

On why Jevtic was adamant about negotiating transfer clauses

With his players that were inside the salary cap, he was very adamant on clauses, in terms of a percentage fee, for the players if they were to be sold to an overseas club. He tried his best to get a minimum sell-release clause. As a club, you try and maximise as best you can, (and) find a middle ground. With the marquee players, he was very clear that it was an open investment for the club and there was no minimum sell-on clause. There was no percentage back to the player. The player was being remunerated for a service rendered as a footballer and if there was a fee to be involved, that would be in line with his ability in an open market.

I think what Dragan understood and demonstrated to us was that a salary-cap system is not an open market. If we're bringing a player from an open market and his ability outweighs the stage on which he's playing, how can we remunerate the player accordingly? If a club from China came in for Ninković, or Japan or South Korea, Saudi Arabia, the United Arab Emirates, there was a percentage that would have gone to Miloš and his family. He'd have received part of the transfer fee. Subsequently, when he became the marquee, all those clauses were removed. He told us that Miloš would be the best player in the competition, but he never once asked for any bonuses. If he was a Johnny Warren Medallist, he said we should upgrade his contract to be a marquee to keep him. History will tell you that's exactly what happened.

On the reaction in the Sydney FC community to Jevtic's untimely passing

I remember it clearly when the tragedy struck, I was actually in South Korea. We were at a Champions League game on the Tuesday night. My role in the Champions

League was to fly in early and make sure the training ground, the hotel, the buses, (and) everything on the ground was in order before the team came in. I remember clearly, we were playing a domestic game against Western Sydney Wanderers. We actually won the game 2–1. Shane Smeltz scored in the last couple of minutes, a half-volley into the top corner.

Then Tony Pignata called me while I was sitting in my hotel room in South Korea to let me know the news. Smeltz was a client of Dragan's as well. We had Dimitrijević, Ninković, Smeltz, and Ognenovski all in the squad. Dragan was their agent. I rang all the boys to see how they were. They were all in shock but the main concern for all the boys was Dragan's wife and his sons. How they were going to be. We reached out to them as a club. It was a terrible thing that happened. It was a real sense of loss for a long, long period of time. But the thing that struck me the most was how the players just wanted to make sure that Dragan's wife and his sons were looked after and that any payments or agent's fees that were still applicable would be paid to them, because they'd lost a father, husband and breadwinner.

On defining Jevtic's impact on the Australian football at the time

He was a very fair and reasonable man. He found a common ground for both his client and a football club to make the situation work. I think the reaction of his players after his passing really resonates with me, as there was a genuine care and a love for him. In football, that isn't always evident. It demonstrated to me that the players had a close relationship with not only Dragan as an agent, but as a man. I think they felt part of his family. When we did a new contract with Miloš, he made sure that part of the payment was still forwarded to Dragan's wife, even though it was a new contract. He didn't even have an agent. The contract was done basically between the club and Miloš himself. But he wanted part of the contract paid to Mariana and Dragan's kids. I think he really appreciated the fact that Dragan had brought him to Australia and provided the opportunity for himself, his wife, (and) his kids, and while he was still playing, he wanted to share some of that financial benefit with Dragan's family. I think that was something quite rare and it touched me a little bit that Miloš had that much respect and love for Dragan.

On Jevtic's agent style

He was very assertive, very assured. He had a lot of confidence in his players. Very, very confident that what he was bringing into the football club would enhance what we already had and improve the environment. He was very good at convincing you that you were doing the right thing.

He had a good understanding of the level here, and had connections around Europe, Eastern Europe in particular. I think he understood not only the individual players, but he also understood the market and the level of the individuals and where he could place them.

Chapter 18:
Reflections of the Hustle – David Valensisi and Peter Paleologos

David Valensisi

From Newcastle to the Illawarra, Geelong to North Queensland, regional Australia has provided significant playing talent to Australian football and the A-Leagues. There is also an Australian agent who emerged from the regions and developed a notable profile. David Valensisi is from country New South Wales. Without the credentials of a professional playing career or significant metropolitan football networks, Valensisi has become an agent who combines country, salt-of-the-earth values with a partiality for opening pathways for emerging talent.

He had a rare insight into agency, having worked for two months in the then Soccer Australia player transfer office under the omnipresent Anne Nicholls who managed the FIFA agent exams and dealt with clubs and agents on player registration and transfer matters. Enchantingly, Nicholls wanted Valensisi to take her job at the then Soccer Australia when she retired.

Background

Valensisi has seen it so many times before. Australian parents or guardians being proactive in trying to organise professional or academy trials for their children in Europe. Sometimes, parents of talented youngsters get lucky through contacts and organise one or two trials. However, if no offer is made, the player is then stuck in Europe in limbo. This is why Valensisi believes that even younger players need an agent to find opportunities. That is what Valensisi does and it is exemplified with the talented Steven Lustica, who was 18 and wanted to try his luck in Europe. Valensisi organised trials for Lustica with Monza (Italy), then in Germany and in England (Norwich City).

Valensisi said, "Steven is one of the best young players in Australia and the fact that Inter Milan wanted him only serves to increase his prestige. He was supposed to begin a period of training with Inter but broke his leg and everything fell through. Now we will go to Monza in Italy, hoping that this will be a springboard for him."[143]

The work that goes into setting up trials for Australian players includes months of planning and building the trust of European scouts, clubs or agents within your network. For Valensisi to get a player to the attention of a club like Inter Milan is a testimony to his hard work and pathway-building abilities.

His understanding of regional and country Australia and its unseen talent that can be overlooked by professional clubs and scouts provides him with an informed perspective on what it takes to create pathways and talent-identification networks in those regions. Interestingly, the Nike "The Chance" trials in Australia in 2010/2011 amplified why regional Australia is getting better at developing their local talent. "North Queensland in particular caught the eye of coach Ron Smith (ex-AIS), who was searching the country for talented youngsters who will be given trials in the United Kingdom thanks to the sportswear giant."[144] Smith's observations confirmed that the talent in football is spread across all parts of Australia, therefore football needs agents and scouts like Valensisi on the ground to unlock opportunities. Especially if you consider the talent that has come out of regional and rural Australia such as Adam Federici (Nowra), Rhyan Grant (Canowindra), Mitchell Langerak (Emerald) and Josh Risdon (Bunbury), who all played for the Australian national team.

In his own words

On how Valensisi become a player agent

My journey is probably a little bit different to the majority of people that are agents. I was born in country New South Wales. Having an Italian background meant I always had a passion for football, getting up early (in the) morning, watching games and playing and participating. I played at a decent level and represented NSW country.

The turning point for me was probably back in the '80s when there weren't too many players going overseas from Australia. There were a few but not many. One of my mates, at about age 15 or 16, won a "Big Brother scholarship" that entitled him to go to Ipswich Town to trial. I think that's when they won the English Championship. They wanted him to stay, but being Italian background and missing home, and thinking another opportunity would come along, he didn't. He probably to this day regrets that decision.

He went on to have a career. He played for Northern Spirit and Newcastle Breakers, then he played with Sydney FC when they won the inaugural A-League with Dwight Yorke and Pierre Littbarski. But his career probably never took off to the heights that it should have. I always wanted to make sure that players, and especially players from the country areas, got opportunities and good advice. Such a small percentage of people actually make it and follow their dreams and make it into the European leagues or national team setups, and country kids are less likely to be identified. I was always about helping players wanting to do their best and I want them to go on to play for Australia. The best thing to do is give the right advice to other young aspiring athletes and try to mentor them and make sure they make the right decisions in their life and career.

On identifying talent from Australia's regional areas

I am based both in the city and in the country and have nine or ten players in the A-League. I still follow the boys in the country and keep an eye out for talented young players. There's one guy now at Sydney FC, a 17-year-old from the country. A few clubs wanted him and he just went away with the under-17 Joey's team.

It is up to him and his talent to get into those national teams, but it also helps having someone in the corner. Let's face it, not many people are going to go and watch games in the country. Back in the day, there was NSW Country, they played against NSW City. Now you've got to be part of the academy setups and it's hard for some of them to get a look in.

On the change to youth pathways by bringing in A-League academies

Academies are always going to promote from within because parents are paying $2,000 to $3,000 for registration fees.

We're lucky in New South Wales because Sydney FC play in NPL 1 and they're quite competitive. Now Melbourne City and Western United have been promoted to NPL 2. Most NSW sides are in NPL 1. They're playing at that higher level and you can't beat that at 16, 17 or 18.

On where the hotbeds of talent in rural and regional Australia are

There's no one country town that you can say has brought the most talent because it's more individuals who have made it to the next level than a whole group from one region or town. So, it's probably hard to say.

I'm from Griffith and we've always produced good young players. In the last four or five years, we've played in (the) NPL (in) Canberra and in the junior ranks up to the 16s and 17s. They've done quite well and actually won the under-18's NPL in Canberra. However, no one was selected to play for the Canberra National Youth League team. It's quite funny, you can win an NPL tournament or be the best team in the league, but no one is selected for the next level. That shows you that no one's really watching the talent. Then you see Alou Kuol, who played in Goulburn Valley in Shepparton. He went on trial at Melbourne Victory and Melbourne City and was overlooked and look at him now. Kuol was on the bench for VfB Stuttgart the other night. There's not a real hotbed, but definitely talented players in your Alburys, your Sheppartons, but I don't think enough people are paying attention. The scene is different to Sydney or Melbourne, that's for sure.

But that's the role of a scout and my enjoyment as an agent is finding rare, unearthed talents and looking at someone and thinking, "I believe in that kid. Let's see how far we can take him or her." That's what I think most clubs should be looking at a lot more — developing the talent and promoting. Ultimately, it makes them a transfer fee, it makes money for their clubs.

It's not just about the parents that have the most money or the ones that make the most noise at the ground. I love to see my clients going well because no one had heard of half of them, they didn't give them a chance. I now look at them playing for Australia national team under-23s, 20s and 17s, and think that is a big tick for my scouting ability as an agent.

On the most rewarding aspects of the agent business

I'm really proud of all my players. They all have different journeys, different stories, like everyone in life. Some of them are probably on different pathways, like Connor O'Toole, who was in Japan at the same school Jason Davidson went to. He was recommended to me by someone.

I sent him to Brisbane Roar because I knew they had no left-back when Shane Stefanutto came to the end of his career. From there he went on trial, got a contract there and won young player of the year. He made his debut and played for Australia under-20s and under-23s but didn't make it to the Olympics unfortunately. They've all got their own stories and journeys, like Lachie Wales, Jerry Skotadis, (and) Jez Lofthouse from (the) NPL, now playing at Brisbane Roar. Rhys Bozinovski of Western United came through the ranks, made it to Australia under-20s and won the grand final in his first season. Matthew Sutton at Melbourne Victory and then Melbourne City. He hasn't played A-League yet but is a young, up-and-coming goalkeeper and it's exciting to see. I like the younger guys because it's like a family environment. I'm there from the start of their journey. Let's take you from the journey all the way from your grassroots, all the way up, and we'll be on this journey forever. It's not work, it feels more like a friendship.

And it's a lot of trust and a lot of companionship with the parents as well. Trust in me. Trust that I'm looking after their child. Because at the end of day, they are 16, 17 and 18-year-old boys and they need someone to guide them.

On the consequences of the lack of a National Youth League has had on Australian player development

It's disappointing because you don't get to see the players playing against the other best youth sides around Australia, not that they played many games anyway. They only played around eight games or something like that. It hasn't probably affected me so much because I'm a football tragic, I'll watch everything. Now that NPL TV is online, it's brilliant. I don't have to watch it all live, I can watch it a couple of days later, but the scouting process hasn't changed that much because I'm always watching, whether it be live or on delay.

On what type of players Valensisi seeks to represent

I go for the more technical kind of player. In today's game, you need a bit of pace and power, but I like the intelligent players because that's harder to learn. When you hit 16 or 17, if you don't have those basics down pat, you're pretty much in trouble if you're hoping to make it as a professional because Australia is one of the only places where 18-year-olds aren't playing regular first-team football. Here we sometimes keep young scholarship players down or else we have to pay them more if they are starting each week. That is wrong and the clubs should be promoting the youngsters because let's face it, you've got to be at that 20 to 21 mark and doing well to be noticed abroad.

I like players that have a bit of character as well. Don't be afraid to express yourself. We're trying to create too many roadblocks with this current development curriculum. Everything is very structured, which is great, don't get me wrong, but you need to express yourself as a player and have a bit of flair. Those moments are the things that catch scouts' eyes, catch coach's eyes. They're the things that change games, (and) get spectators on their feet. It's all about spectators at the end of the day. If you've got that 'wow factor', then people notice. Lachie Wales is a great example. Some people said he was never going to make it, he wasn't even offered a contract at one stage.

Then I had three or four clubs chasing him and he scored against Argentina in the Olympics. He's looking hungry, he's looking fit and is on the fringe of the Socceroos. He was in the final 50-man squad for the last World Cup. He is someone that probably does not have the best technical ability, but he works hard and he has that right character. He has pace and that bit of flair and is prepared to take risks and beat players. That's really why he is where he is today. I don't just pigeonhole and say one aspect or two aspects are important. You've got to see the whole picture — I think that's what we don't do as an Australian football culture. We kind of make everyone robotic in their movements and actions.

On being based in London when doing his agent apprenticeship

I was living in London and I was working for an agent based in Australia. I wasn't an agent, I wasn't registered. So, I wanted to make sure that I was practising the right rules and regulations. So, if anything did happen, I was covered.

I remember going to big exclusive hotels in London. I was with the CEO of Sunderland at the time and we were trying to bring Sunderland to Australia because back then tours weren't really happening. I think Lou Sticca had done many, including Glasgow Celtic. I was trying with Sunderland and that was good because I got to meet the CEOs of major EPL clubs and learnt how to conduct business with them.

I spent a lot of time in Belgium because it was a market that I was really interested in and not many Aussie players had played there apart from Paul Okon back in the day. I've always watched a lot of youth football in Belgium because I liked Anderlecht and the way they brought through a lot of younger players.

The same with Ajax Amsterdam, I think their academies are brilliant and we've got a lot to learn in Australia, the way they're set up and the way they coach them from under-12s and 13 onwards. I spent a bit of time at SC Heerenveen as well. It's just impressive how structured and well-drilled these young guys are. They're very well-educated.

The coaches give them a good education, a good pathway into life and I think we can learn a lot from that in Australia. I did my apprenticeship backwards actually. I got all the contacts first, saw a lot of football; (I) was not actively involved so much on the agent side, but more from the scouting and coaching side. I then worked on the best way (a reengineering essentially) to integrate my skill set and my players into those systems and clubs.

On the most difficult or challenging aspects of the agent business

Probably the most challenging part is when you try to sign the younger players. Some coaches in Australia give them the advice, "You don't need your agent." Coaches have agents themselves, so it's a bit hypocritical in a way because they're obviously trying to decrease the chances of the player leaving.

My advice to young 15 and 16-year-old guys, or to their parents, when people say they don't need agents, is to ignore them and see the (coach's) motivation. It's not all coaches, it's just some.

We're trying to provide other opportunities. If Club A doesn't want you, I'll find you club B, C or D that maybe can give you those opportunities because I think you're good enough. That's why I'm signing you as a client.

The most challenging part is when an ex-professional gives advice (that) you don't need an agent or as a player you approach 20 agents and promote yourself around. That's even worse, because if I'm talking to a club and another person is talking to the same club, it is all too difficult. All you're doing is ruining your own chances of actually getting somewhere. Plus, who's going to work for you if you're not exclusive with that agent? Why would I?

Players only hurt themselves when they have multiple people (agents) working for them. They might not make a decision based on the best for your career or the best for your pay packet.

That's probably the most challenging and frustrating part because I've got the best interest of the player at heart and I'll do whatever I can to make him succeed. But when you've got clubs doing things only for their own interest, they forget that the young kid just wanted an opportunity.

On Valensisi's day to day as an agent and his planning
for the upcoming transfer windows

I'm all about being on top of it (agency) the whole year, being organised with where your players are at. I set many targets for the players and I'll monitor where they're tracking in terms of their progression during the season. Especially if it's contract renewal time or they're going to be off-contract at the end of the year. You want to make sure that they get as many minutes as possible, but also be effective in the games that they play.

Setting realistic expectations of the player is important, because at the end of the day, everyone wants to play for Inter Milan or Barcelona or Australia or whatever. But you've got to set little tasks along the way, and you've got to work hard. I have to work hard as an agent to make sure I keep them realistic. But I've also got to make sure that they're working hard on the park and getting those opportunities as well. Once they have those chances, they've got to take them. Gearing up for a transfer window is making sure that I have all my ducks in a row and knowing what their market value is.

On promoting young Australian players to clubs

I think it's a bit of a tough one because coaches obviously want to do well and clubs need to be successful so they can be more marketable and get more fans at the game. I think there's a lot of young attacking players in Australia that could break into the A-League, yet most of the foreigners are attacking midfielders, wingers and strikers. For young attacking players it's always going to be harder. How can you get to Europe if they're not getting any opportunities in Australia? Most teams in Europe don't really rate Australian football unfortunately.

A lot of them come in and they don't adapt. Sometimes the setups, the facilities of the clubs aren't good enough, so they don't have nutritionists or don't have proper team facilities, but programs are getting better. Some of the clubs are really advanced.

Parents coaching at grassroots level in Australia is also a bit of a challenge. Maybe he or she has watched a lot of football, which is great and is doing a good thing by helping kids play on weekends. But how can you get little Johnny or his mates to the next level and actually teach them something about the game? So (that) when they hit 14 and go to an academy level, they're ready?

I think Football Australia have to look at providing better opportunities for these young people and also coaches. Get them educated so they can promote young players and educate them while they're training them. That's probably the biggest challenge. If you want to send someone to the English Championship but he's not playing in the A-League, why would they even listen? It's just the way it is here. They're going to look at you, (they will) laugh and say, "What are we, a charity?" You've got to be playing to get those opportunities. When the boys get an opportunity,

I really stress to them that you have to take it, you've got to cement that spot. That's yours. You have to make it your own. You have to have that spark about you to get fans excited and then to get the coaches excited about you being on the park and on the ball.

On his agency portfolio

I don't want to have a hundred clients. My approach is quite structured. I work with players that I believe I can assist in getting to where they want to be by the end of their career, whether that be the national team, overseas or whatever their goals are. I want to be able to help them. I want players that I know I can help. It's good for me as an agent to have internationals on the books, but at the same time, I've got to be able to make sure that I can meet their expectations and manage what they need.

It's all about timing, how much time I can devote to them and making sure that I can help them. I'm not going to take on a player just for the sake of it. That's not right. It doesn't help them. I want a good group of young players that are at different levels, under-17s, under-20s, under- 23s and national team level. I don't want to have the whole Australian Joeys team because I'm only going to be pushing them against each other. I've got to make sure that I service their needs properly and that's why I've structured my business in that way, to make sure that I've got the right amount of players that I can assist.

That's why I take them from a young age, because we build up that relationship, trust and friendship from day one, it's not just about making money. They're not a walking dollar sign.

On bringing foreign players to Australia

I get a lot of offers from agents that I work with in other countries and players randomly send their CVs, but I like to do my due diligence on them. Why haven't they been playing for a year? Why have they gone from top division (in) Spain down to Uzbekistan? Why? What's happened? What's changed this year? Has something happened in their personal life? Has something happened in regard to injury?

I'm always a bit wary of promoting players just because their CV looked good three or four years ago. What's happened in the last three or four years that has all of a sudden made Australia their number one destination?

I always like to promote my players from Australia rather than bring in from overseas. That's my way, I'm not too worried about the foreigners that come to Australia, unless it's a big marquee. That's not my main focus.

On any final learnings from the agency business

I think you always learn and every deal is different. Every player's situation is different. As you get older, you mature. I suppose you learn more about yourself, you learn more about the industry, (and) you learn more about the clubs you deal with on a day-to-day basis. I think it's just always being truthful and honest about yourself and your clients' expectations and just having that trust in the working relationships with the club and the player. You can't go wrong from there. There's no bad deal, sometimes you get annoyed and frustrated at the way it's panned out, but again, you learn from it. You've got to take the positives in every deal. If you hold grudges, there's no point. You just won't go anywhere. That's not going to help you, your agency business or your clients.

Peter Paleologos

"Cafés, a fondness for coffee, sitting around hotel lobbies, random (off the cuff) international travel, a well-worked pen and a notepad full of scribbled notes." I used this account of the idiosyncrasies of the agent business recently when speaking to some younger novice agents whom I was assisting with their preparation for an upcoming FIFA agents' exam.

My journey into player agency began to take shape as referee in Melbourne while officiating Super League matches (under-13 to under-16). Some of the best players in Victoria and Australia came out of these junior Victorian leagues during the late 1990s and 2000s. As a referee, I saw from close range the determination and abilities of talented players who were aspiring to have a successful football career. This intrigued me. After completing my law degree, I became involved in the organising committee of the Australian and New Zealand Sports Law Association (ANZSLA) conference in Melbourne, where I managed to secure Les Murray as the main speaker. The conference focused on sports law, sport business and management themes and it was during a coffee with Les Murray and a close friend at the then famous Café Greco in Chapel Street, South Yarra, that my interest in football consultancy and player agency was born.

After sitting and passing the difficult FIFA exam at a university hall in Sydney, I became the only agent that was a former referee and Australian lawyer. It provided me with a point of difference in terms of not just my dealings with players but also with other agents. Outside the PFA, I was the only Australian football lawyer initially, and was able to use this niche offering to provide advisory and consulting services to many other agents who needed player transfer regulatory advice.

I was keen to see Australian football improve and reimagined to reach its potential. I made submissions to the Crawford Report and developed the Australasian Premier League model.[145] The Australasian Premier League was an alternative model to the PFA's Australian Premier League and encompassed franchise teams from Australia and South-East Asia.

Being a lawyer allowed me to also dive into the unique employment contracts laws and transfer regulations in football, which were emerging as distinctive and fascinating areas of law. I was one of the first in Australian and Asian football (and even Europe) to refer to and use the term(s) 'football law' and 'football lawyers' back in the early 2010s, having registered the business name 'The Football Lawyers' in September 2013. Since then, it has been increasingly referenced and is now commonly used in the football agent and sports law industry worldwide, but especially in Europe.

The agency business is about making and building contacts and establishing relationships with clubs and scouts around the world to assist players. Therefore, to kick-start my agent career and network, I attended the inaugural Soccer Expo conference in Cannes, France to meet people and build my knowledge. As Australian Media personality, George Donikian once said that 'they say travelling is education' and I would add to that travelling for an agent (just like meetings in cafes) is fundamental to the agent's business as optics and presence matter.

Reflections on an Australian football agency journey

Player agency does not need to be a capital-intensive business. I must have met over 90 talented players at Café Brunetti in Lygon Street in Melbourne for a conversation over coffee, discussing their career aspirations. For me it's about having a good rapport when dealing with people, finding your agent voice and confidence, and building a track record of player deals. Being in Australia, and far away from the power agency centres in Europe and South America, no Australian agents had any hyped-up men or women behind us when we started out in agency. For most Australian agents, it was all about hard work and hustle and trying to help as many good players as you can.

In terms of player deals, I advised players like Nathanial Atkinson, Lawrence Thomas, Francesco Stella, Brandon Wilson and Tomislav Uskok in their first or early career deals. In essence, opening doors is what agents do. With my well-connected Belgian agent/lawyer associate, we got Mathew Ryan's CV to the Club Brugge sporting director's desk. We heard nothing initially, as the sporting director at the time had left the club. Then in December 2012, former Icelandic player Arnar Grétarsson was appointed the new sporting director. He found Ryan's CV on his desk and contacted Central Coast Mariners directly to undertake a transfer. We missed out on the deal due to a club-to-club agreement, but at least we provided a suitable career launch pad to a talented Australian player.

I was always about having a mix of work as an agent and helping other agents' players when requested. Costa Rican player Carlos Hernandez, ex-Melbourne Victory, is an example. I attended his house (at a time where we could knock on the door without invites) to get his video highlights on a VHS tape to send to a Japanese counterpart (there was no Wyscout, YouTube or InStat back then and he was not my player).

In terms of women's football, I manage Mel Andreatta, the assistant Australian national team coach's contract negotiations with Football Australia. In my conversations with Mel, I always recognise that she has an informed understanding of the Australian women's player development cycle. Mel is keen to see more investment in the A-League Women's and see football stakeholders supporting the key development ingredients that lead to long-term and sustained success for talented players. Like nearly all Australian agents, I did not charge professional women players for their first A-League Women's contracts, as we were well aware of the struggle that many women players were facing.

On a professional level, I have dealt with a plethora of younger Australian male players from the National Youth League (NYL), National Premier Leagues (NPL), and A-League scholarships holders and those who spent time with overseas academies, particularly in Spain, England and Italy. I have seen first-hand how hard it is for young Australian players to make it professionally.

I have an Excel spreadsheet that documents over 800 enthusiastic and talented Australian male players from the NYL and NPL, overseas academies and young tyros (who I have met or dealt with at some level) who never made it fully professionally.

For me, the agency business is about understanding the client and how to react to different types of players from a 19-year-old to a seasoned professional. I am big on preparation, as I try to map out the transfer windows and be prepared to discuss interest in my players on the spot, as there is no linear negotiation in football.

In my view, a good agent can facilitate and open opportunities. The agent's role is to put the player in front of the right coaches, to open trial opportunities with teams overseas and to promote the player. As a representative, "You're there to put the player in front of the right people and advise on the right contract."[146]

A recent trend I have noticed is that players can leave agents easily. Locker-room talk can result in players talking about their agents with other players. It's a small community. Sometimes the player does not fit in a league or club's style or there are agents who want to cut into the deal. I have often been faced with what we call 'grass cutting' and interference by other agents close to the club. It can result in many good agents being left in the dust on player deals.

The emphasis is on maintaining relationships. An agent colleague once said to me in regard to two giant Bulgarian clubs, "CSKA Sofia and Levski Sofia are both alike in dignity" and to never be critical of either club in their derby comparison because you need them both as clients. As an agent it's important to keep neutral and not be polarising to clubs. You cannot always afford to get into a battle of ideas or opinion where it is my philosophy against your philosophy or my arguments against yours. You need to keep good people on side.

It's the regulatory issue again!

When it is time to negotiate a deal, I am well aware of the dual reckoning that is the player contract offer versus the regulatory requirements that need to be met, otherwise a deal can be compromised.

To enhance this process, I developed a depository of templates and player-contract clauses to use, as well a checklist process for all paperwork. Each transfer clause, release clause or sell-on clause that I draft has to be quite tailored and as an agent you need to consider extra add-ons and bonuses.

Dealing with regulatory issues that affect Australian players under the age of 18 transferring overseas is a major issue that I have consistently come across; as not all parents and players understand the regulatory hurdles involved in young players moving abroad.

In a recent interview, I made that point. "Not having the regulatory paperwork in place may result in not being able to take up any offer of a European club scholarship. If a youth player moves overseas, parents need to understand the rules of the national association, FIFA and the leagues."[147]

In addition, FIFA's requirement that training compensation is payable by the engaging club to the player's former club/s is a major issue which blindsides parents and players when they get their first professional offer. "If a young player signs their first professional contract, their new overseas club has to pay training compensation to the previous Australian clubs, including their junior clubs. Many European clubs will not pay training compensation for younger players who are untested at the top level. Also, if a player is a minor — parents must move to the country and do so for non-football-related reasons. Or if the Australian player has an EU or UK passport, the club has to agree and prove that it is providing footballing, academic or vocational training and support to the player and looking after the youngster in the best possible way."[148] The FIFA regulations that apply to training compensation and youth signings can undermine some younger player transfers if not carefully considered and mitigated.

I have acted for many players' behalf in getting a training compensation waiver from a former club or several junior clubs. For one Australian player, namely Curran Ferns, I assisted in getting him an opportunity in Malaysia. I managed to get seven training compensation waivers from his junior, NPL and A-League (youth) clubs, which may be a world record! The Malaysian club was not going to pay any training compensation and at 21, it was perhaps Ferns' last opportunity to become a professional player.

A (somewhat) Mini MBA in Football Agency - Problem-solving, making deals and negotiation strategy

As an agent, I always try to be a problem-solver and achieve a balanced outcome for clients and clubs, as you need to retain these relationships. Your duty is first to your client (player or coach) but I always remember that I may need to deal with the club again, therefore I must manage that delicate relationship. I have been in or assisted other agents in situations where clubs owe players money because I have a legal background. "If a club doesn't pay a player, how do you deal with that situation? If a player is being bullied and ostracised in a team, how do you deal with that situation? There's always the players' union, which does provide advice to players. But then there's also agents, who aren't lawyers or who don't have a legal background, that need advice for players, because for instance, the player wants to get out of a contract, or isn't getting paid. Also, when players go overseas, each country is very different with its own football regulations, employment laws and visa requirements. So there are a lot of challenges there."[149]

In terms of negotiation with clubs, I try to make the first offer as a form of anchoring the parameters of the playing deal. I tend not to have the client in the room when starting negotiations. From there, it is relentless pushing and shoving around my clients' demands for wages, sign-on fees, bonuses and any transfer fee clause that helps them (the club) with their balance sheet long term, due to the potential on-sell of my player. Some of the must-have terms, that I ensure are negotiated into my players' club contracts are in the following list.

- Duration
- Sign-on fee.
- Gross or net basic wage or salary. If net, who pays the tax (e.g., the club?).
- Salary increases during the second or third year of the contract.
- Appearance bonuses, incentive bonuses and first-team clauses.
- Accommodation.
- Relocation and travel expenses.
- Medical insurance and securing any future visa/work permits.
- Image rights/endorsements. Do we require a supplementary contract?
- Allowable player social media use.
- Transfer release clause or buy-out clause.
- Agent fee, including an acceleration clause (i.e., if the club does not pay the first full instalment, the full fee falls due). Further, addressing the issue of 'benefit in kind' that arises from agent's fees (i.e., who pays the tax?)

Besides the traditional player transfer agreement and player contract, I have also negotiated (helped agent associates to negotiate) unique contractual terms or various player or transfer arrangements with clubs which are shown in the following list.

- Player boot deals.
- Transfer agreements including sell-on percentage clauses (to overcome training compensation disputes).
- Player loan agreements with an option to buy.
- Contract renewal clauses based on player performance and number of matches played.
- Release clauses for A-League or overseas club trials.
- Academy and scholarship contracts.
- A payment schedule structured to consist of a much lower guaranteed pay with a pay increase based on performance incentives.
- Release clauses based on playing Asian Champions League or club relegation.
- Avoiding club-favoured unilateral extension options and penalty clauses.
- Player transfer requests.

Image rights — the new state of play

For agents who deal with top players, it is not just about a player's boot deal any longer, but also the commercial deals and image rights' deals that are now available in the football industry.

For professional players heading to the bigger leagues, image rights must be considered. As a player agent and football lawyer, I have advised on some image rights deals which require a three-phase process. In phase one, the player signs an employment contract with a club and they become commercial partners. In phase two, I advise the player to assign his or her image rights to their image rights company (if they have one), and then in phase three, the image rights company enters into a contract with the club and the commercial partners. Negotiations on image rights issues and remuneration and performance clauses depend on the club context and capacity, as well as the local tax office rules. From anecdotal experience, I am aware that many agents like clubs to take on or buy the image rights from players, as they subsequently do less work. However, I believe it is essential that this area is negotiated for the top players.

The agent's agent!

I have been fortunate to gain the trust and respect of many Australian and international agent peers. In my career as an agent I have met, engaged and shared ideas with over 200 agents from over 50 countries. This has enabled me to comprehend the varying cultural/business practices that arise in different leagues. I have experienced a multitude of different agency styles and anecdotal approaches, whether it was dealing with a passionate and deal-driven Spanish agent, the motivated and quick-to-respond Englishman, the powerful and well-connected Italian club agent, the insightful and bravado style of an Argentinian agent, the structured methodical approach of the Japanese agent, the cultivated but direct Dutch agent, the systematic and clarification style used by a Swedish or Slovakian agent, the careful and pleasant New Zealander or dynamic and go-getting American agent. I have appreciated what each one (stylistically) brings to the table.

Further, I have mentored several young agents in Australia and internationally and provided feedback on what factors they need to consider other than just getting a deal over the line. It is good to see some doing very well. This has given me an opportunity to develop cutting-edge agent industry best practice. I have developed precedents on what type of agent contracts are enforceable in different leagues/ countries and have designed a suite of mandates to ensure collaborations with other agents and players are effective. In a way, I have become something of an agent's agent, a consultant and sounding board for agents to overcome their contractual challenges affecting a deal.

15 learnings on my player agent journey

1. Other agents you partner with will work on their players first and will only focus on your players if they have time and are compelling.

2. Not many overseas clubs and agents know the Australian NPL or NYL (now A-League Academy players), as many do not have a Transfermarkt or Wyscout profile.

3. Playing games week-in, week-out is a significant factor in getting interest for a player. Further, players cannot always rely on past merit and must deliver immediately for the new club.

4. There should ideally be two (or a maximum of three) agents involved in an international player deal. Too many agents make it complicated and will end up being a deal-breaker.

5. Players are always being contacted by random agents trying to sound them out or pry them off you.

6. Increasingly, there is a trend that coaches and clubs are going with their preferred agents. Be aware of who is the person from the club who says 'Yes' to signing a player.

7. Don't sign players on an agency contract who you believe will struggle to get a playing deal or opportunity for in the future.

8. If an international agent sends you a long list of available players, be wary that this list may be shopped around by different agents.

9. Overseas agents can unrealistically assume that you can get their players' deals in the A-League. Address their expectations on the salary cap and playing style and show them examples of successful A-League foreign players.

10. Players are a great resource to introduce you to other agents, players, coaches and club directors. Use them.

11. You can easily lose face with clubs or agents if you do not fully control, deliver and gain agreement from the player to get the deal done. Keep comprehensive and up-to-date notes of conversations and WhatsApp messages.

12. Always do your due diligence to control the negotiation for the player. Players may have another agent. Get the mandate or representation agreement settled. No excuses.

13. Always know the dynamics and full picture concerning your competing agents. Get prospective players to tell you which other local agents they are talking to about representation.

14. Link up with a powerful, well-networked and respected European agent if you can. Someone who is one phone call away from a trial, deal or opportunity for your talented player.

15. Make sure you are aware of a players' contract status at all times.

Reflecting on my football lawyer and agents' perspective, it is the mix, excitement and complexity of agency work that motivates and inspires me to keep hustling. From scouting for new talents, finding opportunities for players, analysing the various league and club trends, negotiating career-enhancing contracts, and assessing the value of players and high-stake deals, there is always a stimulating project to chase and bring to (hopefully) a successful conclusion. The beauty of the agent's profession is that it is vast, multidisciplinary and transversal. You must always know the feasibility of a player transfer operation and in particular, the parties involved.

Recently, I am maybe one of the first agents in the world to become a special comments co-commentator on an ad hoc basis (in the NPL 1 Victoria). I have tried to amplify the message that there are many talented NPL players (caveat — I don't manage NPL players) who deserve an A-League shot at a contract.

Chapter 19:
The Agent's Roundtable

"Player pathways are difficult, as is forecasting player careers."
— Jonathan Fadugba, football consultant, writer, scout

Australian agents have an essential and integral role to play in player development, talent identification and the scouting of players. The landscape of Australian football player pathways and the creation of career opportunities overseas has been hugely influenced by agents as Australia simply does not have enough professional clubs. In an age where attention is the new currency, agents can only promote and assist players if they are at the required professional level to pique the interests of clubs. All Australian agents have encountered the up-and-down cycles of player development and are at the cutting edge of keeping international clubs interested in local players.

Agents are always talking about player development. We focus on who is coming through, which club or academy program is developing players and the international trends affecting our Australian players.

I have used a three-part structure in this chapter to explore the Australian player development landscape. Firstly, I look back on the Australian player development scene, the previous Australian Institute of Sport (AIS) development model (which was raised by so many agents I interviewed for this book) and the external view of Australian players during the Golden Generation.

Secondly, I move to the decade just past and look at current player development trends and pathway challenges that Australian players faced, as well as recent Australian football agent reflections.

Thirdly, I provide the results from a 2022 research survey completed by various Australian agents and intermediaries to promote the discussion of where Australian playing talent is now positioned regarding pathways and club requests.

PART A

What we had in Australian football!

As part of my research, I came across an infographic (which I replicate) from an Australian football magazine which featured the Australian male players playing overseas in 2001.[150]

Australian Playing Overseas
(2000-2001-2002)

Austria	England *(continued)*
Frank Bazanno - SW Bregenz	Dimitri Brinias - Bournemouth
Eddy Bosnar - Sturm Graz	Darren Broxton - Southampton
	Mark Bosnich - Chelsea
Belgium	Jacob Burns - Leeds United
Joey Didulica - Germinal Beerschot Antwerp	Adrian Caceres - Brentford
Lorenz Kindtner - KSV Roeselare	Shane Cansdell-Sherriff - Leeds United
Rodrigo Palomino - Francs Borains	David Carney - Everton
Josip Skoko - Racing Genk	Simon Colosimo - Manchester City
Archie Thompson - Lierse	Sean Cooney - Coventry City
	Chris Coyne - Luton Town
Czech Republic	Clint Davies - Birmingham City
Mike Sajrynes - SFC Opava	Gareth Edds - Nottingham Forest
	Michael Ferrante - West Ham United
Chile	Richard Garcia - West Ham United
Marcelo Pena - Everton	Lee Gilman - Norwich City
	Mark Graham - Southampton
Croatia	Scott Guyett - Oxford United
Kresimir Basic - Hrvatski Dragovoljac	John Flan - Blackburn Rovers
	Hayden Foxe - West Ham United
Denmark	Lee Howels - Cheltenham Town
Sasho Petrovski - Viborg FF	Danny Invincible - Swindon Town
Richard Plesa - Aarhus GF	Richard Johnson - Watford
	Brad Jones - Middlesbrough
England	Harry Kewell - Leeds United
Daniel Allsopp - Notts County	Shaun Kilkelly - Sheffield Wednesday
Con Blatsis - Derby Country	Steve Laurie - West Ham United
Jason van Blerk - Stockport Country	Stan Lazaridis - Birmingham City
Jon Brady - Rushden & Diamonds	Jay Lucas - Southampton

England *(continued)*

Scott MacDonald - Southampton

Trent McClenahan - West Ham United

Danny Milosevic - Leeds United

Shaun Murphy - Sheffield United

Kevin Muscat - Wolverhampton Wanderers

Lucas Neil - Blackburn Rovers

Paul Okon - Middlesbrough

David Oldfield - Peterborough United

Andy Peterson - Portsmouth

Tony Popovic - Crystal Palace

Blake Restell - Doncaster Rovers

Jordan Rhodes - Leyton Orient

Matthew Rosier - Southampton

Mark Schwarzer - Middlesbrough

Chris Sharpe - Southampton

Russell Waller - Darlington

Luke Wilkshire - Middlesbrough

France

Mile Sterjovski - Lille

Germany

Paul Agostino - 1860 Munich

Joey Di lorio - Werder Bremen

Frank Juric - Bayer Leverkusen

Joshua Kennedy - VfL Wolfsburg

Goran Lozanovski - Alemannia Aachen

Tony Sekulic - VfR Mannheim

Josip Simunic - Hertha BSC Berlin

David Willey - FC Creglingen

David Zdrilic - SpVgg Unterhaching

Ned Zelic - 1860 Munich

Greece

Ante Covic - PAOK Salonika

Bill Damianos - Kalithea

Kosta Salapisidis - Kalithea

John Tambouris - Kalamata

Greece *(continued)*

Kyriakos Tohouroglou - PAOK Salonika

Michael Valkanis - Larissa

Italy

Ross Aloisi - FC Alzano

Marco Bresciano - Empoli

Vince Grella - Empoli

Adrian Madaschi - Atalanta

Srećko Mitrovic - AC Perugia

Nello Notto - Torino Calcio

Nick Rizzo - Ternana

Daniel Severino - Piacenza

Jess Vanstrattan - Juventus

Japan

Steve Corica - Sanfrecce Hiroshima

Malta

Matthew Galea - Hamrun Spartans FC

Peter Pullicino - Hibernians FC

Netherlands

Jason Culina - Ajax Amsterdam

Brett Emerton - Feyenoord Rotterdam

Zeljko Kalac - Roda JC Kerkrade

Mark Tsiorlas - FC Utrecht

Peter Zois - NAC Breda

Norway

Chad Gibson - Bodo/Glimt

Ante Juric - Molde

Steve Laybutt - Lyn

Anthony Magnacca - SK Brann

Kasey Wehrman - Moss

Clayton Zane - Lillestrom

Portugal

Michael Curcija - Sporting Braga

Romania	Singapore *(continued)*
Joshua Maquire – Steaua Bucharest	Alex Duric – Geyland United
	Josip Kozic – Balestier Central
Scotland	Hrvoje Matkovic – Home United
Ben Honeyman – Brechin City	Darren Stewart – Balestier Central
Stuart Lovell – Livingston	Ernie Tapai – Clementi Khalsa
Simon Miotto – Raith Rovers	Hamilton Thorp – Tanjong Pagar United
Craig Moore – Glasgow Rangers	Nebojsa Vukosavljevic – Geyland United
Mark Robertson – Dundee	Vlado Zoric – Home United
Chris Sweeney – Queen's Park	
Tony Vidmar – Glasgow Rangers	**Spain**
Stuart Webster – Greenock Morton	John Aloisi – Atletico Osasuna
Sean Widera – Hibernian	José Bello Serans – Racing Club de Ferrol
	Cameron Pino – Seville
Singapore	
(The Singapore S-League was at its peak at this time as one of the leading professional leagues in Asia) [151]	**Sweden**
	Luke Casserley – AIK Solna (Stockholm)
Adam Anderson – Woodlands Wellington	Chay Hews – IF Sylvia
Brian Bothwell – Geyland United	
Vlado Bozinovski – Clementi Khalsa	**Switzerland**
Tony Carbone – Marine Castle United	Scott Chipperfield – FC Basel

During this period, Australia was a significant exporter of talent and there was a plethora of Australians playing in big and medium-sized European leagues, including a considerable number of players to the English Premier League.

A few years later in 2006, Australia's football players were among the most successful young Australians, earning millions of dollars each year due to the amount of money on offer in the rich European soccer leagues. More than 20 Australians earned AUD1 million or more, including 12 players who were in Australia's 2006 World Cup squad.[152] Harry Kewell, Mark Viduka, Mark Schwarzer and Craig Moore had been playing in the United Kingdom for most of the past decade.

A significant part of this Australian player development during that time occurred within the National Soccer League, the AIS program, and the various ethnic-supported football clubs in Australia during the 1970s, 80s, 90s and the early 2000s. Young players were getting their first-team opportunity earlier which is exemplified in statistics provided by Andrew Howe, (research specialist in Australian soccer). He clarified, after a request from ex-Socceroo Tony Vidmar[153] that "during the years 1987 to 1998, based on modelling of players that played more than 70 per cent of games during each season, 14.8% of those players were aged under 21." Somewhat earlier in 1991, even agents began to notice Australian talent during the Portugal FIFA World Youth Cup where it was noted that "players like Lorenz Kindtner, Mark Bosnich, Paul Okon, Kevin Muscat and David Seal were all in form as the player agents circled."[154]

Furthermore, John Davidson in his seminal article, "The Socceroos Factories," took readers on a journey through some of the clubs responsible for the production line of talent and asked whether Australia would ever be able to match the talent produced in the Golden Generation era. Davidson highlighted the high bar reached and the track records of clubs like Sydney United, South Melbourne, Adelaide City, Marconi Fairfield, Melbourne Knights, and the Brisbane Strikers in talent development during the late 1980s, 1990s and 2000s. This was indicative of Australia at the time where we were once a hotbed of talent production that produced U-17 and U-20 national teams who gave as good as they got in major World Youth Championships.

This production of talent was characterised by ex-Socceroo Jason Culina who commented that "the players were dedicated and motivated to do our best, to go to Europe." His father Branko was "all for giving young players a chance" and "he gave Mark Viduka his NSL debut at Melbourne Knights." At South Melbourne, coach Ange Postecoglou commented that "there was always a demand for success. Young players knew they had to be at their best to succeed. It attracted the best young players."[155]

Tony Vidmar added that Adelaide City had a great core of young talent. "Now there's more than 150 players overseas. The environment, it had nothing to do with dollars, players just wanted to play. I don't think there's going to be that generation again. They were unique."

"Step back to 2003/04 and, ironically, the old National Soccer League assisted the development of a number of our most talented younger players. By that final season, many NSL clubs were so broke that teenagers were thrown into the first team. It didn't hurt their progress."[156] When the NSL disbanded, it left a major gap, as Ange Postecoglou described as coach of the Australian youth team at the time. "In 2004/05, we didn't even have an NSL (or NSL National Youth League). We came back from the 2003 World Youth Championships having beaten Brazil, and many of the squad came back to play State league football — having just beaten Brazil!"[157]

Coaches like Frank Arok, Raul Blanco, Eddie Thomson, Les Scheinflug and Zoran Matic were also primarily responsible for developing young football talent in Australia.

The Australian Institute of Sport (AIS) football program's role in player development

The AIS football program was another key factor that facilitated Australian football development. Remo Nogarotto, a former chairman of Marconi and Soccer Australia, and former Football Australia Board member described AIS head coach Ron Smith as "the doyen of the football development community in Australia. He introduced science — he didn't try to over-engineer players. He finessed them."[158] The AIS program was also one of the first youth academies worldwide to introduce world-leading sports science and physiological tests, which included the six, 12 and 20-metre sprints, skinfold testing, vertical jump measurements, Vo2 score, the beep test and a focus on player mindset and the speed of the game. Further, the AIS team used to play tour games in South America and Europe.

However, the AIS program did not just focus on science and the player development pathway, it gave players competitive exposure by participating in the National Youth League between 1981 and 2005 where over 400 players went through its ranks. Of the 141 footballers who had gone through the AIS by the start of 1996, 69 went on to play for the National Youth side, and 15 for the full national side. Subsequently, a growing trend emerged for players to be snapped up directly from the AIS before they had ever played for an Australian club. "The AIS was a hive of education, football, and culture, remembered fondly by the alumni. The best of the best teenagers from around the country with immense natural talent, remember the AIS as pure football, and some of the most memorable days of their lives."[159] The program was disbanded by Football Federation Australia in August 2017.

As the AIS was one the world's most elite football academy programs during its era, I interviewed Ron Smith for the player development and pathway research for this book in 2022.

In his own words: Ron Smith (ex-AIS football head coach)

On operating the AIS program

I'll give you a bit of context. It changed enormously when the AIS was taken over by Football Australia. Up until 2008 or around that time, there was no directive from Football Australia about how to run the program. That was my job. The program was run as a professional environment, (with) intense training as well individual training, gym conditioning and sport science, and was geared towards international tournaments. The AIS was at the forefront of innovation, including research into athlete health and performance.

On Ron Smith's football philosophy

It was totally about developing individuals to play within team structure. We tried to teach the players to be adaptable in different systems because they were only with us for 12 to 24 months. Then they would go into senior football, so that was the rule for us.

The most important thing was developing the individual first.

On world-leading sports science and its implementation in the AIS program

We were the first ones not to do anything that you might call formal, physical training. I said to the team sports scientist, "I'm not going to measure anything, you come up with some tests to monitor how fit the players are, we're just going to play football. We're not going to spend a lot of time running around the track or doing shuttle runs, we're going to train with a ball."

We designed practices where everything was done with the ball. I thought we couldn't afford to waste 20 per cent of the training session doing warmups without a ball or running without the ball. We were going to do all that intensity work with the ball, and we did it for ten years.

And then we started to monitor, profile and test players.

The sports scientists said that unless you measure what you're doing, you cannot put more loads (known in sport science as overload) into players' training programs. I didn't care. We were going to develop players and we'd get them fit by playing football.

On developing players for the Australian National Youth Teams

Over a period of a few years, we started to realise who was getting picked for the National Youth Team. I didn't pick them. If I didn't get 50 per cent representation in every youth squad, I faced the sack. If there was a really good kid in the country areas and a really good kid in the city in the same position, I'd bring in the kid from the country, let's give him a chance. Steve Corica was one of those kids. The (city) kid at Marconi was already in Sydney at an NSL club. We tried to do what was in the best interests of as many players as possible. But the philosophy was about developing individuals.

On AIS player trials and talent identification

We used to go all over the country. If anyone ever wrote to me and said their player was the best thing since sliced bread, but didn't get picked in the State team because the coach didn't like him, I would say, "If you want to bring your son, at your expense, I'll have a look at him, okay?" I would never shut the door on anybody, no matter where they were in the country. If they were a long way away, I would make a few enquiries because every State coach was in my network.

For example, I'd ask a contact in Queensland, "What do you know about this kid in Gympie?" He might say, "He's the best player in Gympie, but he's not good enough for your squad." I'd ring the parents and tell them if they want to fly down, okay, if he can survive training, I'll pay for his accommodation for the rest of the week. But if I think he's out of his depth, I'll tell you, and he'll have to come back. So, if they pay anything, I'll try and maximise the benefit for the kid. I had parents come mostly from Sydney, because that's the biggest population. They would come down, do one training session, and I didn't even have to say anything. They would say, "Thank you very much Ron, come on son, we're going home," because they could see the kid was way out of his depth.

On the AIS program getting noticed by overseas academies and clubs

Clubs in England were asking about the AIS because we were obviously producing good players. More and more we were getting contracts in the United Kingdom. Years ago, Joe Simunic told me that what they were only talking about doing in the UK (what) we were doing 25 years before. Player preparation, profiling, training, sport science and testing, etc.

On the AIS influence on State Institute football programs

Rocky (Steve O'Connor) worked with me for nearly four years, (from) about 1990 to 1993. We started to influence State programs with mixed age groups. Then what happens when the international coaches come into Australia to lead the Joeys, under-20s and football development? They basically tell us we are a bunch of muppets, what would you know about football? That was their attitude. They thought, "We'll get rid of that, we'll have academies."

On attending the annual National Youth Championships

They used to be all over the country in different States. To pick the players to come into the AIS, I used to go and watch the under-14 and 15 State Championships. In between that, I used to go to every State when they had their level-three coaching course on at the end of the season. What we used to do was bring in the best 24 youth players, so they would have their own training program while the coaches were working. I was there primarily to recruit kids. By the time we got to an under-15 Championships, I pretty much knew. At the time, if you asked me about any young player, I'd tell you what month he was born in.

On having, in essence, Australia's first player scouting infrastructure

It was my job. I had a great network of people. We brought them into the AIS each year for a week so they could see what was happening.

Final observations

To conclude, the AIS was a unique offering in the world of youth football development, especially under coaches Ron Smith and Steve O'Connor. Youth football analyst Louise Taffa said that "Australia once had a program (the AIS) similar to La Masia (FC Barcelona's academy), in the sense that it gave young players the same seamless transition from youth to first team football."[160] Ex-AIS graduate Craig Moore, who is now a football agent, observed that "I have always known that the AIS produced so many, but this shows how good and creative we were back in the day and how far we have gone off track now. We were known for this program all over the world and have always had the talent."[161]

Invariably, Australian agents and some international agents started to flock to the AIS and the yearly National Youth Championships to scout the talent — sometimes to Ron Smith's annoyance.

Australian State Federation Academies

In 2007 Australian football also had elite, State-based football programs and academies that were funded by both government and the State football federations such as the Victorian Institute of Sport (VIS), New South Wales Institute of Sport (NSWIS), South Australian Sports Institute (SASI) and Queensland Academy of

Sport (QAS). These State-based academies complimented the AIS football program and helped develop a plethora of talented players. Of course, player development can go through cycles, and sometimes you have a select generation or a good group of players coming through at the same time.

The two people who were pivotal in setting up the cutting-edge program at the VIS were Ian Greener and Ernie Merrick. "The pair set up the VIS in 1991, working together for the four years. The VIS has had great success in bringing on excellent young talent. Josh Kennedy, Scott McDonald, Jason Culina, Mark Bresciano, Vince Grella, Ljubo Milicevic and Matt Spiranovic all went through the VIS program."[162] Similarly, the VIS, NSWIS, SASI and QAS participated with their talented squads in the (NSL) National Youth Leagues, which added another best versus best element to the Australian youth player development scene.

Nike — The Chance — a project to showcase unidentified talent

Post-AIS, Australian agents needed more showcase events to identify younger talent coming through the ranks. Then Nike announced its global talent search *The Chance* in the 2010/2011 season. They paid for a group of young, unsigned footballers from around the world to take up a one-year professional contract at the English Premier League-backed Nike Academy. There "the chosen players would experience world class facilities, train with elite coaches, have access to nutritionists, psychologists and fitness conditioners, as well as play matches against elite academies and English Premier League reserve teams."[163]

Former AIS coach Ron Smith (Smith) was appointed as the head scout for first Australasian trials initiative for *The Chance*. Smith travelled across Australia and New Zealand for several weeks, scouting the best young talent to trial at the Australasian final for a place at the final Nike Academy trial in London. To identify talent from a combined athletic and tactical perspective, Smith used elite testing methods, including the "Ronaldo test" where players have to run and dribble with the ball to test their speed, control and ability to change direction. There was also the passing test where players have to hit targets to gain as many points as possible.[164]

After two months of trials and seeing hundreds of players across Australia and New Zealand, the final 27 players were selected by Smith for a three-day, intense camp. Tom Doyle from New Zealand, Tom Rogic, Nikodin Matica, a goalkeeper from New South Wales, and Alon Blumgart, a midfielder from Victoria, were chosen to go to the London finals in 2011. Subsequently in London, Rogic was selected as one of the eight trialists chosen worldwide from 75,000 footballers, thus launching his professional career.[165] Blumgart was very close to being selected in the final eight. The Nike Academy Australasian trials operated until the 2016/2017 season when the Nike Academy in London closed.

PART B

Current player trends and football pathways

Has the game changed or player development changed?

The style of the game has changed in player positioning and the types of players sought by clubs, therefore agents must be able to understand physical, technical and tactical factors. These factors all play a part in player opportunities, as clubs use archetypes to select players with similar characteristics. Athleticism is highly sought after in players. Further, clubs will always assess a player's technical skills, tactical skills, physical skills and psychological (mindset) attributes. With today's players pressed and marked tightly, a player must be a manipulator of the ball and have game intelligence. Further, positioning has changed. For example, the full-back position has 26 different game situations and the game in many countries is played at speed and under pressure with compact and fast transitions.

Many agents and scouts would also say that player development in Australia is not where it was 10 or 20 years ago. Ned Zelic, in his observation of the current state of Australian youth player development, said that during his time, the Australian player template was about a winning mentality, a fighting spirit and technical ability within a very competitive environment. Yet, the current Australian player development playbook is a mixed bag and does not always allow players to take on other players. There is too much talk by some coaches on strict formations and systems.

What is the club and pathway environment and challenges that Australian agents face now in attempting to promote Australian players?

Agents now have to face an even more dynamic and ever-changing suite of variables to place their Australian players abroad, especially when there is no transfer market between Australian A-League clubs, unlike in the NSL days. Former agent and youth player development coach Fabian De Marco stated, "Introducing a transfer system between Australian clubs will give more of an incentive to focus on the development of their players."[166] Agents have the remit to get each player into the right league or market, as no two careers are the same, and these days, clubs and managers covet good character, professionalism, locker room adaptation, personality and hard work, not just talent.

Agents also face a challenge in getting their clients well-paid jobs. Recent FIFPRO research figures from 2022 indicate that the player contract landscape is not very encouraging:

- 41% of players have overdue payables owed to them by their current clubs.
- 45% of players worldwide only earn up to USD1,000 per month
- 21% earn less than USD300 per month

The global football market is also not growing the number of well-paid opportunities, with only new professional clubs in the USA and Canada expanding their major contract opportunities. Further, most good Australian players have only one or two options or offers at any one time.

The transition to the NPL has basically not worked

Two decades ago, there was the AIS program and other State academies like the Victorian Institute of Sport. Now players have a suite of academy offerings, including overseas academies, where parents pay to send their kids abroad. In Australia, we also have local academies, yet there is not enough measurable information and data available about how many first-team players they produce.

The A-League's raison d'etre is now seemingly aimed at retaining more of those late-teens and twenty-something Aussies in Australia, and A-League clubs have entered teams in the National Premier Leagues (NPL). However, the NPL, which was partly set up for youth development, has missed the mark due to the high costs to play and there has been no plan to combat unintended consequences. It may be that there are too many talented players with many simply fading away as opportunities do not present themselves.

One quote from Arthur Kiousis best describes the current issues with Australian youth pathways from NPL to professional football. "We keep hearing about pathways in today's football world. But where are the destinations? Every year over 2,000 players finish under-20 NPL. Where do they go next?"[167]

What happened to the National Youth League?

Interestingly, John Boultbee of Football Australia said in 2009 that a proposed youth league would be a vital tool in halting the talent drain.[168] The subsequent Youth League's framework was drawn from a talent development review by former NSL stars Alistair Edwards and Andy Harper, who investigated similar structures in Brazil, Argentina, Japan, USA, France, England and the Netherlands.[169] Boultbee commented at the time that "the FFA is hoping the Youth League will not only raise the playing standard, but bring about increased competitiveness internationally."

Yet the Youth League has been on hiatus for a long period of time, thus curtailing player pathways. Agents have been denied seeing new A-League youth talent benchmark themselves against their peers in the National Youth League or former Y-League. This is at the time where the demand by European clubs and scouts for the broadcasting of competitive youth leagues and tournaments to identify unseen talent is skyrocketing.[170] Funnily enough, the regionalised NSL National Youth League (which the AIS had teams in and ran from 1984 to 2004) was considered one of the most outstanding youth leagues in the world and a producer of talent.

Making it as a professional player — a new reality

Australian agents must manage the expectations of players and parents, as the number of players making it to the top five world leagues or in other significant European leagues is very low. The PFA's 2017 research indicates that 80 per cent of Australian players who go overseas are back in Australia within 3 years and only four out of every 100 Australian players who go to Europe make it a long-term career stay (over 10 years).

In Germany and England, less than one per cent of the young talented players at club academies make it to a professional level. In fact, fewer than one per cent of the 10,000 boys at English club academies are going to make a living from the game.[171] Two-thirds of those awarded a professional contract at the age of 18 abandon the sport by age 21. There is also the issue of clubs having so many players on their books that there are many professional players available for loan. Further, if you look at all the professional footballers in the world, only two per cent play for national teams.[172] Playing in the Champions League means you're in the top 0.0001 per cent of footballers globally.[173] In fact, over the last 10 years, 83 per cent of players in the European Champions League quarter-finals had all played first-team football by age 17.[174] This is not happening in the A-League.

Moreover, research undertaken by FIFPRO into the UEFA Youth League (under-19's elite competition) observes that of the quarter-final squads from 2015 to 2017 (270 players), 11 per cent are unemployed, 83 per cent are playing outside the top 5 European leagues and/or outside the First Division in their countries.[175] These are worrying figures. Further, of all the winning squads of the first 11 editions of the FIFA U-20 World Cup, only 22 players have had a high-level career at the top level.[176] There are also limits to development opportunities worldwide, with only half of the 50 top FIFA- ranked nations having more than two elite youth competitions. The figures and research reflect that the professional playing career pathway ahead is extremely challenging for any talented Australian male youth male players, and for many, potentially unreachable.

Then there is the contemporary positional demand context that all agents must understand. The following table provides a summary.[177]

Playing position	Demand by Clubs
Goalkeepers	Least in demand due to shortage of positions – local players preferred in many countries.
Full-backs	Less demand compared to other playing positions unless they are a very effective dual defensive/attacking wing-back.
Centre-backs	Always sought after especially if they are very athletic and technical. Left-sided ones are gaining real popularity.
Defensive midfielders	Supply is high but demand for this position is average – those who can also play centre-back can be preferred.
Central midfielders	Supply is high but demand for this position is average.
Attacking midfielders	Highly coveted for their creativity and football-playing IQ and are high in demand.
No. 10 or Playmaker or False 9	The most complete, creative and versatile playmakers are in huge demand by elite clubs who play with a free-roaming playmaker. In Italy they are called "fantasista" or "trequartista." In Argentina, this position is known as the "enganche."
Strikers	Very good ones are always in demand everywhere – during recruitment periods these players are a priority signing for clubs.
Wingers (can be wide or inverted)	In demand, especially with a good goal- scoring record and goal-assist repertoire.
Head coach	Quality of supply is fairly low worldwide and the sacking or churn rate is very high.
Assistant coaches	Very rarely sought after as they usually arrive with the head coach.

Note that very high-quality players, most top 40 FIFA ranking national team players, upcoming starlets, most top 5 European league and x-factor players always stand out to clubs regardless of their current positional demand.

The Australian player profile and the timing of moves

Not many overseas clubs and agents know local Australian players, as many do not have a Transfermarkt or Wyscout profile, and limited minutes in the A-League is simply not enough to get noticed. This leaves it up to Australian agents to work tirelessly during transfer windows, undertake pre-planning for 30 plus hours a week and spend dozens of hours on mobile phones, Zoom, Teams, Messenger or WhatsApp to try to get an opportunity for an Australian player. Many Australian agents undertake a return on investment analysis to put to clubs, pitching that their player has a lot of upside and can give better outcomes for the club than many of the players they already have.

Then, all good agents get asked the following question: Should talented Australian players go overseas at a younger age or should they try to go through the A-League pathway?

Former Socceroo Jim Patikas has warned youngsters that Europe will not be any easier to conquer than Australia, despite the fact that there are more opportunities overseas. "If you play for an Australian National Youth team and a club comes along and they want you, then it's okay" to go overseas.[178] Former Socceroo and Sydney Olympic star Peter Katholos, who has been involved with coaching at youth level, a player adviser and also scouted for overseas clubs, states that "if players want to make it at an overseas club, they need to leave at 13–14 years of age to have a really good opportunity to make it. Things have changed in Australia. We don't develop our players the way they do in Europe. We don't have the coaches or the development standards to get our players at the right level".[179] Katholos' view mimics the perspective of many Australian agents; that Australian players are very good by world standards until their mid-teens but sometime after that, are negatively affected by weaker pathways and structures.

PART C

The Agent's Roundtable –
The current Australian player development landscape

Although Australian agents have been at the pointy end of Australian football player development outcomes, no one has conducted a roundtable with them on their views and what changes and initiatives should be considered. Agents are at the heart of advising on talent development and are in the player promotion business, therefore their well-informed and unique view must be considered.

Consequently, I conducted a research survey during October and November of 2022 with a cohort (over 25) of other Australian agents and intermediaries. I sought to obtain their views on:

Australian football player development over the last 2-3 decades;

Whether talented Australian male youth footballers have adequate pathways in order to become a professional club player; and

What talent identification methods are used by agents to scout and/or discover talented players.

The results are produced in the following table.

The Australian agent view on Australian football player development over the last few decades (up to 3 answers could be chosen by each agent)

Answer choices	% of Agents who agree with answer
It has declined significantly due to various factors including not enough experienced youth coaches, training and curriculum issues, generational lifestyles and the cost of playing.	80.77%
Australia has lagged behind other Asian countries and even the United States in investing in youth player development.	61.54%
The lack of a National Youth League has eroded player development in Australia.	46.15%
Generally, we have lost the Australian footballer DNA where physicality and combativeness were at the forefront.	42.31%
Australian clubs don't tour Europe enough to play youth tournaments and provide a benchmark comparison to their players.	42.31%
The previous National Soccer League (NSL) developed better younger players than the A-League as it gave opportunities and promoted talent.	34.62%
Other answers including a lack of incentive to develop youth, a need for more top world- class players playing in our stadiums and training with our younger players, and the fact that the NPL system does not facilitate a best vs best junior competition.	26.92%
It is cyclical. A-League academies are starting to produce more young talented players.	7.69%
We are developing better technical and tactical players than ever before.	0.0%

The Australian agent view on the pathway available to talented Australian youth footballers must become professional club players (up to three answers could be chosen by each agent)	
Answer choices	% of Agents who agree with answer
The lack of a national Second Division inhibits player pathways.	50%
The Australian A-League clubs and NPL clubs are not incentivised enough to focus on player development and pathways.	35%
In Australia generally, clubs and coaches are risk averse, therefore delay in promoting younger talent to the starting first team.	31.5%
No, we have been left behind as there are not enough A-League clubs to provide professional opportunities.	26.5%
Talented Australian youth players do not play enough international tournaments which attract scouts and talent identification networks.	18%
Other answers included there are not enough professional clubs, we have an unrefined scouting system and more National Youth Championships are needed.	18%
Australian agents are the main drivers for creating player pathways but cannot do it alone.	17%
Australian players just do not have the opportunities to showcase their talent as there is a huge surge in the number of talented players worldwide.	15.5%
Australian clubs do not have enough collaboration with overseas clubs in order to loan players.	14.5%

What methods do Australian agents use to scout or to identify talented players?

Answer choices	% of Agents who agree with answer
Word of mouth. I receive information from my football network.	46.15%
I am the scout therefore I attend games in person.	42.31%
I use trusted referrers like ex-professional players or part time scouts to bring players to my attention.	34.62%
I use platforms like Wyscout, InStat, Transfermarkt or other analytical tools.	26.92%
I watch games on TV, Facebook or NPL YouTube TV.	26.92%
I have coaches bring players to my attention.	26.92%
Other methods including a combination of the above.	15.38%
I have private football academies refer players to my attention.	11.54%

The results in the three tables indicate that from an agent's perspective, there has been a significant decline in men's player development in Australia in the last decade or so. Further, there is a key message from agents that there is a lack of professional opportunities for young Australian male players. This is also exacerbated by the Player Points System (PPS) used in the NPL State leagues. It was put in place to stop players changing clubs and give younger players chances. However, ex-Socceroo Sasa Ognenovski (who is now a coach and club football director) is leading calls for an overhaul of a PPS policy that he believes threatens to cost Australia another generation of potential young footballers. "It does not work, it's absolutely doing the opposite. The A-League (and NPL) youth boys are close, but not getting senior games anywhere. The PPS does not help. If they don't play (NPL 1), they go down to NPL 2 or NPL 3, (and) lose their passion for the game."[180]

It should be noted that the momentum currently growing around the set-up of an Australian National Second Division or B-League may be game-changer for player development and opportunities.

Anecdotally, most agents use word-of-mouth or scout in person for players. A significant survey concern is that no agent agreed with the proposition that "Australia is developing better technical and tactical players currently than in previous decades." This proposition is supported by Professional Footballers Australia's insightful study into Australian football's Golden Generation, namely "Culture Amplifies Talent," which found that "there's no sugar coating the data — at the elite level, across the big five leagues of world football, Australians just aren't mixing it. From 29,735 in 2003–04 to 3,817 by 2014–15, there has been an 87% decrease of minutes played by Socceroos in the top flights of England, Germany, Spain, Italy or France. As the study points out, "our net production of [elite] talent has declined over the past 10–20 years" … "Yet at the same time, junior participation rates among boys aged five to 14 have boomed from 208,000 in 1997 to 531,000 in 2017."[181]

In my 2022 survey, I sought to also identify the current thinking of Australian agents on what initiatives and ideas should be implemented to improve Australian football player development. I have compiled their responses in the following table. These remarks, suggestions and proposals should be contemplated by all stakeholders in Australian football.

Initiatives suggested by Australian agents to be immediately implemented in order to improve Australian football player development

Better educated and paid coaches at elite/ NPL level. Not specific to any curriculum but focus on the development of the individual. Creating more thinkers, ideas and more importantly, opportunities for players to develop solutions.	Cost of playing should decrease immediately; soccer should be free up to under-12s at least.
Youth player salary cap exemptions like MLS, rewards for playing young players to promote the domestic transfer market.	Collaboration with Japanese teams to learn their strengths in youth development.
Implement a Second Division and further expansion of the A-League.	Concentrate the talent pool of NPL junior clubs, by bringing back the under-13 to under-16 Super Leagues.

A-League Academies to start at earlier ages, with specialised academy programs.

Incentivise NPL 3 teams. Players can't be older than 28.

NPL 2 clubs must have five U21's in the first eleven and five on the bench.

NPL 1 clubs must have three U21's in the first eleven and three on the bench.

A-League teams must have two U21's in the first eleven and two on the bench.

Youth cup featuring the best 19-23-year-olds playing against each other and setting up more player trials and combines.[182]

Pick a consistent style of Australian football first. Build an Australian playing philosophy and the Australian way.

Bring coaches in from Europe under Australia's successful immigration system to train players and coaches.

Although it is still quite early research, experts recommend that children and young people try to participate in a variety of sports and physical activities to maximise life-long sport participation, enjoyment and engagement.

New B-League clubs to collaborate with Universities (facilities, investment, fan engagement)[183]

A loan system for younger players between A-League clubs, B-League and NPL clubs[184]

Cap international footballers playing in the A-League to 4.

Send a group of the best players from the A-League Academies to shadow and play competitive friendlies with UEFA Youth League teams or base youth teams in Europe to enter leagues or competitions.

Hopefully the Socceroos' brilliant performance at the 2022 World Cup, the Scotland Premier League pathway and the emergence of the talented under-17 Joey's team recently will add to the Australian player reputation and brand, and potentially unlock further opportunities. Excitingly, Australian football is possibly on a cusp of a new generation of talent development with a growing trend of younger Australian players transferring from the A-League to European clubs. At the time of writing, younger Australian players who have had been part of recent major transfer deals include Jordan Bos (Westerlo) and Marco Tilio (Celtic on loan to Melbourne City), Anthony Pavlesic and Nestory Irankunda (Bayern Munich) and three young A-League goalkeepers (Joe Gauci, Steven Hall and Henry Blackledge) in the January 2024 transfer window. It can confidently be said that Australia has consistently produced good talent in the goalkeeper position.

The women's professional playing pathway looks much more positive, as talented Australian women players and coaches are in strong demand worldwide and agents are increasingly involved in the women's football transfer space.

Where are the player contracts?

As agents we must also always understand the current state of demand and requests for Australian talent in international football leagues and club transfers. This may include whether clubs can give players a clearly agreed pathway, the personalities of players that clubs seek, and if the player is a natural fit for the club. Over the last two to three decades, Australian agents have experienced a moving set of factors and trends in the international demand for Australian players in both the men's and women's games, as the following tables demonstrate.[185]

Men's Professional Football	
Very good opportunities in the past however demand has somewhat declined (due to salary changes and the type of players now requested).	China, Thailand, Spain, Malaysia, Singapore, Indonesia, Greece, South Korea, Turkey, Portugal, Switzerland, Qatar and the United Arab Emirates.
Traditionally a drawcard market with ongoing opportunities (Australians have consistently done well in these countries leagues).	England, Croatia, Belgium, Netherlands, Italy, Germany, Japan, Austria and Denmark.
Current markets in demand (attracted to the profile and attributes of Australian players).	Scotland, India, Norway and Sweden.
Recent growing trend of opportunities (markets beginning to be attracted to the Australian player profile).	United States (MLS/USL/NWSL), Canada, Iceland, Mexico, Egypt, Uzbekistan, South Africa, Czechia, Finland, Hungary, Lebanon, Ireland, Iran, Poland, Argentina (youth development), Baltic States (Lithuania, Latvia, Estonia), Ireland, Armenia and Slovenia.
Difficult markets (due to the significant ratio of local talented players, passports required, language or solely seeking top range experienced players).	France, Serbia, Cyprus, Chile, Vietnam and Saudi Arabia.

Women's Professional and College Football

Very good opportunities in the past, however demand has somewhat declined.	National Women's Soccer League (United States).
Traditionally a drawcard market with ongoing opportunities (Australians have consistently done well in these country's leagues).	Norway (Toppserien), Sweden (Damallsvenskan), USA College scene namely the National Collegiate Athletic Association (NCAA) and the Netherlands.
Current markets in demand (attracted to the profile and attributes of Australian players).	England (Women's Super League and Women's Championship) and Scotland.
Recent growing trend of opportunities (markets beginning to be attracted to the Australian player profile).	Iceland, Mexico (Liga MX Femenil), Spain (Liga F), Denmark, Portugal, Italy and Austria.
Difficult markets (due to the significant ratio of local talented players, passports required, language or solely seeking top- range, experienced players).	France (Division 1 Feminine), Germany, Japan (The WE League) and Brazil.

Overwhelmingly, Australian agents are a player's means of extracting the most out of themselves and a crucial necessity for the completion of the player's club transfer. The player transfer canvas is getting tougher compared to a few decades ago. Having to work directly with players and their pathways, agents have seen and felt the ups and downs of the Australian player development landscape. Therefore, their views on player development, pathways, scouting and talent identification must be both at the forefront of any future football youth development policy and the transfer strategy of clubs, players and coaches.

Chapter 20:
The Agent Game of Two Halves –
Conclusion

"There are a lot of agents that are incredibly hard-working, brilliantly networked, hard negotiators, and have spent a lifetime recruiting good players that they believe will ultimately deliver on the pitch."
— Daniel Geey, partner in the sports group at Sheridans law firm (London) and author of *Done Deal*.

I contend that there have been two significant and distinct phases of the Australian agent's industry — pre-2015 and post-2015.

Pre-2015 Australian agent experiences — evolution and opportunity

At the time of Australia's 'Golden Generation' playing in the FIFA World Cup in Germany in 2006, there were 28 licensed Football Australia agents. Australia was a small market with only one newly emerging professional league.

A London-based magazine article written in 2004 identified an intriguing trend that the "number of Australian players in Britain has turned from trickle to flood, fuelled by an army of agents. Australia at the time named a full-strength squad (against England) in a friendly, of which 13 of the 19 players included hailed from United Kingdom clubs. Away from the Socceroos, Australian players are popping up throughout the British leagues, many of them emerging talent brought halfway round the world to finish their football education. Managing established players and locating and dispatching the youth is a battalion of Australian agents. Currently, there are 30 of the latter registered with FIFA, compared to Norway's 21, Sweden's 16 and Denmark's 13; an amazing statistic for a country with a domestic football scene characterised as being semi-professional at the time."[186]

The pre-2015 agent's business featured several elements that either do not exist or cannot be observed in the Australian football market today. Firstly, the existence of the AIS football program (as well as State Institutes) provided a huge pipeline of talent for Australian agents to scout and represent. Greg Blood in his seminal article[187] entitled *Remembering the contributions of AIS Men's football to the Socceroos*, observed that under the control of head coaches Ron Smith (1986–1996) and Steve O'Connor (1996–2008), the AIS program had immediate results in developing national players for the Young Socceroos, Olyroos, and longer term, the Socceroos. In fact, the 2006 and 2010 Socceroos World Cup teams included former AIS players — John Aloisi (1992 scholarship), Marco Bresciano (1997), Brett Emerton (1995–996), Joshua Kennedy (1998–1999), Mark Milligan (2002), Craig Moore (1992–1993), Lucas Neill (1994–1995), Josip Skoko (1992–1993), Mile Sterjovski (1996–1996), Mark Viduka (1992–1993), Luke Wilkshire (1998), Vince Grella (1996–1997), Carl Valeri (2000–2001), Nikita Rukavytysa (2005–2006) and Dario Vidosic (2005–2006).

Additionally, as Canberra-based former Socceroo Andrew Bernal stated to me during my research of Australian player scouting, agents went to the AIS and National Youth Championships to scout potential players. In a recent presentation to football coaches, Ron Smith said, "Agents affected the AIS program by telling players to go overseas." Smith also stated that the AIS saw more agent visits and scouting trips per capita than anywhere in the world. In the early years and prior to the A-League, many AIS graduates gravitated to the National Soccer League (NSL) before transitioning to European or Asian leagues. As football in Australia was mainly semi-pro and the NSL clubs were giving younger players opportunities, agents at the time were very focused on the overseas market to obtain professional opportunities for Australian players.

The pre-2015 period was also influenced by Professional Footballers Australia (PFA), headed by Brendan Schwab (a world leading sports labour rights lawyer) who would host annual roundtable meetings with licensed agents. These roundtables would be brisk and robust meetings where the PFA staff and agents would debate regulations, contract issues and disputes, and player trends. Each agent attendee would receive a large folder with various information, contract clauses, collective bargaining agreement updates, Socceroo entitlement information, player welfare information and other informative tools provided by the PFA. It was quite a unique offering at the time that did not happen in other parts of the world and it gave many Australian agents an understanding of regulations and insights that most international agent counterparts were not privy to. Finally, pre-2015 agents could take their Australian contractual dispute matters to Football Australia through the grievance procedure. This was an invaluable dispute resolution forum for Australian agents that was removed post-2015 and it has only recently scheduled to come back in 2023.

Post-2015 Australian agent experiences — from regulation to an open, chaotic market and back

The FIFA regulations that changed agents to intermediaries and removed agent licences in 2015 opened the player agent market in Australia and internationally to what many interpreted as chaos. The removal of barriers of entry (including the exam, the need for professional liability insurance and low registration fees in Australia) meant there was a huge proliferation of intermediaries who came into the market with little training. The FIFA deregulation meant that there were too many agents (intermediaries) and the observation that "everyone is an agent these days" was heard within Australian circles. On average, just two A-League players were available for each Australian registered intermediary to manage post-2015. Further, there was no real enforcement by FIFA as a regulator and conflicts of interest were not always properly controlled.

Post-2015, with the growth of player transfers and more money in the game, the market felt saturated with opportunistic agents/intermediaries.[188] The change also created a trend where five to ten agents in Australia did most of the business and the rest were mainly part-time operators.

The post-2015 period also resulted in many European markets being controlled by European agents because an Australian agent now must register to operate in each country. Registering in each country was an expensive proposition. Therefore, it became harder to open doors for players unless you had a direct contact on the ground. It could be argued that FIFA's change in 2015 may have inadvertently resulted in changing the player landscape considerably, where "the world of agents and fees and all that stuff is designed in a way to make it harder for talents from more obscure countries to kind of pave a path to the big leagues in Europe."[189]

Even the PFA expressed their concerns in 2019 that the loose regulations have created a minefield at the sub-professional level, especially for young talented players coming through the National Premier League (NPL) and academy systems. As current Melbourne Victory CEO John Didulica (who was CEO of the PFA at the time) stated "you hear of agents signing up a raft of young players, who don't know enough to know otherwise, and then not proactively progressing their careers but they end up shackled to a three or four-year contract. This is where the PFA tries to help players."[190]

Alarmingly, in 2018 one in four of the 147 legal cases brought by the PFA involved an agent, whether they were disputes between players and agents or disputes between agents in multi-party club and transfer transactions. The outcome of these concerns was that the PFA expanded its own remit to advising young players before they enter into agency agreements.

Final thoughts

I hope that through the 25-plus interviews and the researched observations in this book, I have presented a case for Australian agents to feature at the forefront of Australia's football industry development. Australian agents have left their undeniable mark in representing the game's talent in both the A-League and on the international scene.

Australia has always been blessed with well-credentialed player representatives who love the game and are passionate about opening the elite European, North American and Asian club markets to Australian players. The tyranny of distance provides a challenge for Australian agents to hold onto client talent and deal with the powerful European clubs on a day-to-day basis. However, with different strategies like Buddy Farah being based partly in Europe, Miro Gladovic flying internationally every other month and John Grimaud with his partner on the ground abroad, Australian agents can also have a considerable presence in the European markets. Perhaps it is the Australian agent's experience of operating in a multicultural and cosmopolitan country like Australia that gives many of us the unique insights and understanding of cultural nuances necessary to work effectively in the international agency business.

Australian agents have shown we have strong player portfolios and credentials, the passion to be effective agents, the understanding of regulations, and the language and cultural affinity to speak to the right decision-makers to do player deals. We have a 360-degree view of the game, along with experienced, well-informed opinions, perspectives and solution/ideas to improve the Australian talent development ecosystem and player/club pathways.

There was more robust agent regulation pre-2015 and there were more Australian players at big European clubs between 1990 and 2012. As agents, we had more importance in football, the sense that you had a licence you could show in Asia or Europe to open club doors. That was different to the somewhat tangled disorder that agents faced recently where a multitude of individuals can pursue the agency game and there was a need to register in multiple markets. Hopefully the recent FIFA licensing changes will be positive for all.

Australian agents via hard work, transparency, and reputation must continue to put forward good players to ensure they are enticing coaches, international clubs and other partner agents. The agency world is now varied, and agents must either have a suite of offerings for clients or work effectively in niche markets. Coupled with this is the challenge that agents now face in holding onto players who can have their heads turned very easily, especially if their career is not going well. Many players will make decisions to change their agent after being influenced by social media, close entourages, family and other players in the dressing room. With all these challenges, good agents need to rely on the loyalty of the player, along with their exceptional communication and deal-making abilities.

Football agency is a relationship-driven, dynamic business and it is always exciting to work in the fast-moving and evolving player representation scene. Australian agents work within two pull factors: local players want to work with agents and most want to head overseas. Eddie Krncevic best encapsulates that reality. "The young ones with stars in their eyes, and the older players with financial carrots dangling in front of them, will always be tempted to leave these shores and chase their dreams overseas."[191]

I hope this book has presented the positive side of the agent industry and respected the Australian protagonists. Despite all the apparent challenges, Australian agents have shown excellence in football player agency. Consultants prepare once and sell the same product multiple times, while football agents need to prepare each time and promote players individually. With each player and club transfer being an individual project, the ability of agents to shape, shift and connect deals, and find a pathway for talented players is their prime motivation and reward in "The Agents' Game".

Bibliography

Caioli, Luca, Messi – Neymar – Ronaldo (Head to head with the World's Greatest Players), 2014, Icon Books Ltd, London, United Kingdom.

Calvin, Michael, The Nowhere Men (The Unknown Story of Football's talent spotters), 2014, Arrow Books, London, United Kingdom.

CIES Football Observatory, Exclusive report on football agent activity, February 2012. https://www.cies-uni.org/en/international/news/cies-football-observatory-exclusive-report-football-agent-activity

Colucci, Michele and Bellia, Ornella Desiree (Editors), Transfers of Football Players (A practical approach to implementing FIFA rules) – Volumes 1 and 2, 2020, Sports Law Policy Centre, Press Up s.r.l, Italy.

Colucci, Michele (Ed), The FIFA regulations on working with intermediaries (Implementation at national level), Issue 1-2015, Sports Law Policy Centre, Press Up s.r.l, Italy.

De Marco, Nick (Ed), Football and the Law, 2018, Bloomsbury Professional, Haywards Heath, United Kingdom.

Fédération Internationale de Football Association (FIFA), Football Agents in International Transfers Report, released December 2023.

Football Legal, The journal dedicated to international football law, Bordeaux, France.

Geey, Daniel, Done Deal (An insider's guide to Football Contracts, Multi-million-pound transfers and Premier League big business), 2019, Bloomsbury Sport, London, United Kingdom.

Heitner, Darren A, How to Play the Game (What Every Sports Attorney needs to know), 2014, American Bar Association (ABA Publishing), Chicago, United States.

KEA European Affairs, Study on Sports Agents in the European Union, November 2009, A study commissioned by the European Commission.

Macguire, Kieran, The Price of Football, 2020, Agenda Publishing, Newcastle upon Tyne, United Kingdom.

Murray, Les, By the Balls, 2011, Random House, Sydney, Australia.

Postecoglou, Ange (with Andy Harper), Changing the Game - Football in Australia through my Eyes, 2016, Penguin Random House Australia, Melbourne, Victoria.

Smith, Jon (with James Olley), The Deal (Inside the World of a Super-Agent), 2016, Constable, London, United Kingdom.

Stensholt, John and Mooney, Shaun, A-League (The inside story of the tumultuous first decade), 2015, Nero, Collingwood, Melbourne, Australia.

Wilson, Jonathan, Angels with Dirty Faces (The Footballing History of Argentina), 2016, Orion Books, London, United Kingdom.

ARBITRAL AWARDS

Court of Arbitration for Sport, Professional Football Agents Association (PROFAA) v. Fédération Internationale De Football Association (FIFA), CAS 2023/O/9370, July 2023

In the matter of an Arbitration Under Rule K of the Football Association rules between CAA Base Limited, Key Sports Management Ltd (T/A Wasserman), Stellar Football Limited, Areté Management Limited (Claimants) and The Football Association Limited (Respondent) and Fédération Internationale De Football Association (Participant) — Partial Final Award, December 2023.

EBOOK

Wyscout — Helping Football Intermediaries Thrive, at All Levels of the Game, 2020.

FIFA AGENT PLATFORM

FIFA Agent Platform and Portal @ https://www.fifa.com/legal/football-regulatory/agents/agent-platform

FIFPRO

FIFA Agent Regulations Reforms — FIFPRO Presentation at the PFA Player Agents Conference, 15 November 2021.

PODCASTS

Ashley Morrison Media podcasts #12 and #13, Ashley Morrison with Peter Paleologos on the agents' industry, https://ashleymorrisonmedia.com/category/peter-paleologos/

The Gab and Juls Show (Gab Marcotti and Julien Laurens), 22 December 2021, podcast interview with Italian super-agent Giovanni Branchini to discuss his career in football.

The Transfer Window podcast with Ian McGarry and Duncan Castles, featuring Bernie Mandic as a guest on 12 July 2019 and 31 March 2020.

The Agents Angle — The World's Premier Football (Soccer) Agent Show with Jonathan Booker and Peter Paleologos.

WEBINARS

World Football Summit webinar, 'Setting the Record Straight: Jonathan Barnett and Mino Raiola defend the role of Agents', 4 January 2021, World Football Summit YouTube channel.

Wyscout Forum 2021, 'Exploration of the new FIFA proposed reform on Agents' by Stefano Malvestio (International Consultant at Bichara & Motta Advogados) and Luis Villas-Boas Pires (Head of Agents at FIFA), https://www.hudl.com/blog/wyscout-forum-2021-fifa-reform-agents

Procuratore Calcio.com, 'Free mini course - How to become a Footballers' Agent in Italy' (Mini Corso gratuito — come si diventa agente di calciatori in Italia), 27 February 2024, https://youtu.be/lWcznIyNHy8?si=CXpchWQKkvp4ouo7

Endnotes

1   World Football Summit webinar, 'Setting the Record Straight: Jonathan Barnett and Mino Raiola defend the role of Agents' 4 January 2021, World Football Summit YouTube channel

2   The term 'lofting' refers to sharp practices engaged by clubs like a player being dropped from the main squad to train alone.

3   FIFA Legal Digital Hub, https://digitalhub.fifa.com/m/1b47c74a7d44a9b5/original/Regulations-on-the-Status-and-Transfer-of-Payers-March-2022.pdf

4   Green, Michael and Ghaye, Tony, 'The Emergent Practices of English Football Agents,' Journal of Global Sport Management 2023 https://pure.hartpury.ac.uk/ws/portalfiles/portal/28161392/The_Emergent_Practices_of_English_Football_Agents.pdf

5   Sports Agents – History and Law https://sportslaw.uslegal.com/sports-agents-and-contracts/sports-agents-history-and-law/?amp

6   Holt, Matthew, Michie, Jonathan and Oughton, Christine, 'The role and regulation of agents in football' A report for the Sports Nexus, August 2006.

7   Fitzpatrick, Richard, 'The Machine of '87: Messi's Boyhood Teammates Recall Early Signs of Greatness' https://syndication.bleacherreport.com/amp/2717227-the-machine-of-87-messis-boyhood-teammates-recall-early-signs-of-greatness.amp.html 23 June 2017

8   Fédération Internationale de Football Association (FIFA), 'Football Agents in International Transfers Report' released December 2023.

9   These 1994 regulations were the subject of a successful complaint by Laurent Piau, a French players' agent, lodged before the European Commission which resulted in the need for them to be modified.

10   KEA European Affairs, 'Study on Sports Agents in the European Union' November 2009, commissioned by the European Commission.

11   Ibid.

12   Ibid.

13   This agent licence expired after five years. Agents who wished to continue in the industry were subject to re-examination (if the national association required it).

14   In the Case T-193/02, Laurent Piau v Commission of the European Communities and FIFA, 26 January 2005 https://curia.europa.eu/juris/document/document.jsf?text=&docid=49878&pageIndex=0&doclang=EN&mode=lst&dir=&occ=first&part=1&cid=4269906 and KEA European Affairs, 'Study on Sports Agents in the European Union' November 2009, commissioned by the European Commission.

15   Parrish Richard, 'Working with Intermediaries – Reform of the players' agent's system' www.fifa.com, January 2018.

16   France kept their own agent rules and did not recognise the status of the FIFA intermediary regulations.

17   McGregor, Andrew, Brabners law firm, August 2019, FC Business magazine, 'Rebuilding the relationship between clubs and agents.'

18   Jorge Mendes quoted on CNN at https://theathletic.com/1374316/2019/11/20/jorge-mendes/

19   World Football Summit webinar, 'Setting the Record Straight: Jonathan Barnett and Mino Raiola defend the role of Agents' 4 January 2021, World Football Summit channel on YouTube.

20   Financial Times, 5 September 2014, 'Jorge Mendes, power broker behind football's elite' https://www.ft.com/content/6eb42db4-3427-11e4-b81c-00144feabdc0

21   Smith, Jon (with James Olley), 'The Deal (Inside the World of a Super-Agent)' 2016, Constable, London, United Kingdom.

22   Fuentes, Ramon, iusport website, 1 September 2015, 'Representatives and intermediaries, the other great football business' (translated from Spanish), https://iusport.com/art/9787/los-representantes-e-intermediarios-el-otro-gran-negocionadel-futbol (This article originally appeared on the iusport website. TEJ has authorisation for its publication).

23   Harvey, Alex, Sheridans sport lawyers, Twitter 2019.

24   The term 'baller' has come into football from the United States, where it was mainly National Basketball Association agents who coined this term for super talented players.

25   FIFPRO report, 'Working Conditions in Professional Football' 2016 https://fifpro.org/media/xdjhl-wb0/working-conditions-in-professional-football.pdf

26   Ibid.

27   Lipman, Matias, intermediary, South America, LinkedIn.

28   Francis, Stijn, CEO, agent and sports lawyer, Stirr Associates, Belgium, X (Twitter).

29   Johnson, Bradley, professional footballer, LinkedIn.

30   Echeverri, Felipe Toro, lawyer, LinkedIn.

31   Ripoll, Enric, founder of ER Sports Law & Arbitration, X (Twitter).

32   Harvey, Alex, Sheridans sport lawyers, Twitter 2019.

33   Shea, John, Lewis Silkin lawyers, LinkedIn presentation.

34   Ioannidis, Gregory, sports lawyer, professor and attorney at law @ Kings Chambers, England.

35   Union Royale Belge des Sociétés de Football Association ASBL v Jean-Marc Bosman (1995) C-415/93 (known as the Bosman ruling) [1] is a 1995 European Court of Justice decision concerning freedom of movement for workers, freedom of association, and the direct effect of article 39[2] (now article 45 of the Treaty on the Functioning of the European Union) of the TEC. The case was an important decision on the free movement of labour and had a profound effect on the transfers of footballers within the European Union (EU).

36   Brand, Gerard, Sky Sports, 'How the Bosman rule changed football – 20 years on' 15 December 2015 https://www.skysports.com/football/news/11096/10100134/how-the-bosman-rule-changed-football-20-years-on

37   http://www.ozfootball.net/studsup/dtrh/dtrh97.htm

38   The World Game website, SBS TV.

39   Football Nation Radio, Melbourne, https://soundcloud.com/fnr_footballnationradio/fnr_football-football-extra-27-march-2018-george-christopoulos

40   My interview with George Christopoulos was held at one of his popular hospitality venues at Port Melbourne, Australia. The intermittent noise and interruptions slightly affected the taping of the interview. Therefore, based on both a review of my extensive scribbled notes and a transcript of the recorded interview, I have amended the grammar and improved the expression flow for this chapter.

41   Finkelstein, Eric, 11 February 2021, 'Soccer Family Agent Hopes to Elevate US Soccer to Prestigious Level'. http://sportsagentblog.com/2021/02/11/soccer-family-agent-hopes-to-elevate-us-soccer-to-prestigious-level/

42 Ergic was a standout player in the AIS side that won the National Youth League and with Perth Glory, scoring 10 goals in 23 appearances in the 1999–2000 season. He was signed by Juventus at just 19-years-old. He went on to make over 200 appearances for Swiss club Basel and represent Serbia and Montenegro at the 2006 World Cup. Ergic has since become a poet and writer for Politika, the Serbian national daily.

43 Ormond, Aidan, FTBL, 25 June 2020, 'An Agent's life behind the transfers, stars and-glamour' https://www.ftbl.com.au/news/an-agents-life-behind-the-transfers-stars-and-glamour-549692

44 Ibid.

45 Prichard, Greg, SBS The World Game website, 18 February 2017, 'Mooy's agent reveals: 'They thought I was dumping treasure in the swamp.'

46 Ibid.

47 Peacock, Adam, Fox Football podcast, 8 January 2020, 'A player agent explains transfer windows and player movement — Paddy Dominguez.'

48 The Independent Soccer Review Committee published a report in 2003 on the governance of soccer in Australia.

49 Ormond, Aidan, FTBL website, 27 February 2007, 'Deal or No Deal' https://www.ftbl.com.au/feature/deal-or-no-deal-74120

50 FTBL website, 11 April 2009, 'The Men who made Harry' https://www.ftbl.com.au/feature/the-men-who-made-harry-142237/page0

51 Ibid.

52 Ibid.

53 The World Game website, SBS Television,15 July 2019, 'Mandic reveals why Kewell turned down Barca, Arsenal and Chelsea for Liverpool.'

54 Alleyne Richard, The Telegraph, 10 June 2005, '£2m for taking a couple of phone calls' https://www.telegraph.co.uk/news/uknews/1491739/2m-for-taking-a-couple-of-phone-calls.html

55 Professional Footballers Australia, PFA website, 19 August 2008, 'Players Turn to PFA in Off-Season' https://pfa.net.au/news/players-turn-to-pfa-in-off-season/

56 Bernie Mandic appeared on two podcasts being 12 July 2019 and 31 March 2020 (The Transfer Window podcast with Duncan Castles and Ian McGarry (featuring 'The Agent View' with Bernie Mandic).

57 The Age, 19 July 2003, Two minute interview (with Bernie Mandic) https://www.theage.com.au/life-style/two-minute-interview-20030719-gdw2jw.html

58 Ormond, Aidan, FTBL website, 27 February 2007, 'Deal or No Deal' https://www.ftbl.com.au/feature/deal-or-no-deal-74120

59 Professional Footballers Australia, PFA website, 19 August 2008, 'Players Turn to PFA in Off-Season' https://pfa.net.au/news/players-turn-to-pfa-in-off-season/

60 AAP, ABC News, Australian Broadcasting Corporation website, 23 November 2011, 'Kewell appoints his own coach' https://www.abc.net.au/news/2011-11-23/kewell-appoints-his-own-coach/3689776

61 Bucci, Nino, Inside Sport, 5 July 2011, 'The man behind Harry Kewell: who is Bernie Mandic?' http://forum.insidesport.com.au/1125407/ThemanbehindHarryKewellwhoisBernieMandicNinoBucci-fromTheAge#bm1125418

62 The Sydney Morning Herald, 3 January 2003' 'Demise of the goose that laid the golden egg' https://www.smh.com.au/sport/cricket/demise-of-the-goose-that-laid-the-golden-egg-20030103 gdg1z5.html?fbclid=IwAR00B4uLBg8_xe05SwPt9BgsuE3DhMwk9P46oLSFGjCwzK-Ct59qR85mNck

63 Hassett, Sebastian, The Age, 7 June 2011, 'Lifestyle the lure for Kewell' https://www.theage.com.au/sport/soccer/lifestyle-the-lure-for-kewell-20110606-1fpbt.html?js-chunk-not-found-refresh=true

64 The Age, 19 July 2003, 'Two minute interview' (with Bernie Mandic)' https://www.theage.com.au/lifestyle/two-minute-interview-20030719-gdw2jw.html

65 Ibid.

66   Hinds, Richard, AFP and The Daily Telegraph, 18 February 2022, 'Western Sydney Wanderers coach Tony Popovic could be the A-League's first $1m manager' https://www.foxsports.com.au/football/a-league/western-sydney-wanderers-coach-tony-popovic-could-be-the-aleagues-first-1m-manager/news-story/2390aa93e5f1f53fb0d6fcd1c821b649

67   Mandic, Bernie,12 July 2019 (The Transfer Window podcast with Duncan Castles and Ian McGarry (featuring 'The Agent View' with Bernie Mandic).

68   Ibid.

69   Mandic, Bernie, 1 April 2020 (The Transfer Window podcast with Duncan Castles and Ian McGarry (featuring the Agent view with Bernie Mandic)

70   Sempre Inter website, 15 March 2022, 'Inter to Announce Extension of Marcelo Brozovic's Contract Before Fiorentina Clash, Italian Media Report' https://semprinter.com/2022/03/15/inter-to-announce-extension-of-marcelo-brozovics-contract-before-fiorentina-clash-italian-media-report/

71   SBS website, 3 February 2013, 'Australia well served by K-League' https://forum.insidesport.com.au/1648366/AustraliawellservedbytheKLeague

72   Ibid.

73   Ormond, Adrian, FTBL website, 27 February 2007, 'Deal or No Deal' https://www.ftbl.com.au/feature/deal-or-no-deal-74120

74   When Saturday Comes website, February 2004, 'Up from down under' https://www.wsc.co.uk/index.php?option=com_content&view=article&id=2194/29&catid=

75   Ibid.

76   Stensholt, John, Australian Financial Review, 14 September 2006, 'Top of the Table' https://www.afr.com/companies/top-of-the-table-20060914-kab9v

77   Smithies, Tom, The Daily Telegraph, 1 January 2016, 'A-League clubs wasting cash on marquee signings says man who brokered Alessandro Del Piero deal' https://www.dailytelegraph.com.au/sport/football/a-league/aleague-clubs-wasting-cash-on-marquee-signings-says-man-who-brokered-alessandro-del-piero-deal/news-story/8c72431e5ed4e7a856fcb87310551020?nk=5dafece34af17c51ea823afb36624143-1564891043

78   Stone, Kathy, FTBL website, 9 October 2012, 'Turning Dreams into the real deal' https://www.ftbl.com.au/news/turning-dreams-into-the-real-deal-318490

79   Ibid.

80   SBS The World Game website – 'Bundesliga released data Wyscout stat analysis on Matthew Leckie.'

81   Lewis, Dave, SBS Sport website, 29 October 2018, 'Meet the Bundesliga Scout looking for Leckies' https://www.sbs.com.au/topics/sport/football/article/2018/10/29/meet-bundesliga-scout-looking-more-leckies

82   Rugari, Vince, The Sydney Morning Herald, 5 August 2020, 'Let them pay what they want: Agent calls for A-League salary cap floor to go' https://smh.com.au/sport/soccer/let-them-pay-what-they-want-agent-calls-for-a-league-salary-cap-floor-to-go-20200805-p55iwd.html

83   Stensholt, John, Australian Financial Review, 14 September 2006, 'Top of the Table' https://www.afr.com/companies/top-of-the-table-20060914-kab9v

84   Aidan Ormond, FTBL website, 27 February 2007, 'Deal or No Deal' https://www.ftbl.com.au/feature/deal-or-no-deal-74120

85   SBS The World Game website (no author) feature on Gary Williams.

86   Davutovic, David, Perth Now website, 2 October 2016, 'ECU Joondalup forges sister-club arrangement with English Premier League side Burnley' https://www.perthnow.com.au/sport/soccer/ecu-joondalup-forges-sister-club-arrangement-with-english-premier-league-side-burnley-ng-8d05918e-724ae31f0f1af0953432e2f4

87   Ibid.

88   Hinton, Ritchie — 'Seven things you did not know about being a player agent,' ITYS e-mag, 2008.

89   Greco, John, My Football website, 24 September 2015, 'Hyundai A-League star linked with EPL

leaders' https://www.myfootball.com.au/news/hyundai-a-league-star-linked-epl-leaders

90   Lewis, Dave. SBS website, 29 June 2019, 'Ange the inspiration as Muscat looks to make his mark overseas' https://www.sbs.com.au/topics/sport/football/article/2019/06/29/ange-inspiration-muscat-looks-make-his-mark-overseas

91   Davutovic, David, Perth Now website, 4 February 2018, 'Karrinyup-raised Frank Trimboli is a respected king maker in the world of soccer' https://thewest.com.au/lifestyle/stm/karrinyup-raised-frank-trimboli-is-a-respected-king-maker-in-the-world-of-soccer-ng-b88701834z

92   From Vince Grella interview with Peter Paleologos via WhatsApp on 20 March 2020.

93   Fuentes, Ramon, iusport website, 1 September 2015, 'Representatives and intermediaries, the other great football business' (translated from Spanish), https://iusport.com/art/9787/los-representantes-e-intermediarios-el-otro-gran-negocionadel-futbol

94   Davutovic, David, Perth Now website, 4 February 2018, 'Karrinyup-raised Frank Trimboli is a respected king maker in the world of soccer', https://thewest.com.au/lifestyle/stm/karrinyup-raised-frank-trimboli-is-a-respected-king-maker-in-the-world-of-soccer-ng-b88701834z

95   McHugh, Joe, Video Celts website, 8 February 2022, 'Charlie Nicholas stumbles over Celtic's low-key Recruitment Agent that has transformed the club' https://videocelts.com/2022/02/blogs/latest-news/charlie-nicholas-stumbles-over-celtics-low-key-recruitment-agent-that-has-transformed-the-club/amp/

96   Davutovic, David, Perth Now website, 4 February 2018, 'Karrinyup-raised Frank Trimboli is a respected king maker in the world of soccer' https://thewest.com.au/lifestyle/stm/karrinyup-raised-frank-trimboli-is-a-respected-king-maker-in-the-world-of-soccer-ng-b88701834z

97   Ibid.

98   Ibid.

99   Ibid.

100 Base Soccer, Contribution to the Parliamentary Review, 22 December 2020, 'A best practice article to United Kingdom Parliamentary Review' chaired by Rt Hon Lord Eric Pickles and Rt Hon Lord David Blunkett, Retrieved from https://www.theparliamentaryreview.co.uk/organisations/base-soccer

101 Ibid.

102 The World Game website – interview with Vincenzo Grella (undated).

103 Football Bosses with Tony Pignata and Michael Zappone' FNR Football Nation podcast, 24 January 2018, 'Vince Grella on Football Bosses' https://soundcloud.com/fnr_footballnationradio/fnr_football-vince-grella-on-football-bosses-24-jan-2018

104 Ibid.

105 Davutovic, David, Optus Sport, 14 May 2021, 'The perfect place to launch your career, Australia's proud history in Belgium' https://sport.optus.com.au/articles/os25639/australia-history-with-belgium

106 Higgs, Paddy, GOAL.com Indonesia, 28 November 2012, 'Australian Nathan Hall is in line to win the coaching position at Indian I-League club United Sikkim' https://www.goal.com/en-au/news/4024/aussies-abroad/2012/11/28/3561604/australian-coach-nathan-hall-nears-indian-i-league

107 The Nation Thailand, 18 April 2017, 'Dunga's agent says Thailand job second choice' https://www.nationthailand.com/life/30312619

108 Rajan, K, The Malaysian Star, 13 April 2015, 'FAM scouting for more foreign players with Malaysian parentage' https://www.thestar.com.my/sport/football/2015/04/13/fam-fishing-for-more-foreign-players-with-malaysian-parentage

109 Dasey, Jason, The Sydney Morning Herald, 3 December 3, 2015, 'Gary Phillips' and A-League quartet revamp Malaysia's Negeri Sembilan' https://www.smh.com.au/sport/soccer/gary-phillips-and-aleague-quartet-revamp-malaysias-negeri-sembilan-20151203-glecnt.html

110 I did not interview Tony Rallis for this book. Tony has made over 80 A-League player deals and has so much content to discuss that I could not include his story as it would need a whole tome.

111 'Top 20 Highest Paid Footballers in China 2017' https://financefootball.com/2017/01/06/top-20-

highest-paid-football-players-in-china-2017/

112   Postecoglou, Ange, The Sydney Morning Herald, 12 December 2013, 'World Cup draw stirs fond memories of the boys from Brazil' http://www.smh.com.au/sport/soccer/world-cup-draw-stirs-fond-memories-of-the-boys-from-brazil-20131212-2za6a.html#ixzz2nG4wkQuv

113   Slevison, Andrew, FTBL website, 9 October 2011, 'Melbourne Heart's Terra almost signed for Suwon Bluewings' https://www.tribalfootball.com/articles/melbourne-heart-s-terra-almost-signed-suwon-bluewings-835721

114   Ormond, Aidan, FTBL website, 18 November 2008, 'Why Fred signed for Phoenix' https://www.ftbl.com.au/news/why-fred-signed-for-phoenix-128669

115   Migliaccio, Val, The Advertiser, 5 December 2012, 'Talented Latinos ready to strut their stuff' https://www.perthnow.com.au/news/nsw/talented-latinos-ready-to-strut-their-stuff-ng-64183f3d74a1464b-b2aafec8614e77d8

116   Migliaccio, Val, The Advertiser, 5 June 2014, 'Foreign legion to target the A-League after World Cup' https://www.adelaidenow.com.au/sport/football/a-league/foreign-legion-to-target-the-aleague-after-world-cup/news-story/81d3d38595d886dae5f9217fed9784f3

117   Zelic, Lucy, SBS The World Game podcast, 7 October 2020, 'Agent Buddy Farah, Joey Lynch, Ross Aloisi.'

118   Weiner, David, Optus Sport, 31 January 2020, 'Buddy Farah — Inside the world of transfers: What really happens?' https://sport.optus.com.au/articles/os4714/inside-the-world-of-transfers-what-really-happens

119   Ibid.

120   Gatt, Ray, The Australian, 27 January 2016, 'Dutch to blame for Australian Euro exile' https://www.theaustralian.com.au/sport/football/dutch-to-blame-for-australian-euro-exile/news-story/1c1a498ae44cbe49a500e9d959a680d3

121   Ibid.

122   Ibid.

123   Rugari, Vince, The Sydney Morning Herald, 18 June 2020, 'It's surreal: Carpenter's Lyon move unmatched in Australian soccer' https://www.smh.com.au/sport/soccer/it-s-surreal-carpenter-s-lyon-move-unmatched-in-australian-soccer-20200618-p553zi.html

124   Rugari, Vince, The Sydney Morning Herald, 'Wanderers win FIFA case over Olyroos star's Danish transfer' 11 December 2020, https://www.smh.com.au/sport/soccer/roar-sydney-wanderers-win-fifa-case-over-olyroos-star-s-danish-transfer-20201211-p56mqp.html

125   Samios, Zoe, Australian Financial Review, 20 July 2023, 'Meet the million-dollar Matildas (both of them).' https://www.afr.com/companies/sport/sam-kerr-is-female-soccer-s-3-3m-superstar-no-one-else-comes-close-20230718-p5dpa4

126   Bloomberg LLP report – 'A soccer player export boom in Portugal.'

127   Tito, Clement, FTBL website, 25 June 2017, 'Ansell chases Socceroo dream via Portugal' https://www.ftbl.com.au/news/ansell-466329

128   Lynch, Michael, The Sydney Morning Herald, 8 February 2013, 'Victory's humble man of steel' https://www.smh.com.au/sport/soccer/victorys-humble-man-of-steel-20130207-2e1j2.html

129   Professional Footballers Australia (PFA), PFA website, 19 August 2008, 'Players Turn to PFA in Off-Season' https://pfa.net.au/news/players-turn-to-pfa-in-off-season/

130   Ivanov, Boris, 'TF14 Player Management,' Twitter, 23 January 2017.

131   Davidson, John, SBS Sport website, 4 January 2021, 'Brexit blues: New rules to block Australian talent heading to Britain' https://www.sbs.com.au/sport/article/brexit-blues-new-rules-to-block-australian-talent-heading-to-britain/fzafain2v

132   Kulas, Damir, The Corner Flag website, 6 December 2017, 'What Australian football can learn from the German experience' https://www.cornerflag.com.au/what-australian-football-can-learn-from-the-german-experience/

133 Dasey, Jason, ESPN Football website, 23 October 2014, 'Feyenoord youth academy looking for new frontiers in Southeast Asia' https://www.espn.com.au/soccer/blog/name/153/post/2100337/headline

134 Davidson, John, SBS Sport website, 26 February 2021, 'Aussie keeper's wild adventure from Toowoomba to England, Portugal, USA' https://www.sbs.com.au/sport/article/aussie-keepers-wild-adventure-from-toowoomba-to-england-portugal-usa/mc6klu3gl

135 Davutovic, David, The Sunday Telegraph (published on the Fox Sports website), 12 September 2022, 'Croatia raiding Aussie kids' https://www.foxsports.com.au/football/a-league/croatia-raiding-aussie-kids/news-story/8bdb5b357b78c75a3f4f117a03ea6b67

136 Goal Weekly! 'Krncevic's Krunchlines' Season 2 : Issue 28, 21 August 2006, page 29.

137 Goal Weekly! Krncevic's Krunchlines' Season 2 : Issue 10, 10 April 2006, Page 22

138 Goal Weekly! Krncevic's Krunchlines' Season 2: Issue 26, August 2006, Page 29

139 Parkin, Richard, The Guardian Australia, 14 March 2019, 'Behind the football: the uncertain role and influence of agents' https://www.theguardian.com/football/2019/mar/14/behind-the-football-the-uncertain-role-and-influence-of-agents

140 Bossi, Dominic, The Sydney Morning Herald, 21 March 2016, 'Sydney FC squad reeling from death of popular player agent Dragan Jevtic' https://www.smh.com.au/sport/soccer/sydney-fc-squad-reeling-from-death-of-popular-player-agent-dragan-jevtic-20160321-gnnnd4.html

141 Lewis, Dave, SBS The World Game website, 23 March 2016, 'Hersi saddened by the passing of 'honourable' Jevtic.'

142 Ibid.

143 Slevison, Andrew, Tribal Football website, 2011, 'Aussie youngster Lustica to trial with Inter Milan, Norwich' https://www.tribalfootball.com/articles/aussie-youngster-lustica-trial-europ-an-clubs-231744

144 Ormond, Aidan, FTBL website, 1 September 2010, 'A-League African draft camp' https://www.ftbl.com.au/news/a-league-african-draft-camp-230660

145 Australasian Premier League, (Libero Consulting) http://www.ozfootball.net/ark/Bookshelf/Misc/AustralasianPremierLeague-LiberoConsulting.pdf

146 Stogiannou, George, Neos Kosmos, 9 March 2017, 'The current play of player agent industry' https://neoskosmos.com/en/2017/03/09/sport/football/the-current-play-of-player-agent-industry/

147 Stamocostas, Con, Neos Kosmos, 19 December 2018, 'Revealed! The secret to making it as a professional footballer' https://neoskosmos.com/en/2 018/12/19/sport/revealed-the-secret-to-making-it-as-a-professional-footballer/

148 Ibid.

149 Stogiannou, George, Neos Kosmos, 9 March 2017, 'The current play of player agent industry' https://neoskosmos.com/en/2017/03/09/sport/football/the-current-play-of-player-agent-industry/

150 Australians playing overseas infographic 2000–2001 season (The Clean Sheet Twitter account — August 2021). This information was cross referenced with data available at https://www.ozfootball.net/

151 Duerden, John, Lions and Tigers: The Story of Football in Singapore and Malaysia, Paperback, January 2018

152 Stensholt, John, Australian Financial Review, 14 September 2006, 'Top of the table' https://www.afr.com/companies/top-of-the-table-20060914-kab9v

153 Exchange between Andrew Howe (Australian statistician and Tony Vidmar), Twitter.

154 Studs Up – Australian soccer fanzine – Issue 38, March 1999.

155 Davidson, John, FTBL website, 7 December 2010, 'The Socceroo factories' (This article appeared in the December 2010 issue of FourFourTwo magazine) https://www.ftbl.com.au/feature/the-socceroo-factories-240764/page0

156 Ormond, Aidan, FTBL website, 'Youth development: The lost boys,' 31 October 2007 https://www.ftbl.com.au/feature/youth-development-the-lost-boys-95832/page0

157 Ibid.

158 Davidson, John, FTBL website, 7 December 2010, 'The Socceroo factories' (This article appeared in the December 2010 issue of FourFourTwo magazine) https://www.ftbl.com.au/feature/the-socceroo-factories-240764/page0

159 Gorman, Joe, SBS Sports, 'AIS to Champions League – Ergic and Milicevic's parallel careers,' 31 July 2018,https://www.sbs.com.au/sport/article/ais-to-champions-league-ergic-and-milicevics-parallel-careers/r28672p2x

160 Taffa, Louise — X (Twitter) account.

161 Moore, Craig — Twitter, 31 March 2019.

162 Ormond, Aidan, FTBL website, 'Youth development: The lost boys,' 31 October 2007 https://www.ftbl.com.au/feature/youth-development-the-lost-boys-95832/page0

163 Ibid.

164 FTBL website, 27 August 2010, 'Coach wowed by Aussie talent' https://www.ftbl.com.au/news/coach-wowed-by-aussie-talent-230156

165 False Nine on Twitter — 'Nike — The Chance analysis'

166 de Marco, Fabian, (former intermediary) — LinkedIn account.

167 Kiousis, Arthur on Twitter, 4 July 2019.

168 Davutovic, David, The Sunday Telegraph (published on the Fox Sports website), 12 September 2022, 'Croatia raiding Aussie kids' https://www.foxsports.com.au/football/a-league/croatia-raiding-aussie-kids/news-story/8bdb5b357b78c75a3f4f117a03ea6b67

169 Hassett, Sebastian, The Sydney Morning Herald, 19 September 2008, 'New league the missing link for young stars' https://amp.smh.com.au/sport/soccer/new-league-the-missing-link-for-young-stars-20080919-gdsvjg.html

170 SportTechie webinar, 1 December 2022, 'The World of Global Football getting smaller: How data, devices and digital video are improving talent discovery.'

171 Kelner, Martha, Sky Sports News, 24 February 2021, 'Youth football: What happens to those who don't 'make it'?' https://news.sky.com/story/youth-football-what-happens-to-those-who-dont-make-it-12226577

172 Perlemuter, Jerome (of the World League Forums) presentation to AIAF.

173 Lokaj, Jan, calculated and published by Ben Littleton on Twitter, 31 July 2018.

174 Geey, Daniel, (football lawyer) on X (Twitter).

175 Bielefeld, Alexander of FIFPRO, FIFPRO research into UEFA Youth League.

176 Tancredi Palmeri, Italian football lawyer on Twitter, 30 October 2017.

177 Rahman, Abidu, 'Football positions in demand' – LinkedIn, 9 February 2024.

178 Stamocostas, Con, Neos Kosmos, 19 December 2018, 'Revealed! The secret to making it as a professional footballer' https://neoskosmos.com/en/2018/12/19/sport/revealed-the-secret-to-making-it-as-a-professional-footballer/

179 Ibid.

180 Davutovic, David, Optus Sport, 'It's the worst thing I've ever seen, the stupidest system in the world.' 22 March 2023 https://sport.optus.com.au/news/australian-football/os15697/australia-grassroots-problems-youngsters-feature

181 Parkin, Richard, 'Where next in Australia's pursuit of football's next golden generation?' The Guardian Australia, 31 October 2019 and Professional Footballers Australia – Culture Amplifies Talent report, https://pfa.net.au/wp-content/uploads/PFA-Golden-Generation-Report_DIGITAL.pdf

182 A 'combine' is the American term for what is essentially soccer/football trials or try-outs for professional team contracts. Trial and draft combines are used to assess and scout college and academy players in the USA to select rookie players for Major League Soccer and National Women's Soccer League club contracts.

183 Rallis, Tony, Soccer Stoppage Time, 11 September 2017 (idea also raised on radio show)

184 Ibid.

185 This information was cross referenced with the CIES Football Observatory's 422nd edition of their Weekly Post presenting the studies of the presence of expatriate footballers at international clubs.

186 When Saturday Comes website, February 2004, 'Up from down under' https://www.wsc.co.uk/index.php?option=com_content&view=article&id=2194/29&catid=

187 Blood, Greg, The Roar, 27 April 2017, 'Remembering the contributions of AIS Men's football to the Socceroos' https://www.theroar.com.au/2017/04/28/remembering-contributions-ais-mens-football-socceroos/

188 Murphy, Chris, football agent — England, X (Twitter).

189 Mikdadi, Bassil — The Asian Game podcast episode 87, 23 June 2022.

190 Parkin, Richard, The Guardian Australia, 14 March 2019, 'Behind the football: the uncertain role and influence of agents', https://www.theguardian.com/football/2019/mar/14/behind-the-football-the-uncertain-role-and-influence-of-agents

191 Goal Weekly!, 2010, Issue 1.

Acknowledgements

Writing a book on Australian football agents was much more challenging than I anticipated and more rewarding than I could have imagined.

It is a rare opportunity to bring together the often unknown stories of fellow Australian football agents and amplify their importance in growing football in Australia. The agent industry is highly competitive, and the sharing of inside information, business models, player deals, and intellectual property is extremely rare.

I must begin by thanking Jade Lo for advising me on keeping the manuscript succinct and relevant. Likewise, to Ivan Donato, Greg McCleod and Jonathan Booker for reviewing and suggesting ideas for some key chapter drafts. Further, thanks to Nanette Walsh for patiently transcribing over 25 recorded interviews and podcasts.

I'm wholeheartedly grateful to all the Australian football agents, scouts and intermediaries featured in this book who took the time to share their stories and allow me to interview them. I hope my book does justice to their stories and positive contribution to football.

I would also like to thank Terry McFlynn, whose views and perspective were invaluable.

Ron Smith and Lou Sticca could write their own memoirs but were open to sharing their stories with me. Ron Smith gave me insights about the success of the Australian Institute of Sport's (AIS) football program, and Lou Sticca about his epic journey in the game. I am grateful to be able to include what are only small parts of their respective compelling stories. As many journalists observe, interest in the subject makes for a better interview. It was an honour to interview and listen to all the agents and intermediaries, their fascinating stories and different perspectives.

Thanks to everyone from Fair Play Publishing who helped me so much. Special thanks to Bonita Mersiades, the ever-patient publisher and advisor, as well as her editorial and design team.

Yet this book would not have been possible without the clubs, fellow agents, coaches, football directors, club presidents, scouts, sponsorship departments, brand managers, player union delegates, football lawyers, parents and players who I have met, conversed with, debated, advised, collaborated with, represented and had dealings with during my international agent journey over the years.

Finally, thanks to all those who have been a part of my transition into the industry, particularly George Apostolou (RIP), John Tzitzios and Anthony Phaesse.

About Peter Paleologos

Peter Paleologos founded Libero Consulting, an Australian-based football player management agency. He is passionate about facilitating the improvement of the Australian and World football agent regulatory environment. Peter is the author of the Australian Youth Footballer Regulatory Guide, a licensed FIFA Football Agent, and a football lawyer.

Peter is President and Secretary of the Australian Football Agents Association Inc. He is on the editorial committee for Football Legal, the international journal for football lawyers, and has written over 32 articles on Australian, Malaysian, Indonesian, Jamaican, Fijian and New Zealand football law matters.

Peter has a Master's in Sports Business and completed the Business of Entertainment, Media and Sports Executive course at Harvard University Business School. He is a FIFA-appointed pro bono counsel who provides legal aid services to players and coaches at disciplinary hearings.

In 2023, Peter completed the first edition of the FIFA Executive Programme in Football Agency, and he has given presentations at various football agents' conferences. He is the co-founder and co-host of the only international niche football agents podcast, namely 'The Agents Angle'.

MORE REALLY GOOD FOOTBALL BOOKS FROM FAIR PLAY PUBLISHING

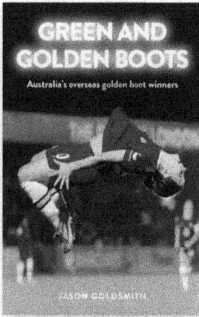

Green and
Golden Boots

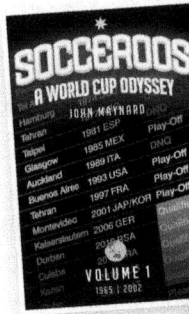

Socceroos – A World Cup Odyssey,
1965 to 2022 Volumes 1 and 2

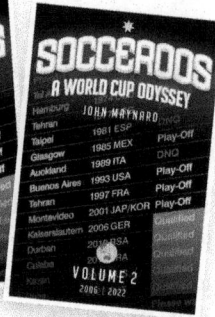

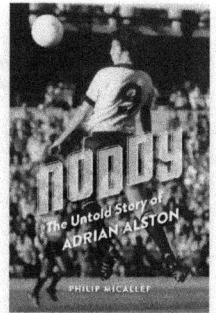

Noddy, The Untold Story
of Adrian Alston

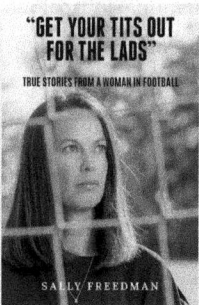

"Get Your Tits Out
for the Lads"

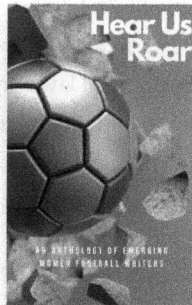

Hear Us Roar
– An anthology of
emerging women
football writers

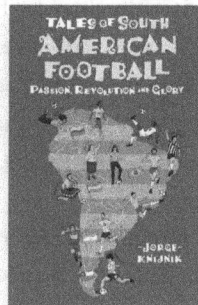

Tales of South
American Football –
Passion, Revolution
and Glory

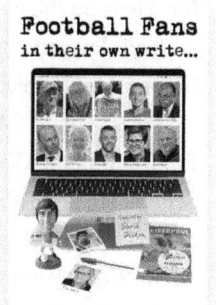

Football Fans
in their own write...

Available from fairplaypublishing.com.au

and all good bookstores

FAIRPLAY
PUBLISHING

9 781925 914733